Practical Computer Cost Accounting

Practical Computer Cost Accounting

Kenneth M. Sullivan

VNR VAN NOSTRAND REINHOLD COMPANY
NEW YORK CINCINNATI TORONTO LONDON MELBOURNE

Library of Congress Catalog Card Number: 82-11025
ISBN: 0-442-27961-2

Manufactured in the United States of America

Published by Van Nostrand Reinhold Company Inc.
135 West 50th Street, New York, N.Y. 10020

Van Nostrand Reinhold Publishing
1410 Birchmount Road
Scarborough, Ontario M1P 2E7, Canada

Van Nostrand Reinhold
480 Latrobe Street
Melbourne, Victoria 3000, Australia

Van Nostrand Reinhold Company Limited
Molly Millars Lane
Wokingham, Berkshire, England

15 14 13 12 11 10 9 8 7 6 5 4 3 2 1

Library of Congress Cataloging in Publication Data

Sullivan, Kenneth M.
Practical computer cost accounting.

Includes index.
1. Electronic data processing departments – Cost control. 2. Cost accounting. I. Title.
HF5548.2.S837 1983 658'.054'0681 82-11025
ISBN 0-442-27961-2

To Stephanie

Preface

Computers are fascinating machines. Many people are drawn to them, and some even develop lifelong relationships that rival human friendships. Perhaps we favor these machines because they come so close to us, in terms of flexibility and usefulness.

The problem is that in our enthusiasm for computers we tend to become overindulgent with them. We forget that these devices cost a great deal of money. And; like all other assets, they must be carefully controlled and must deliver an adequate return on their invested costs.

This book is about the control of computers. But not the kind of control requiring esoteric devices such as price/performance curves, system flow diagrams, or a thousand and one other techniques dreamed up by people trying to sell computers. Instead, we will be concerned with cost, and with how to make sure that each hardware dollar is wisely invested.

Real control of computers is a bit like worrying about the nuts and bolts that hold a complicated machine together. Somebody must check the fasteners periodically to make sure none of them has jiggled loose. This isn't flashy or exciting work, but when done consistently ensures that the machine will keep on functioning.

Control of computers requires attention to detail. That detail must be logically and systematically accumulated. And that detail must be turned into value.

One benefit derived from attention to detail is that those who honestly accomplish it are more likely to truly understand what computers are, how they operate, and how they can most effectively be used.

It is not enough that we can acquire computers and program them and produce solutions. It is more important that we know *when* to acquire these machines, where to use them, and how to prevent excessive or ineffective applications.

There is no doubt that the future holds an important place for computers. It is obvious that these machines are becoming more important to all of us as we function in the world. We are committed to data processing, and that committment will grow.

It therefore follows that those who understand computers will have an insurmountable advantage over everybody else. This is as true for individuals as it is for companies.

Whether you know much about accounting or not, whether you like it or dislike it or have no opinion, the fact is that this well-developed methodology offers the only viable way to control computers. Therefore, all practitioners having a long-term interest in computing should develop a complementary knowledge of accounting. Accounting helps to control, and it also helps provide a better understanding of computers and their operations.

Most of the ideas in this book are not original, although many of them have never before appeared in print. These ideas are a synthesis of the thoughts expressed and developed by many of my associates in the computer field.

I have had the good fortune to work for many years with a company that is in the forefront of computer technology, as well as in computer accounting. This relationship has certainly made my task easier since I have virtually lived through many of the concepts about which I have written.

Special thanks to Dick Roth, whose basic thoughts on simplified mainframe accounting are incorporated within. Rufus White's enthusiastic concepts also helped. And Ralph Lawrence, a pioneer in computer accounting, deserves thanks.

The physical act of writing a book is very time consuming. For help with this I must thank my employer, McAuto, who allowed me unlimited use of a sophisticated word processing system. Without that machine, my burden would have been very heavy indeed.

Contents

Practical Computer Cost Accounting

Part I
Computers and Accounting

Chapter 1.1
The New Computing

CONTROL AND THE COMPUTER

A high-powered Chief Executive Officer who controls a major corporation begins his periodic nationwide facility tour. He is a dynamic man and likes to personally visit each of his many plant sites as often as possible to get a feel for how things are going throughout the country. He likes to mingle with the workers.

This executive has been a very busy person, so it has been about two years since he last paid each of his divisions such a visit. Still, he is not anticipating any significant changes in the way his company is operated.

His first stop is the engineering design facility in Chicago. After that he will visit fourteen other plants in as many days. His tour will be packed with visual experiences, and little else.

The Chicago facility hasn't changed much physically during his two year absence. The general atmosphere is quiet and academic. Offices are laid out with research in mind.

Interspersed among the engineers' desks he sees many new pieces of equipment – what look like small computers, complete with video screens, printers, and other computer-like features. When the CEO stops to examine one of the devices, an enthusiastic engineer gives him a quick demonstration of the graphic design capabilities of that particular machine. The small processor beside the engineer's desk performs like any other computer the executive has ever seen, although his experience in that area is quite limited. The engineer is very proud of his computer and points out that it has no connection with the large, centrally located processors elsewhere in the building.

Something about the proliferation of these small machines bothers the executive. Their presence stays in his mind.

Twenty days later, after he has had time to digest his trip, the CEO asks an aid to check into the situation at Chicago and find out what all those small computers are being used for.

The aid personally visits the Chicago facility, talks to many practitioners, and conducts a thorough investigation. When he returns to headquarters, he explains to the Chief Executive Officer that the Chicago engineers are in the process of adopting a form of decentralized computing using 35 newly purchased minicomputers.

The executive remembers allocating a healthy share of his capital budget to the purchase of a new generation of large computers for the Chicago plant several years ago. Does the Chicago organization still have those large computers?

Yes, the aid replies, they have a large, sophisticated computer center that has been built up over the past twenty years. The data center currently has three large mainframes, with full complements of disk devices, tape drives, and other peripherals. The central computer operation is considered the most sophisticated in the company. The engineering group has always made a heavy use of computers, thus this center is considered substantial. It has an annual operating budget of about $45 million.

Well then, why do they have minicomputers too? Are the small machines doing something the central computers can't?

No, it doesn't appear that the minicomputers can do anything more than the central facility. Minicomputers are generally inferior in capability. But the engineers seem to feel that these small machines are easier to use and more reliable. Minis appear to be very popular, and additional units are being acquired almost monthly. Everybody seems to want a minicomputer.

What are we getting with these small computers? Have they improved productivity? Is more design work being done with fewer engineers? Is there a decent return on investment?

Nobody has thought about productivity or R.O.I. The machines seem to be acquired because they are popular and fashionable. And it appears that total engineering output is about the same now as it was several years ago, before any minicomputers were acquired. The Chicago facility has been a stable performer for years. A few of the engineers were interviewed and they seemed to feel that minicomputers improved productivity, but there was no financial analysis to back up these feelings. In fact, there seemed to be a general lack of quantitative analysis for all aspects of minicomputer acquisition.

Are the engineers turning out better designs using all this additional capability?

The engineers have been turning out high quality designs for decades. A check with other divisions showed that the general quality of design effort has remained at the same high level for years.

Are these minicomputers saving the company money?

Nobody really knows. The machines have been purchased one or two at a time for the past several years, with no overall plan in mind. There are a wide variety of makes and models. Nobody has attempted to standardize. Some of the engineers have been experimenting with a communications link that will hook several of the small computers together, but there is no clear objective behind this linkup. It hasn't been very successful to date. And it is not clear who authorized this effort, or who is paying for it. But it does serve as an example that this equipment is handled on a very informal, casual basis. Nobody is keeping records of anything.

How much have these 35 machines cost us?

It's very hard to be precise about that. To get around acquisition rules set up by the central computer facility, these small machines have been purchased as everything from calculators to machine tool controllers. Each purchase is relatively small, but additional equipment seems to be constantly needed and acquired. Perhaps $2 million of original equipment was actually purchased. At least that much additional equipment is acquired each year.

You mean we have spent at least $2 million on top of the $45 million we already spend each year for the central facility and there's no tangible payoff, or at least no way of measuring the payoff?

It could be worse than that. Some of the minicomputers have grown to the point where they use full-time operators. And many of these machines require specialized programming support, so programmers have been hired. Some of the computers have full time managers. Frankly, many engineers now seem to be busier operating and programming minicomputers than designing products.

THE DIRECTION OF COMPUTING

Where is the physical act of data processing headed? Will a minicomputer eventually be placed on everyone's desk? Can such competition drive centralized mainframes from existence? Will somebody arbitrate this potential fight between modes of computing, or will change occur naturally, without planned direction?

As our fictional CEO discovered, minicomputers have a way of quickly infiltrating modern corporations until they become as ubiquitous as pencil sharpeners. Minicomputers have an advantage over their larger counterparts. The mini often starts as a relatively low cost, low capability machine. By adding features, they can be built into sophisticated processors with abilities close to those of large centralized mainframes. Of course, as capability is increased, cost also goes up.

In many companies, it took decades to build centralized computer facilities but only a few short years to acquire scores of small computers. The combined processing capabilities of these smaller machines can easily exceed the power of the central computer operation. Yet while most large computers must be heavily justified before acquisition, minicomputers can often be acquired with petty cash or with very little formal justification.

Computing has come to a crossroads. Various data processing choices have become available. It is no longer necessary to restrict usage to large, centralized computers operated by highly trained staffs. Individuals can now acquire their own small computers, program and operate them, and develop local processing capabilities tailored to their precise needs. The local control is very appealing to many people.

When a number of these small computers are located within a single company, they can be linked together with data lines to form distributed networks. Computational capabilities can be developed that were never before available.

Should a company allow new forms of computing to proliferate without restraint? Is restraint even possible, considering how inexpensive and easily obtainable many of these devices are?

Companies today have a number of ways that they can satisfy their data processing needs. Because of these hardware alternatives, two questions emerge:

- What is the right form of computing for a company?
- What is the most cost effective form of computing?

The right form of computing might not be the most cost effective. But whatever the choice, a company would not be treating itself or its stockholders fairly unless it clearly understood the costs involved with computing.

Answering the above two questions takes something more than gut feel. As our CEO and his aid found out, people will attempt to justify their preferred mode of computing using nebulous terms such as increased productivity and better local control. Perceptions and attitudes are not adequate representations of computer cost effectiveness. Because a form of computing seems right, or is popular, doesn't mean that it is best for the company, or the least expensive choice. To determine what is best, we must begin with quantification. From numbers we can draw conclusions. We can meaningfully compare and contrast. Personal opinions and preferences can be tested.

Many people today don't really understand the computer. Lack of understanding makes these individuals uncomfortable and unwilling to implement simple controls that most other assets within the company must meet.

A century ago, Lord William Kelvin, the famous British mathematician and physicist, wrote the following about quantification:

> I often say that when you can measure what you are speaking about, and express it in numbers, you know something about it; but when you cannot express it in numbers, your knowledge is of a meager and unsatisfactory kind; it may be the beginning of knowledge, but you have scarcely, in your thoughts, advanced to the stage of science, whatever the matter may be.

Computers are not toys or playthings or diversions. Within a company they are purchased to do a job and to make the company more profitable.

Regardless of the form that computing takes, it must be quantified in some systematic manner so that its value can be measured.

Effective principles of measurement are brought together in a discipline known as accounting.

THE PURPOSE OF ACCOUNTING

Regardless of appearances, costs associated with computers are, and will continue to be, significant. Although the initial purchase price of a minicomputer is sometimes relatively small, there are many more components to total cost than just the hardware. It is the job of accounting to accurately uncover all costs and present them in a logical and meaningful format to decision makers. When this is done properly, it is called *cost accounting.*

Very few computer organizations, large or small, have ever thought much about accounting. Statistics will be introduced later to prove this point.

When people deal with computers, thoughts are typically centered around hardware operation or programming. Little consideration is given to whether or not the operation is cost justifiable. There are too many other more interesting things to explore. After all, it's fun to operate computers.

Computer power today is proliferating throughout all organizations in ways that were not even contemplated ten, or even five, years ago. What began as inadequate accounting has therefore deteriorated even further as entirely new modes of computing have been introduced. Consequently, few corporations today know what computers are really costing them. They have no idea of whether or not these machines are enhancing profits. To paraphrase Lord Kelvin: Since these companies cannot quantify their position in computers, they know little or nothing about it. Yet computer acquisitions can demand a very significant portion of the annual capital budget.

Are minicomputers or large centralized processors the best choice? Should everybody who needs a personal computer have one? Should everybody be forced to use terminals connected to large central mainframes? Is it an either-or situation?

These are the gut issues that face both managers and users of computers. It has to do with the form that computers and computing will take in the decades ahead. Every corporation must obviously choose its own path. But making a choice without reasonable amounts of cost information is foolhardy and dangerous. This is particularly true if the company makes a poor choice of computers while a competitor makes the right choice. An unwise acquisition of computers could tip the scales in favor of the competition.

It is not enough today to simply *feel* that a method of computing is right, or accept a single hardware vendor's point of view. If a computing approach has merit, numbers will prove it out. Otherwise, the approach might eventually become an expensive waste of precious corporate assets.

In this book we will not attempt to prejudge any form of computing, nor choose one superior mode. Some methods of data processing have been around a long time while others are so new that nobody has uncovered their true potential, nor has anybody put them to practical use. Neither longevity nor newness can guarantee superiority, though.

A set of tools will be provided that can be used to quantify all forms of computing in a consistent, straightforward fashion. Using these tools as a start, or baseline, practitioners can closely examine the makeup of their own computers or contemplated systems. With this information, they will be in a better position to confront and examine the quickly changing technology that will inevitably appear in the next decade.

Accounting is an old tool that has been perfected over many centuries. This time-tested methodology can be adapted quite easily to the new world of computers. The fast-paced, fluid explosion of processing power can be subdued and controlled using some very ancient financial techniques.

Chapter 1.2
Why Worry About Accounting?

Computer accounting and chargeout have been around in various forms at least since the mid-1960s. Over the years, many progressive installations have had time to develop sophisticated forms of computer chargeback. As a result, responsible corporations today expect their centralized processing facilities to charge users in some way for computer services rendered.

Computer costs have been accumulated into such things as cost centers and profit centers. Chargeback from these accounting categories occurs through the use of utilization measurement. Most computers can be made to automatically measure resource consumption as each program is processed. These utilization statistics form the basis for various types of job chargeback.

Installations that had early accounting on their computers will find that most utilization schemes were developed by technically oriented people such as systems programmers. When computers first appeared, there weren't many other people around with enough perception to realize that computer accounting was important.

Systems programmers understood computers and realized that such major resources were too valuable to simply give away. They correctly noted that when a computer was free, its resources were quickly filled to capacity. It was logical to deduce that much of this usage was trivial and nonproductive. By establishing job chargeback, users would be forced to place natural limits on their computer demands, and only process work that had an economic payback.

Systems programmers thus began developing accounting methods. Most of these schemes were created from a technician's viewpoint. This was understandable since technicians, being human, naturally believed that their viewpoints were more valid than any other viewpoints. As a result, we got accounting techniques based on such technical concepts as byte transfer, channel program executions, disk rotational delay, task control block time, system resource block time, and I/O waits. All of these measurements are beyond the average computer user's comprehension. Accounting systems were therefore built around concepts that could not be grasped by the general user population.

Richard Nolan, in his book *Management Accounting and Control of Data Processing* (National Association of Accountants, 1977), explored the relationship between the large computer center and its users. He carried out indepth interviews with the managers and users at 56 computer installations in major corporations throughout the country. One of his basic conclusions was that in all cases technicians or systems programmers who began computer accounting systems made invalid assumptions about things like cost allocation techniques and utilization measurement. Their methods may have been technologically elegant, but they made no sense in terms of real cost or user understandability. As a result, most users made no attempt to control computer usage or costs. An overwhelming 84% of computer users questioned had little or no understanding of computer accounting and chargeback. Only 16% felt they understood costs and could adequately project future impacts.

What technicians often don't realize is that one of the most fundamental concepts of accounting is that the end result must be *understood* by the people for whom it is intended, or it is worthless. Even when information is conceptually correct, if its presentation is poor or confusing, then there is no real value to its substance. People do not have the time or inclination to sift through what appears to be meaningless data. They simply ignore it.

It is unlikely that computer accounting has improved in the years since Nolan conducted his study. Major user groups such as IBM's SHARE publish papers on accounting from time to time. Most of these papers are written by systems programmers. The same old complex schemes are dredged up over and over again. For example, there are concerns over accounting accuracy down to the microsecond, which most users can't relate to. Or there are suggestions that the user can somehow build transaction accounting schemes within his own application programs (which is equivalent to the electric utility sending you a bill with no dollar values, but the message: "Send us what you think you owe.") In all cases, these methods continue to be complex and incomprehensible, or incredibly expensive to implement. Technically oriented people, such as systems programmers, simply do not approach accounting from a practical, common-sense viewpoint.

Complexity does not guarantee equitability. And equitability is the primary goal of accounting. In the end, users must pay a fair price for what they consume.

PROFESSIONALISM

Although well meaning technicians have developed a variety of computer accounting methods, most companies would be much better off if chargeback systems were developed by professional accountants. These people view accounting from a user's standpoint, and their minds are not clouded with the technical jargon of computing. Accountants have been trained to simplify. They certainly understand cost, and how it should best be presented to users.

There are really no overwhelming challenges presented by computer accounting. The basics of machine architecture are straightforward and easy to grasp. Many of the fundamental design concepts have been around for decades and can be successfully explained to children in grade school. Why, then, is there any reason to create complex or hard to understand measurements?

With the right approach and attitude, computer accounting can be made simple and easy to understand. And simplicity makes accounting inexpensive to live with.

The complex assumptions used to develop initial accounting techniques must be abandoned. They no longer serve any useful purpose. Although computer technicians justify complex accounting because they feel that nothing on earth approaches the complexity of a large central processor and its software, the fact is that there are many other activities in this world that actually exceed this complexity. Yet their ultimate costs are simple and easy to understand.

Imagine, for example, the incredible array of functions that go into producing gasoline – everything from initial exploration to drilling to refining to distribution through many levels ending at the local gasoline pump. Political overtones influence such things as wellhead prices, modes of delivery, and usage. Yet the unit of measurement called a *gallon* brings that long chain of events down to a simple, understandable unit of value. Everybody can understand the measurement and can relate to the price that is applied to it. From apparent complexity emerges simplicity of measurement.

Surely the internal and external operation of a computer is no more complex than what it takes to produce a gallon of gasoline. Centralized computers should also have simple, straightforward chargeback schemes that users can easily grasp and understand.

UNIFORM ACCOUNTING

Centralized processing, using large mainframes, is no longer the only form of computing available to the average user. New modes of processing have appeared and are based on the smaller minicomputer. These modes break down into four categories:

- Minicomputers operating as standalone units.
- Networks of minicomputers linked together with communications lines, forming distributed computing systems.
- Turnkey minicomputer systems.
- Various modes of office automation.

Office automation is actually a subset of turnkey systems, but is isolated because of its unusual characteristics, which will be explored in a later section.

The introduction of relatively inexpensive minicomputers has been made possible by semiconductor technology, which allows a great deal of processing power to be put into a small package.

Minicomputers are difficult to define. It is foolish to use capacity or speed measurements to describe them because barriers are constantly being torn down as technology swiftly advances. All we can really say is that minicomputers are smaller than central mainframes. As minicomputers get more powerful, mainframes also become more powerful. Both modes share in the same technology.

Minicomputers today are powerful enough to support many different applications at one time, thus they take on aspects of centralized mainframes. Many mini installations have the same types of problems that mainframe installations have had over the years.

Because minicomputers are small, people have suggested that accounting for them is not worthwhile. Proponents of this attitude claim that accounting is senseless if:

- The device is of relatively low value to the company.
- The physical act of accounting would severely reduce the amount of resources left for productive work.

These are powerful arguments against accounting for minicomputers. These arguments must be defused before accounting can be seriously considered. Both arguments will be dealt with throughout this book.

In response to the first argument, it will be shown that minicomputers are not actually *relatively* inexpensive, but represent major investments by any corporation. These investments grow at a surprisingly fast rate. And there are hidden costs that many people either ignore or fail to consider.

The second argument can be countered with the development of simple, inexpensive accounting. If the utilization measurement is very straightforward, it will also be undemanding from a resource consumption standpoint. In fact, some very good accounting methods don't require any computing resources at all.

There is a simple rule of thumb that resource requirements are directly related to accounting complexity. If we expect many things to be measured, then large amounts of computer time will be needed. But if we can keep the accounting system simple, we will require very little from the computer in terms of critical resources such as CPU, memory, and nonvolatile storage space.

If we implement accounting on minicomputers, and if we already have accounting on the large mainframes, can the utilization measurements be standardized and made uniform? Although this is a possibility, most major installations are not ready for absolute simplicity and require a certain amount of complexity because of the diverse range of services they provide. This is not entirely satisfactory, but is realistic. In other words, there are limits to the amount of simplicity that can be achieved on mainframes. But there is no limit to the simplified techniques that can be developed for minicomputers. We can therefore use these small machines to learn about the equality of simplified accounting techniques. Minicomputers can pave the way in development of simple accounting, which can later be adopted by the big mainframes when practitioners fully understand the benefits.

There is more to accounting than utilization measurement. Costs associated with the computer operation must be collected. The ironic thing about cost collection is that if a centralized computer operation has been doing a good job of collecting costs, it may suddenly find itself at a competitive disadvantage with the newer forms of minicomputers. Cost for a small computer is generally considered to be only the value of hardware. Sophisticated large computer operations take the full cost approach, which includes additional items such as labor, supplies, utilities, and facility costs. Similar expenses actually exist for the small computer, but people choose not to recognize them. Comparisons between the two modes of computing are therefore unfair, but done all the time. The minicomputer inevitably looks cheaper.

All costs associated with computers must be collected. Here, a very uniform methodology can be developed for use by both central computers and minicomputers. Once done properly, the costs of processing in different modes can be fairly compared. If a problem can be solved using one of several different modes of computing, the different costs can be analyzed and contrasted using the basic assumption that costs for each alternative have been gathered in the same way. Accountants call this consistency. It is a disciplined approach that computing must adopt without question because too many alternatives now exist. Choosing the best computer alternative is a matter of cost comparison. If you know your costs, you understand your direction.

COST GROWTH

When compared to central processors, the relative value of a single minicomputer may seem small. This is misleading, however, because although unit cost may be low, the cost of all installed minicomputers can be considerable.

An analogy can be used as an example.

Large companies have large workforces. But the cost of a single individual is small for most corporations. Multiply the unit labor cost by thousands upon thousands of employees, however, and total wage expense generally becomes the most significant value that most companies have. Corporations therefore spend a great deal of money accounting for and charging back labor. This is proof that labor cost, while trivial at the individual level, is a cost that is significant and must be reckoned with. Consequently, countless numbers of employees fill out timecards that record their weekly activity, and which feed into a labor cost accounting systems (the labor/payroll system is often the single largest user of the centralized computer facility).

In most corporations, minicomputers are proliferating today and will continue to proliferate in the future. All indications are that the rate of installation will increase. If total minicomputer costs are not yet substantial, they certainly will be considerable very shortly. Accounting at the individual unit level is as appropriate with these machines as it has been for labor.

Taming the Revolution

People within the computer trade are constantly predicting breakthroughs and revolutions for the process of computing. There are constant claims of more processing for less money.

But it is hard to pinpoint a major computer revolution since the 1950s, although there has certainly been swift technological evolution. Nobody can deny that computers have become so popular and ubiquitous that they have changed the shape of society. Computers have given us a much different world, primarily in the way we interact and use information. And information has become the blood of society.

The prophets of computer revolution may have a valid point when it comes to considering minicomputers. What is so significantly different about these small computers is that they are so easily available. They can be packaged in many different ways, and delivered in forms that often hide the fact that they are really computers. Vendors knowingly do this to broaden markets and sell to people who have never before considered computers.

Word processors are an excellent example. They are sold as typewriter replacements, and are used by a category of worker who has generally had little contact with computers. Word processor vendors have literally created a new market for automation products that the large computer manufacturers overlooked. As a result, powerful CPUs are being installed beside secretaries to perform routine clerical chores. It is easy to be misled into thinking that these new tools are not really computers. But they are. At bottom there is a central processing unit just like all other central processing units. The way the CPU is packaged is what tends to mislead.

We must draw back from the bewildering array of hardware devices available and observe that computers are simply hardware/software combinations that provide solutions. If we do this we will find that most corporations have many more computers than they often think they have.

Capturing all computer costs while the mini phenomenon is relatively young will help set a foundation for control. There is no longer any time to debate the merits of central computing and minicomputing. Minicomputers surround us and are proliferating rapidly. People have had some experience with these small machines and they like what they see. Vendors will continue to package creatively in an attempt to open up more and more markets to automation. The costs associated with this explosive growth will have to be recorded so that control can be established. Adequate cost accounting techniques must be implemented now. Procrastinating will lead to poor control over an asset that may some day rival the cost of labor in most corporations.

Chapter 1.3
A Definition of Profitability

Although there are many reasons why corporations exist today, there is one objective they all have that is dominant. That objective is profit. Profit is a reward for taking risks. Without profit a company cannot attract equity financing from investors, nor does it have funds to reinvest in projects that will become future products or services. In the long run, any company that cannot make a profit will cease to exist through the mechanism of bankruptcy.

Most people understand the basics of profit, but it is still a very elusive phenomenon in the everyday world of work. Not very many employees within the typical corporation know how their company produces a profit, nor how they as individuals can influence that profit. Various schemes, often called profit sharing plans, have been used by corporations to try and instill within individuals a profit making attitude. But, except on the production line where people actually touch and add value to products, profit orientation is almost impossible to develop. How does a manager or a secretary or an engineer or an accounts payable clerk relate his or her job to profit? In most companies these non-production employees make up the bulk of the work force.

Perhaps the clearest understanding of profitability occurs in sections of the accounting department and in top management. Accountants calculate profit and top managers owe their continuing jobs to it, so both must understand how it is calculated and why it changes.

Whenever a new project or product or acquisition is contemplated, management first tries to assess the impact that action will have on profits. No rational company would ever proceed with any project without the belief that overall profits would eventually be increased.

The only exception to profit seeking motivation is government legislation. Government can force companies to do things that are not in their best financial interest, such as clean up pollutant emissions, pay for certain employee benefits, and produce "safer" products. But, in the long run even these actions are passed along to the consumer as price increases, which can increase profits.

Computers represent a major investment to most companies. The acquisition of data processing hardware can affect profitability. There are many forms of computing today, each with its own unique set of benefits and detriments. The ultimate test of any computer's effectiveness is its impact on profitability. If a computer can increase profits, it is a good investment. If a computer has little or no effect on profitability, then its acquisition is questionable.

CALCULATING PROFITS

Companies generate revenue through the sale of goods or services. From this gross revenue, two general items must be deducted before profit can be achieved. These two items are:

- Cost of Goods (or Services) Sold.
- Other Operating Expenses.

The basic calculation is shown in Figure 1-1. Accountants call this list of calculations an Income Statement. The bottom value, double underlined, is net income, or profit. In our example, a company with $100,000 of annual sales shows a net profit of $15,000, or 15%.

The income statement displayed, often called the Short Form, summarizes much detail. Revenue, being most important, is listed first. Cost of Goods Sold is second in importance, and the major deduction from Revenue. Other Operating Expenses is generally of least importance, and is the final deduction from Revenue.

Cost of Goods Sold is highlighted because it is made up of items that are closely associated with the generation of Revenue. Cost of Goods Sold are directly related to Revenue. For a manufacturing concern, typical items making up Cost of Goods Sold would include:

- Direct labor.
- Raw material and finished goods inventories.
- Direct equipment.

GROSS REVENUE	$100,000
LESS: COST OF GOODS SOLD	50,000
OPERATING INCOME	50,000
LESS: OTHER OPERATING EXPENSES	35,000
NET INCOME	$ 15,000

Figure 1-1. General profit formula.

Only labor, equipment, and inventories classified as *direct* can be included in Cost of Goods Sold. There are many types of labor, but only a few of them are direct. There are secretaries, managers, office workers, janitors, procurement specialists, accountants, and engineers. But only those people who work directly on or with the product or service can be considered direct. Somebody who assembles a part, or packs it into a box, or forklifts the container onto a truck can be considered direct. A secretary typing a memo or an accountant adjusting the books are not considered direct, because they have no physical contact with the company's goods or services.

The essence of Cost of Goods Sold, then, is that it represents expenses that are directly related to the creation of goods or services.

A characteristic of this value is that it tends to be variable. As production increases, Cost of Goods Sold also goes up. As production declines, Cost of Goods Sold goes down. The sincere hope of all managers is that production, and revenue, will increase at a faster rate than Cost of Goods Sold. Economies of Scale and the Learning Curve are two principles that take effect to lower the cost of production as volume increases. The production line becomes more efficient and people get better at their assigned tasks as they gain experience.

The second deduction from Revenue, often called Other Operating Expenses, is an accounting classification that includes all costs not directly related to the production function (note that we use the terms Expense and Cost interchangeably, although from a technical standpoint, expense is an expired cost). In well run companies, Other Operating Costs are much lower in total than Cost of Goods Sold. This is as it should be. Indirect costs should never be higher than direct costs.

Some examples of Other Operating Expenses are:

- Utility expenses not related to production.
- Insurance expense.
- Interest expense.
- Office facility expenses (rent, depreciation, etc.).
- Computers.

Computers are a very typical and representative member of Other Operating Expenses. All of these expenses tend to be fixed and not very dependent on the production rate.

The classic relationship between Other Operating Expenses and Revenue is shown in Figure 1-2. In this representation, Revenue grows over time, but the dollar value of Other Operating remains constant. Conversely, Cost of Goods Sold would tend to follow the Revenue curve. Because of these relationships, Cost of Goods Sold has come to be known as Direct Cost, while Other Operating is generally called Indirect Cost.

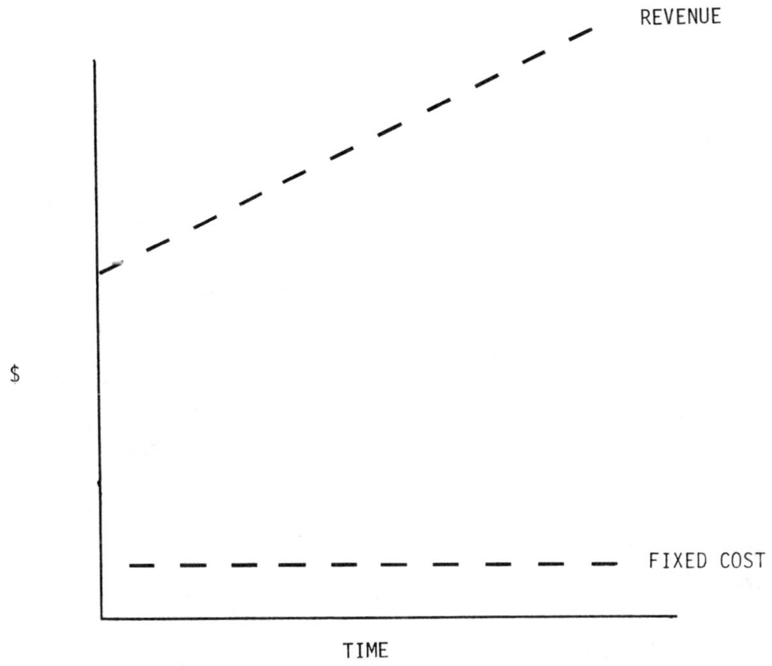

Figure 1-2. Revenue vs. Fixed Cost.

The curve in Figure 1-2 is theoretical, however, and represents an ideal situation. Figure 1-3 is more realistic. Here, Other Operating Expenses are fixed over a short period of time, but then increase in a stair-step fashion as more capacity is needed to support higher revenue levels. Obviously if revenue is headed down, appropriate reductions would also occur in Other Operating.

It is not the object of this book to dwell on all of the Other Operating Costs. We are primarily interested in one of its significant members, which is Computer Expense. Industry averages show that most companies spend at least 3% to 6% of gross revenue on computer and computer related expenses. This classifies Computing as a major component of Other Operating Expense, and as a major cost within most modern corporations.

In recent years computer costs have not acted as classic Other Operating, increasing and decreasing in stair-step fashion. Computers have become so ingrained and popular with most companies that expenditures have continually increased, regardless of revenue levels. Today, we often find a situation such as that shown in Figure 1-4. Here, revenue fluctuates erratically, with peaks and valleys. True direct costs fluctuate with revenue, as would most indirect costs. But computer expenditures simply increase, regardless of revenue level. In

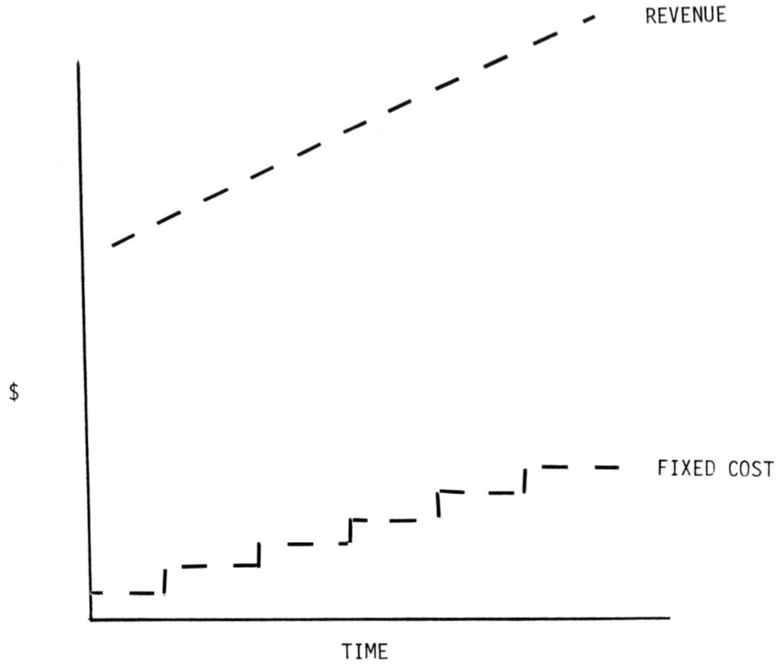

Figure 1-3. Revenue vs. Realistic Fixed Cost.

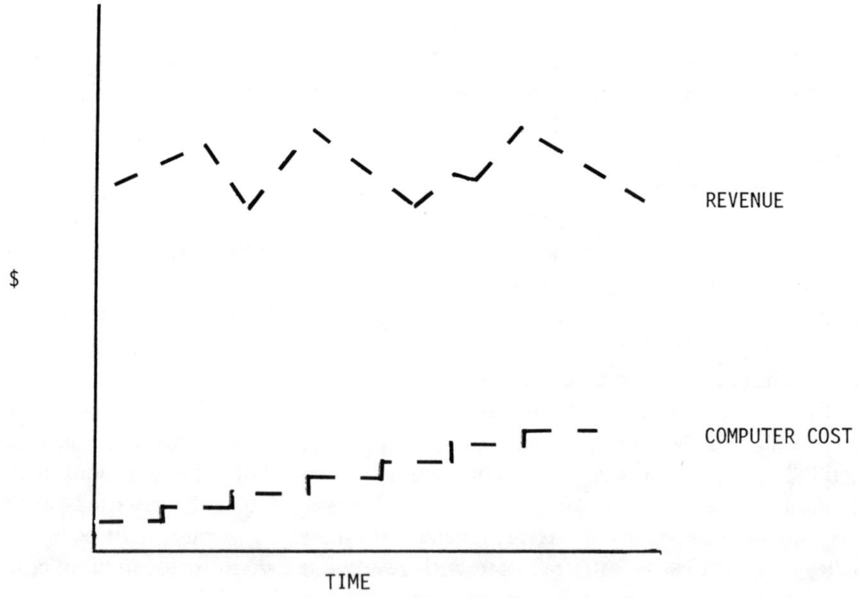

Figure 1-4. Realistic Revenue vs. Realistic Computer Cost.

certain cases, computer costs could be significant contributors to declines in net income, or even help cause losses.

It has always been easy to match labor cost with revenue levels. When sales are up, companies hire more people. When sales are down, workers are laid off. The same flexibility is not available with computers. Their presence is relatively fixed. Just because business is down, you don't simply pull the plug and toss out the computer. Instead, you work the computer at lower than optimum capacity.

CONTROL

Because functions within Other Operating Expenses are not directly related to production levels, they tend to be harder to control than direct functions. For example, what level of computer services is affordable at a given production rate?

Nobody really knows. While an engineer can quite accurately predict the number of labor hours necessary to fabricate a part, nobody can do much more than guess at how many computers are necessary to support a company's production activity. Industry averages don't mean anything.

We will try to answer this question in part seven. The answer depends on how thoroughly we understand the real costs behind computing.

Because of the indirect relationship between the category called Other Operating Expense and a company's total revenue, these indirect expenses have a tendency to easily get out of control. Costs such as travel, entertainment, seminars, and outside training are obvious candidates for abuse. Employees treat many of them as "perks." Companies therefore set up rules and regulations to force employees into following certain standards. For example, a firm may not allow entertainment reimbursement if company employees are the only people being entertained. There is no clear relationship between that kind of entertainment and increased revenue.

Other Operating Expenses must be controlled for one simple reason: There is no relationship between these expenses and the generation of profit. A certain level of these types of cost must be incurred to stay in business, but levels of expenditure must be kept to a minimum.

The best method of achieving control over Other Operating Expense is to use the techniques of cost accounting. Simply stated, cost accounting is a procedure that takes any identified expenditure and charges it back to the individual who authorized it. Using reports, this chargeback is made visible to various levels of management, also. Cost accounting data gives managers a chance to decide when expenses are too high, find the offending parties, and implement restraints. If somebody is spending too much money entertaining, for example, that expense will stand out as large when compared with entertainment expenses of other employees. The individual can then be told to cut back in his use of entertainment. Failure to do this could then lead to disciplinary management action.

Ultimately, control of Other Operating Expenses leads to the maximization of profit. The control is relegated to first line managers who are close to what is actually happening and can relate cost to benefit.

A well managed company is made up of cost controllers who make the small, relatively insignificant decisions that in total keep costs in line with revenue. When these managers do their jobs well, the company is profitable and successful. If they don't practice good cost control, the company risks failure.

COMPUTERS AND PROFITABILITY

As with all of the Other Operating Expenses, if there is a relationship between computers and profitability, it is unclear. This is true despite the fact that computers are tightly entwined within the workings of most major corporations.

It is reasonably safe to conclude that most companies could not exist today without computers. Data bases have proliferated and companies have learned to depend on them. For example, once a company goes on-line with any form of data, it has essentially eliminated the old way of doing things. A return to manual methods is unlikely without substantial disruption to operations.

But regardless of how important computers are to the company, they do not usually generate any form of revenue. In most cases, they generate information about the production process, or aid in the design of future products. Neither of these activities is directly related to producing the current line of products and services.

Centralized mainframes represent major company investments. Minicomputers, in total, are also significant in cost. When management made the original decision to invest in these items, it must have had some idea of future payoff. Or did management simply acquire computers because everybody else was getting them? Is there any relationship at all between computers and profits?

Unfortunately, there is no simple answer. When computers first became widely used, and for a number of years after that, it was quite fashionable to predict that they would significantly improve profits. The principal reason was thought to be that computerized systems could reduce labor requirements. This attitude, more than any actual layoffs, caused many labor unions in the early 1960s to express concern about automated data processing and its potential ability to eliminate jobs. In a very few cases this actually occurred. Linotype operators, for example, found their jobs ending as type could be set automatically by newspaper reporters sitting at city room desks and entering text into typesetting computers.

But in the vast majority of corporations, computers began producing large amounts of information without displacing anybody. And a whole new staff of programmers, operators, and keypunch clerks was created. The real benefit was that the corporation was provided with information that helped it operate more efficiently, or faster, or more accurately. But no money was saved.

Another way of looking at this issue is from a very broad perspective. According to Commerce Department figures, after-tax profits of all U.S. businesses grew from $100 billion in 1970 to $350 billion in 1980. These numbers are adjusted for the effects of inflation on plant assets and inventories.

This growth in profits comes to slightly over 12% per year, on a compounded annual basis.

During that same decade, dollar shipments of large computers has grown at a compounded rate of about 20% per year. And mini/micro computer shipments have grown in excess of 30% per year from mid decade on.

By the late 1960s computers were common in most corporations. The growth in computers has therefore been absorbed by companies that were already sophisticated in their use. It would therefore appear that business is acquiring computers at a rate which is faster than the growth in profits.

In an actual set of studies, the Diebold Group published statistics in 1971 that indicated that at 245 companies questioned, roughly 1% of revenue was devoted to computers. A decade later, that number had risen to between 3% and 6%. And these numbers are suspect because most companies don't know what their true computer costs are. Nontheless, the numbers show that business is acquiring computers at a faster rate than overall revenue is growing, and correlates with our previous observation concerning profits.

From these figures we can conclude two different things:

- The ten year growth in profitability was aided by the significant growth in data processing devices acquired. In other words, profit wouldn't have grown at 12% without the help of computers.
- Profits would have been even greater if data processing had not grown so fast.

These conclusions are exact opposites and illustrate the confusion over profitability. Computers may have helped profitability or they may have hindered it. Nobody really knows whether computers increase or decrease earnings, at least in the aggregate. A case may be built that shows how a particular computer acquisition will increase profitability. But justifications can be developed in which anything can look good. Our aggregate numbers can just as easily suggest that computers haven't helped profitability at all, since computer growth has been nearly double that of profit growth (20% or more per year for computers versus 12% per year for profits). Such a generalization may also be weak. The only thing we can be sure of is that there is no easily developed correlation between computers and profits.

As the Nolan study pointed out in the last chapter, more than three quarters of all companies have no clear understanding of what computers actually cost. Most computers are probably purchased on blind faith and trust, and a doctored up cost savings proposal provided by the computer vendor. Obviously the computer will save money and improve profitability, according to the vendor. But the financial proof he presents may be more like slick advertising than good accounting. Does anybody realistically expect a computer supplier to say his computer won't save money?

If, however, 6% or more of a company's total revenue must be allocated to computers, and that percentage appears to be growing, then the time is right for implementation of meaningful controls. This is what cost accounting can do.

Computers undoubtedly offer profound intangible benefits. But intangibles must be turned into real cost benefits. That is the first step in relating computers to profitability.

Whether or not a particular computer is acquired depends on the judgement of managers. The tools of accounting can be used to help management decide on the best course of action. Management may choose to disregard the numbers and acquire hardware based on some other factor, such as what the competition is doing. That is a risk management is paid to take. But no manager would be doing his job without looking at some form of financial analysis. Meaningful, believable numbers must be supplied to decision makers.

Chapter 1.4
The Challenge of Inexpensive Computers

Computer costs are declining while processor power is increasing. This trend has been observed for years. But the trend hasn't really helped most companies that have already made major commitments to computers. For them, about all we can say is that computer power is increasing faster than computer costs. Computers costs seem to continuously increase, year after year. Companies have an insatiable need for more processing capability. The observation that these computers are fully used is interesting, but of no help to the corporate controller who is strapped for cash or suffering through a short-term sales decline. Every dollar that goes into computers is a dollar that won't go into improving the production line, or beefing up the sales force, or many other worthy causes.

It is remarkable that the U.S. has been able to absorb as much computer capability and power as it has.

- The Univac I performed 2000 instructions per second, stored 12,000 digits and cost $750,000. The Intel 8080 introduced 21 years later performed 200,000 instructions per second, stored 64,000 digits, and cost $175 in 1953 dollars.
- In 1965, $20,000 bought two thousand bytes of main memory. Now, it buys several million bytes of memory, and the dollars are worth less than half of their 1965 value.
- Since 1960, costs of the CPU have been decreasing by an order of 100 every 10 years.
- Ahmdahl Corporation says that by the late 1980s, average computers will execute well in excess of 30 million instructions per second, which is a tripling of speed in less than 10 years.
- Breakthroughs in computer architecture allowed IBM to announce in formal presentations that in 1980 as many MIPS (Millions of Instructions per Second) had been put on the market as in the prior 30 years, and that the number was doubling at least every two years from that point on.

All of this increased power and speed is being absorbed by *average* users, not be nuclear scientists or weather prognosticators. The payroll programs, and inventory programs, and parts tracking systems are being updated and brought online and using up all of this enhanced computer power.

But as computers have been getting larger and more powerful they have also been getting smaller. Reduction in component size created the minicomputer. Inexpensiveness of the components made these small computers relatively cheap.

Many people prefer compact, portable computers that they can control at the local level. These machines are much lower in price than large mainframes, yet they retain significant processing capabilities.

Because of their small size, minicomputers are hard to control. Their low unit value means that they can be acquired with little or no managerial approval. But their costs can grow quickly as various special interest groups acquire them. And they have the following unique problems:

- There are hidden costs associated with all minicomputers. A major portion of this book is devoted to systematically uncovering these costs.
- When minicomputers are strung together using telecommunications networks, the total costs can equal or exceed the costs of a large centralized processor. Yet the network of minis may have far less capability.
- All computer technology is volatile. But minicomputer changes are very frequent because of the keen competition between manufacturers. Hardware can literally become obsolete overnight. This can lead to a constant replacement and upgrading of equipment.
- Computing and the use of computers is attractive to many people. The easy availability of minicomputers can lead to a significant danger from computer hobbyists, who are out to build their own private computer centers at the expense of the corporation. These people may do good things, but what happens when they leave? Will others continue the operation with equal enthusiasm? Or will the operation tend to fall apart?
- There is always the danger that a company can become overcomputerized with small machines that were purchased with little justification and no central planning.

Minicomputers look deceptively simple. What looks simple is often complex, and this can be the case with these small machines. Users looking for a quick, easy solution can find themselves with hardware that is constantly changing and ever more expensive to acquire. Minicomputers offer people the chance to get in over their heads. They can create a system that grows beyond their limited ability to control.

Small computers therefore ultimately qualify for the same kind of accounting controls that are used for large machines. Small size and apparent inexpensiveness are misleading.

Because minicomputer hardware is relatively inexpensive, accounting must also be inexpensive. Additionally, accounting for small computers must be:

- Easy to administer.
- Understandable.
- Reasonably equitable.

Cost accounting must be used to meet the challenge of proliferating small computers. The accounting approach can be simple and direct, but also effective.

The goal, of course, is to keep minicomputers from building in numbers to the point where they seriously endanger profitability. When the cost damage is obvious, then things have gone too far. Cost accounting must be used as an early warning system that indicates when there are too many minicomputers.

Chapter 1.5
What is Computer Cost Accounting?

In a future section, cost accounting concepts will be discussed in detail. It will be shown that cost accounting makes a very good fit with the operation of computers and computer centers. But it will be useful at this point to review some of the principles of accounting to develop a preliminary understanding of this unique and valuable field.

From an accounting standpoint, we must do two things to any computer operation before we can honestly conclude that we have developed financial control. First, we must determine the total value of the installation. This is not an easy task because so many values tend to be hidden within the larger accounting system of the parent company. These costs must be segregated into meaningful categories, often called *accounts* and *pools.* This activity is called *general accounting.* Second, we must devise a method of charging the collected value back to users who receive benefit from the computer. This is called *cost accounting.*

GENERAL ACCOUNTING

All computers, regardless of their size, are configured somewhat similarly. The basic hardware usually consists of a CPU and memory, mass storage devices, input and output devices, and communications links. The computer consumes various types of supplies, such as magnetic media and paper. The computer must be programmed and operated by people, and the entire facility must be managed. Also, the computer uses various occupancy type items such as electricity, heating and cooling, and facility modifications to securely enclose and protect it. These cost characteristics are true for all machines, from the smallest minicomputer to the largest mainframe supercomputer.

These various computer related expenses come from three different sources:

- Costs based on invoices that are paid directly to various suppliers (or depreciation expense on purchased items).
- Labor payrolls, which include fringe benefits.

- Various allocations representing bills paid by the parent company and allocated back to the computer operation.

All of these costs are segregated into special categories that are called *accounts.* This account accumulation is a natural byproduct of the accounting system that already exists in all companies. One account may be used for hardware rent. Another account might represent operator labor. A third might be made up of allocated charges such as electricity expense.

Accounts serve two purposes. They collect costs into meaningful categories that can be controlled. And they provide an audit trail, so that expenditures can be traced back to the entity that caused the expense, such as an individual computer installation.

In theory, the use of an intricate structure of accounts is an excellent way of tracking and controlling costs. But most computer installations make very poor usage of this accounting data. The irony is that it is so easy to obtain and use accounting data in virtually every company in the country. The accounting profession has seen to that. A self-imposed, standardized accounting structure is used by all members of the accounting profession.

Pulling together all computer related costs is not a hard task, but it requires time and a cooperative parent company accounting department.

In a later section we will discuss how to approach the accounting department, and what to ask of it. The result will be the collection and reporting of all costs associated with a computer operation.

COST ACCOUNTING

When considering whether or not to adopt accounting, the size of the computer installation is not material. Costs can be collected for a large centralized computer operation, or a small desk-sized minicomputer.

Each operating entity is called a *responsibility center.* These are the fundamental building blocks of cost accounting.

Responsibility centers represent a controllable activity, such as an independent computer operation. Costs, by account, are charged to the responsibility center. Those who use the services provided by the responsibility center are charged, using cost rates. If everything works correctly, total costs coming into the responsibility center equal total costs being charged out to users.

Developing a chargeout method has aspects of a pricing activity. The computers and related items within the responsibility center must be analyzed to determine an effective chargeback method. This usually consists of some form of utilization, such as hours, transactions, or units.

When total responsibility center costs are divided by total utilization, a rate is developed. This rate represents the cost of doing business with the responsibility center. It is similar to the prices we see all around us for products in the marketplace.

As each user comes in to process on the computer, he is charged for the service. This is accomplished by measuring the amount of work he does, developing some form of utilization, and multiplying by a cost rate. The product becomes the cost of processing. This processing cost works its way into the parent company's accounting system. The parent is then in a position to track and analyze computer expenditures. Budgets can be established for each user.

The basic cost accounting process is outlined in Figure 1-5. Conceptually, this illustration shows that cost accounting is a very simple process. Like so many technical areas, cost accounting can be developed into complex and convoluted schemes. But in this book we will consistently strive for simplicity.

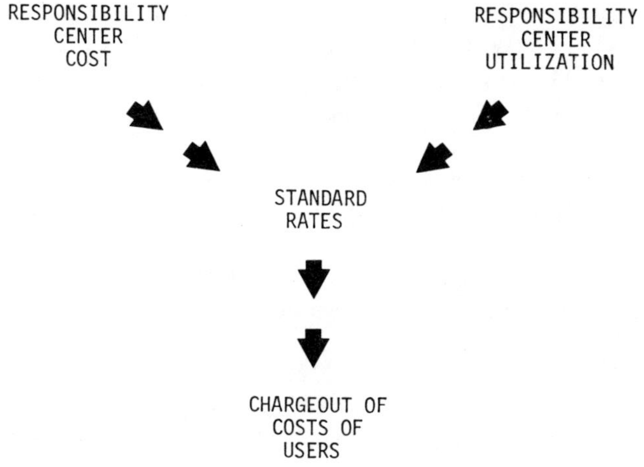

Figure 1-5. Cost accounting structure.

Goals for Cost Accounting

Cost accounting, when it is practiced, is often criticized by those who are affected by it. A common complaint is that all of this paper manipulation is like dealing with "funny money." Since there are no real dollars involved, people find it hard to relate to the numbers they see. Not helping the situation is the common problem of abstract and poorly thought out accounting methods. Complex accounting is worse than no accounting at all.

But behind the basic concepts of cost accounting are some very important potential achievements:

- By going through the entire process of collecting costs, building rates, and charging back for services, the responsibility center learns a great deal about what its costs are and where they come from.
- Cost accounting forces users to pay for the services they require, which means that they must place a value on what they get.
- Cost accounting provides the tools for sophisticated financial planning and control.

Cost accounting provides the quantitative values asked for by Lord Kelvin in the opening chapter of this section. If we follow his logic, and carefully account for computers, we will at last reach an understanding of what they are and how much they help us.

Part II
Modes of Computing

Chapter 2.1
Introduction

Once, explaining the general components of a computer and how each of them operated took little effort. There was only one basic mode of computing. It was called centralized processing. It consisted of physically large central units, called mainframes or CPUs, surrounded by banks of tape and disk units, printers, and card handling equipment. Operators sat at large consoles, monitoring arrays of blinking lights. Others loaded decks of cards into readers or reels of tape onto drives. Still others separated and delivered individual reports as they came off printers.

These fundamentals of centralized computing haven't changed much since the mid 1960s, when IBM brought out the System 360. That model line introduced the concept of multiprogramming, which allowed for a much fuller utilization of CPU, memory, and peripherals.

Changes to the 360 type of architecture have been more evolutionary than revolutionary. Equipment has become faster and more flexible. Software has become more friendly to the user. But the facilities available and the way in which they interact with each other have not changed very much over the years.

Centralized computing is still a viable, healthy method of computing. Nearly all large and medium sized companies in the country have one or more central processing centers. In the early days, they were proudly arrayed behind large glass windows, were spectators could watch operator activity. Now, computers are generally encased behind thick walls. Security problems have forced companies to seal off their processors. This is because most corporations could literally be shut down if substantial damage occurred to their computers. And computers are not very interesting to look at anymore, anyway. Most functions have been internalized within electronic circuitry and taken away from human operators. There is simply no thrill in watching a metal box sit there and hum.

Centralized computing operations offer a variety of services. In most cases, they attempt to be all things to all people. They offer timesharing to small, remote users who use low speed terminals. They offer real-time graphics capabilities to those using CRT screens. And they offer conventional batch or on-line processing against huge data bases. These systems handle everything from a small FORTRAN compile step consuming a fraction of one processor second, up to large payroll·programs processing tens of thousands of checks and consuming hours of processing time.

To effectively handle trivial and complex processing jobs at the same time required computers with substantial flexibility. This flexibility first appeared with the introduction of the transistor which reduced complex computers down to sizes that were reasonable and manageable. By the mid 1960s most computers were built entirely with transistors. Main memory was composed of metallic rings called core. Because core was wired by hand, it was extremely expensive, and tended to limit the size of machines.

Transistors evolved into integrated circuits, often called silicon chips, which began with a density of about 4000 circuits per chip, and have doubled in capacity about every two or three years. Processing logic, arithmetic functions, and memory could be placed onto these chips. The chips were easily mass produced and could be turned out for pennies per unit. Thus began what may be the only true revolution in computers since 1950. These chips gave large computers the capacity and capability to support all classes of users, regardless of their size, for an ever decreasing cost. An added bonus was that the chips significantly increased reliability.

While chips enhanced the capabilities of central hardware, they also spawned minicomputers. Although small computers had been around for many years, they did not become truly accepted until semiconductor technology was incorporated into their processing units. This allowed sizable amounts of computing power to be packaged into tiny boxes. It is ironic that just as significant increases in central computer power and flexibility were achieved, a potential rival, in the form of minicomputers, was created.

The minicomputer is a true computer, and can be configured identically to larger centralized processors. Minicomputers can take on many other forms, too, which opens up the possibility of distinctly new modes of computing.

The dollar value of a complete, full function minicomputer is obviously much lower than the cost of a large, centralized processor. But growth trends indicate that by the end of the 1980s, the dollar value of minicomputer shipments will probably exceed the value of large computer deliveries. Minicomputers are on a growth curve while central processors appear to be maturing, thus installation of new equipment is slowing.

Many employees within modern corporations have done considerable experimenting with minicomputers. This is probably because the basic machines are relatively inexpensive and easily obtainable. The problem is, of course, that most companies don't realize the extent to which minicomputers have been adopted within their facilities. Employees who want these small machines will generally find a way to get them.

As small computers have become more common, it is now clear that computing is heading in four basic directions:

- Large, centralized mainframes
- Decentralized minicomputers that can be considered standalone
- Distributed minicomputers
- Turnkey systems

Each of these categories has its own unique characteristics and each will require a specially tailored accounting approach. Because of that, the next several chapters will discuss, in general terms, the makeup of each of these computer categories. The discussion will be limited to technology. Accounting approaches will be developed in later sections.

Chapter 2.2
Centralized Computing

Centralized computing started the computer revolution. It has been the predominant form of data processing since the early 1950s. Most large companies employ this form of computing, and have become highly dependent upon it. Whether or not it will remain as the premier form of computing is a subject of much debate among practitioners. Depending on where your vested interests lie, it will either continue to flourish for many years, or its days are numbered because it will become a victim of its own size. As in most situations, the truth is probably somewhere in between the two extremes.

Centralized processor installations may not grow as fast as they did in the 1960s and 1970s because so many alternative forms of computing are available. But centralized machines will continue to play an important role in the processing needs of most corporations. Too much momentum has been established by the centralized approach, and it is unlikely that replacements will be found for many years into the future, if ever.

The basic concept of central operating systems supported by various peripherals has not changed much since the inception of IBM's third generation of computers introduced around 1965. Improvements since then have amounted to refinements of operating system software, higher speeds produced by semiconductor technology, and faster peripherals. Reliability has also improved significantly.

The earliest type of central machine consisted of a large operating system that supported a batch stream of jobs handled in a serial manner, one at a time. Third generation improvements introduced multiprocessing. Jobs were scheduled in such a way that maximum usage of the peripherals and CPU were achieved. While one job was transferring data from disk to memory, another job could actually be processing within the CPU. In this way, slower peripherals did not degrade the performance of the CPU. Timesharing was then introduced so that direct interaction with the CPU could be offered to individual programmers, and, later general users. Data base software then became available. Large files of data could be stored, manipulated, or queried in an on-line or off-line mode.

It has been a characteristic of centralized processing that over the years more and more on-line interaction has been offered to both programmers and application users. Direct human to computer interaction has become desirable as an aid to productivity improvement.

THE ENVIRONMENT

Centralized processing began with an active machine room. This was particularly true in the earliest days of computing when the operating of a computer was very informal. But even with second generation gear the machine room continued as a beehive of human activity, with operators and programmers hovering around the equipment. Jobs started as decks of cards that were loaded through card readers into a job queue. Special magnetic tapes had to be mounted with additional job instructions and data bases. Final reports were printed at a local printer, and output cards were punched. The whole process was quite labor intensive. This was primarily because data was stored off-line, either as decks of cards or as reels of magnetic tape.

These input/output oriented operations no longer exist. The typical centralized operation is displayed in Figure 2-1. A central host, which can consist of one or more CPUs, along with some tape drives and printers, and many disk drives, is attached by telecommunications lines to a wide variety of interactive devices.

These connected devices break down into two basic categories: Remote Job Entry Stations and Interactive Terminals.

Remote Job Entry Stations (RJEs), continue the classic batch processing functions, but place the labor intensive operations at the remote site. They generally consist of a card reader/punch, high speed printer, and a small CPU. The primary function of the RJE is to access the resources of the large computer where the actual processing is accomplished, and then provide print capability for output. Data files are stored on tape or disk at the central site. Job functions, such as initiation and termination, are the responsibility of the remote user. The central site merely insures that a computer is operating and available, and mounts magnetic tape and setup disk when needed. Since most data is usually stored on nondismountable disk, little operator intervention is really necessary.

Interactive terminals, which make up the other principal form of computer access, have expanded into a wide array of services in recent years. The first interactive terminal was little more than an electric typewriter with communications capability. CRTs were then developed and have led to various graphic devices. And terminals have been given intelligence, which allows some processing functions to be performed directly at the terminal. Interactive terminals require very little operator support from the center. The terminal primarily makes use

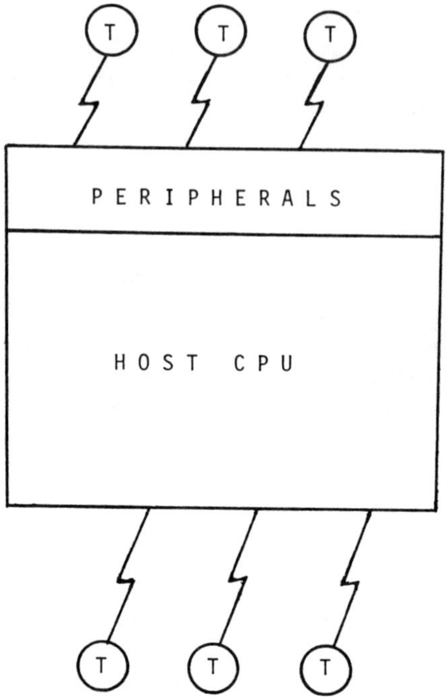

Figure 2-1. Typical RJE to host configuration.

of the CPU, memory, and disk storage. Printing is handled remotely, at the terminal site.

As the trend has been to on-line interaction between user and computer, it has caused the computer room to become rather passive, from a labor standpoint. Many computers can be run by just a few operators. The operator's primary function is to intervene when trouble occurs, such as when hardware fails. Other than outages, the machines basically take care of themselves.

MULTIPLE TASKS

The multitasking abilities developed for computers allowed a wide array of services to be offered. Timesharing, for example, could be intermixed with conventional batch processing. This flexibility required huge amounts of central memory. Semiconductor technology made memory cheap and plentiful. Memory contention was a real problem in the early 1970s. Memory is no longer considered a constraint to the processing of jobs.

With the growth of timesharing and data base systems, the computer bottleneck has become disk storage. Most modern operations have more difficulty controlling the use and growth of disks than of any other resource. Everybody wants on-line data. These days, machine room expansion is caused by the need for additional disk units. Memory and CPU have actually gotten smaller over the years.

The large physical space required by central computer systems is often used as a criticism. When one CPU fails, it blocks access to many large data bases. Such drastic blockouts can cause serious hardships to many companies. Critics therefore contend that huge multitasking systems are simply trying to do too much for too many people. It becomes very hard to achieve optimization because so many things seem to go wrong. Nobody is able to get completely satisfactory data processing service.

JUSTIFICATION

The principal justification of centralized processing has always been *economy of scale.* This concept, which has developed over the years, states that for every additional dollar of processor that is purchased, a two dollar increase in productivity will occur. Stated another way as Grosch's law: "A one percent increase in computer rent is associated with a 2% increase in computer power."

The concept of economy of scale was used for many years to justify larger and larger central computer facilities. But economy of scale has been attacked in recent years, particularly by proponents of minicomputers and small, decentralized systems. Their reasoning is that centralized computers reach a point where they become too big and too unmanageable. CPU power is drained off by overhead and software housekeeping functions necessary to schedule, load, and execute each job. At some point, the amount of work per additional dollar of equipment actually declines. The computer system becomes so large and unmanageable that it begins to literally trip over itself.

While there have been formally stated proofs of concepts such as Grosch's law, the converse attitude is more of a feeling than a quantified argument. People "think" that a computer system is too large. They "sense" that uptime, even at 96% or 97%, is not good enough. Because computers are not capable of remaining operational 100% of the time, they are not satisfactory tools.

Those who feel that large computers are past their prime are speculating. We need more research in this area before any kind of conclusion can be reached.

Aside from economy of scale, points in favor of centralized processing are:

- Centralization reduces the duplication of storage.
- Centralized machines have a diverse user population, which leads to full use of all resources.

- Centralized machines are efficiently operated and maintained through the use of highly trained operators and systems technicians.
- Centralized computers offer a wide variety of software services and special functions.
- Vendor support of central computers is excellent.

Probably the most distinctive aspect of a centralized computer operation is the professionalism of its operators and management. Keeping a large computer running requires a constant stream of supplies, a well organized library of tapes and disk packs, and an organized method of delivering output. Data communications expertise is needed to connect interactive terminals with the mainframe. Contingency plans are used when equipment fails, so that computer power is available to users for long, uninterrupted periods of time. People have to be organized to perform all of these tasks, and that organization is just as important as the hardware.

TYPICAL CONFIGURATIONS

Very few machine rooms operate with only one CPU. Two or more processors are generally latched together using high speed channels. One master CPU acts as a scheduler and controls all other processors. A certain amount of redundancy backup is obtained by such an arrangement. The functions on a disabled machine can be rolled over to another processor in emergency situations. If this processor sharing is highly developed and planned by the computer center, then a high standard of computer operations can be met. If the planning is poor or if adequate computer power is unavailable, then downtime will inevitably result.

Downtime is probably the single biggest criticism of central computer operations. When one large CPU goes down and cannot be backed up, hundreds or even thousands of users are left stranded. This is usually a very serious situation. Yet it is becoming less and less tolerable as computer dependency grows.

When there are multiple CPUs, they usually share common banks of disk drives, tape units, and printers. Figure 2-2 shows the basic concept, with common peripherals feeding into a high speed bus which is attached to three CPUs. In this way data bases can be accessed from any CPU.

These sophisticated computer arrangements require sophisticated support organizations. Hardware is no longer operated as it was in the early days of computing. Back then, operators often participated actively in the execution of various jobs by monitoring the work as it progressed through the system and performing various control and check functions. As job failures occurred, operators would attempt to restart or rerun. If the system was big enough, a programmer was often called in to make quick fixes so that processing could continue.

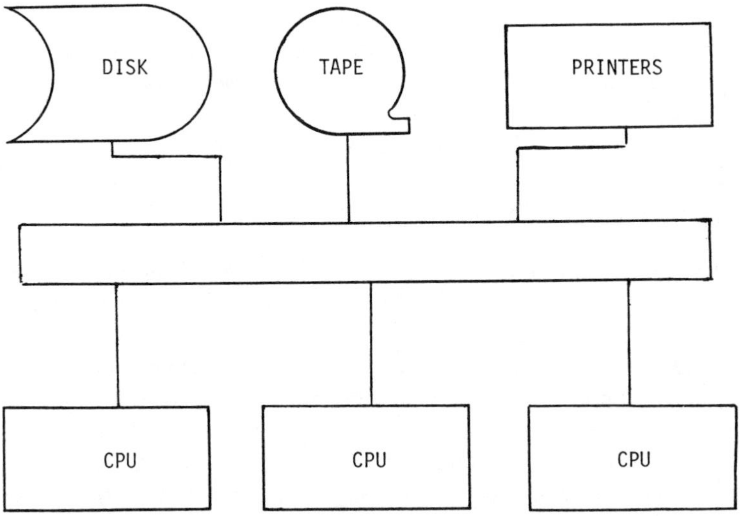

Figure 2-2. Multiple CPU Configuration.

Modern hardware processes all jobs automatically, with no operator assistance. Tape and disk mounts are called for by the system over terminals, and operators need only acquire the specified tape or disk and mount it on the appropriate device. Other than that, operator intervention is unnecesary.

Centralized operations maintain large tape libraries because many programs are still tape oriented. Although there are many different ways to store data, the dependability of tape is still very attractive. Tape is the least expensive storage medium available, even when the costs of the physical space are included. As an archive storage device, when data must be safely stored for long periods of time, tape has no equal. Mechanical mass storage units are available. They use small tape cartridges housed in honeycombed machines. As thier reliability improves, they may eventually replace reels of tape. Mass storage's biggest benefit is that it eliminates human operators.

Large computers perform efficiently only when the environment is carefully controlled. This requires special air conditioning and, in some cases, chilled water supplies for internal cooling. Electrical power must be conditioned, often with motor generators, and sometimes must be backed up with batteries. The walls, ceilings, and floors surrounding the hardware must be strengthened for security purposes. This means that the facility costs associated with centralized processing are significant. Computer rooms are the modern equivalent of well protected fortresses.

Such a large investment in hardware, facilities, and labor necessitates a three shift operation to improve investment payback. This is not very hard to achieve, however, since most installations have evolved a two-tier level of support. The fisrt shift is dedicated to interactive processing that occurs during the normal workday. The second and third shifts handle data base updating, batch processing backup activity, and various program maintenance activities. Systems programmers also do much of their work at night.

INVESTMENT

Centralized processing organizations have developed over many years. It is doubtful that anyone knew how large most computer centers would eventually become.

The investment in computers made by most companies occured in a haphazard way, generally following the direction dictated by major hardware suppliers. Most companies cannot say that there was very much sophisticated planning that went into the long term growth of centralized computing. Users simply wanted more and more computing power, and DP facilities grew to meet those demands.

From today's perspective, was the investment in large-scale computing worth it? Minicomputer proponents would probably argue that much of the money was wasted on experimentation and poorly thought out hardware configuring. Central processing advocates would generally conclude that every penny spent on computers was worthwhile.

But past costs are water over the dam. Today, the costs of a centralized facility are visible and certainly significant. Whether or not these costs are excessive depends on what alternative modes of computing cost in comparison.

Chapter 2.3
Decentralized Computing

INTRODUCTION

People tend to use the terms decentralized and distributed interchangeably. Although this may be acceptable practice for an advertising copywriter trying to sell hardware, the differences between the two modes of computing are significant. These differences add variety to the task of cost accounting, as we shall see in a later chapter.

A decentralized computer is a miniaturization of the mainframe type of operation discussed in the last chapter. A decentral system consists of a minicomputer and related peripherals that are placed in the user's area. No attempt is made to communicate with central mainframes or with other minicomputers.

The decentral minicomputer is configured to support a known group of users. Following the same trends observed in centralized computing, most of these users will process interactively with the mainframe. Because the nature of the workload and its volume are known, the computer can be configured quite precisely.

Decentral operations take two basic forms:

- Generalized systems supporting one large application or several small, unrelated users.
- Turnkey systems that support one common application and many users.

Decentralized computing has become quite popular since the development of powerful minicomputers. Decentral systems offer a true alternative to shared mainframe. The user can run his application on a dedicated system and avoid many of the problems associated with large central systems. He has complete control over his environment and destiny. If there are problems, they are of his own making, and not something created by a distant, faceless central machine room. Self-created problems are always easier to accept.

Advantages of decentralized systems are:

- Computing is placed at the data source.
- Sophisticated communications systems are eliminated.
- The user only pays for the hardware and software that he needs.
- Control is personalized.
- Hardware is relatively inexpensive.

PROCESSOR SIZE

Decentralized processors come in many sizes, extending from relatively large machines that approach the power of low-end central mainframes, down to microcomputers capable of performing limited tasks. We will limit our discussion of minicomputers to a few basic types of machines because the variations are nearly endless. The two basic classes of decentralized computers that will be considered are:

- Relatively large machines powerful enough to support multiple users through timesharing access.
- Dedicated turnkey systems performing a single task for multiple users through timesharing. The basic CPU is of medium to large capability.

By choice we have dropped from consideration microcomputers and very small processors of the home or hobbyist variety. Companies may acquire both of these small types of hardware, but their value is relatively trivial and generally not worth sophisticated accounting effort.

Figure 2-3 shows a representative minicomputer configuration that could be considered general in nature. The minicomputer is relatively large, supporting 10 terminals and two printers. The terminals are divided between two different applications that have nothing in common with each other. The mini itself has dedicated disk storage, which may be a combination of floppy diskettes and rotational packs. When applications are large, disk packs are more practical than floppies.

The configuration in Figure 2-3 closely resembles a typical centralized operation. The mini has been configured to support general applications. Many of the support functions, operating procedures, and facility arrangements will be similar, although on a smaller scale, with those of the central operation. The minicomputer may even require full-time operators and administrators.

Once a minicomputer operation is established, it is common for application usage to grow until the natural limits of the system are reached. This phenomenon is no different than on large computers. Good computer response times en-

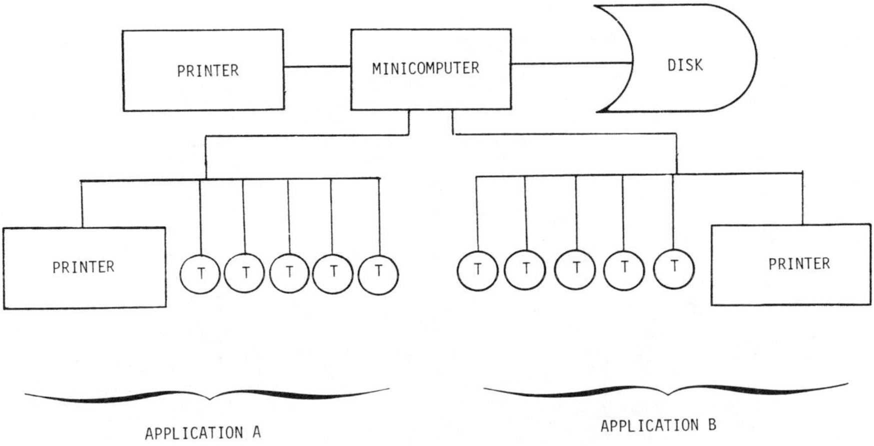

Figure 2-3. General minicomputer configuration.

courage users to seek more and more computerization. Since minicomputers are small to begin with, hardware limits can be reached quickly. This growth is often encouraged by those who have responsibility for the computer operation. Large, busy computers mean more importance and, perhaps, a promotion or two for those who control the minicomputer. Running a large computer operation can be fun too.

This kind of growth is haphazard and poorly thought out. It is not necessarily in the best interest of any company to allow minicomputers to grow in an unrestrained manner. What gets put on those computers may be poorly designed and documented. Data is certainly isolated on a decentralized system and difficult to blend into other programs elsewhere in the company. This data lockup can lead to duplication when several different minicomputer systems need the same source data.

Figure 2-4 represents a second, and quite different, form of decentralized computing. It is sometimes called turnkey. Such a computer system is a hardware/software combination packaged and delivered by a single outside contractor.

Turnkey systems have one outstanding characteristic. That is, the user population is very homogeneous. All users have the same data processing needs.

A common set of software is provided. All users seek essentially the same types of solutions. If, for example, the turnkey package performs graphic mechanical engineering functions, then the users will tend to be mechanical engineers attempting to design parts. Or, if the system performs clerical activities such as text editing, then users will primarily be secretaries performing word processing activities, such as typing memos and reports.

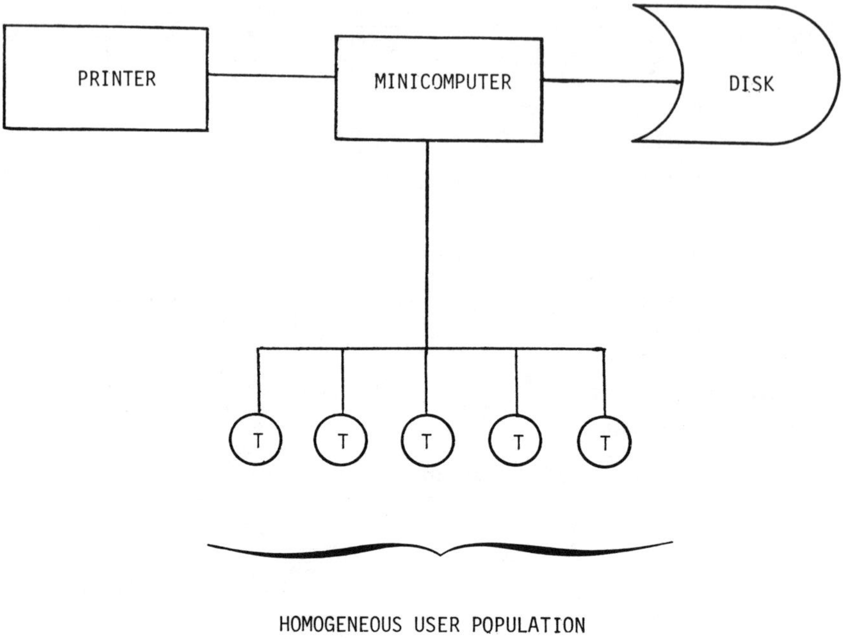

Figure 2-4. Turnkey/office automation configuration.

Turnkey systems are not generally multipurpose. The hardware is closely sized to the needs of the software. There is normally a finite limit to the number of active concurrent users.

Because turnkey systems are so specialized, there is no need for an operations staff. The hardware is usually packaged so that very little environmental change is necessary. There are limits to how much work the computer can handle, and when those limits are reached, another complete system must be obtained.

Turnkey systems are not as likely to be abused as the general purpose minicomputer. While the general machine can grow into a sophisticated operation, turnkey systems tend to be used as tools. They are obtained to solve a specific problem, and little or no future growth will occur.

ENVIRONMENTAL CONSIDERATIONS

New forms of computing, such as minicomputers, occur because people want them. Conditions must be right before individuals will make the extra effort to acquire new computers, and take on the responsibility for operating and maintaining them. Minicomputers were available for many years before they became truly popular. Their time came when prices were competitive and when frustration with the centralized approach rose to an intolerable level.

This condition is somewhat similar to the choice between mass transit systems and the personal automobile. Using mass transit is certainly simple. Somebody else acquires the vehicles, maintains them, hires operators, and establishes routes. All the patron needs is enough money for the fare. The automobile is not quite so simple. The user must assemble a large amount of his own capital for the purchase, or be willing to take on a great deal of debt. He must acquire insurance. He is responsible for periodic maintenance and must purchase fuel. And he has to operate the vehicle himself, and be willing to accept a considerable amount of risk that an accident can occur.

If a visitor from a foreign country where advanced transportation did not exist was presented with these two alternative modes of travel and told the requirements for both, he would probably conclude that mass transportation would be the choice of most people, because of its relative simplicity and lack of commitment from the user. As we know, he would be very wrong. Because conditions were right in this country, the majority of people chose the automobile as their transportation preference. The committment in terms of human resources and capital has been enormous. Yet, right or wrong, the automobile is an irreplaceable part of our society.

The current computer environment is one of similar change, as many people switch from centralized computing to minicomputers. Examining some of the characteristics of this environment will help in understanding just how considerable this change is.

General Purpose Minicomputers

General purpose minicomputers come closest to directly replacing centralized computers. An application that runs well on a central machine can usually run just as effectively on a general minicomputer.

The creation of generalized minicomputer systems is not an easy task. People must be highly committed and motivated to make this kind of system work.

Operating and supporting a minicomputer can be complex. Trained operators must be designated. They may be casual or full-time, but they must be thoroughly familiar with the intricacies of starting, running, and stopping a complex collection of hardware and software. Somebody must also take the time to coordinate maintenance support, order supplies, clean disk packs, develop terminal communications interfaces, and mediate when various vendors begin bickering over who was at fault in causing the inevitable failures. And somebody must be concerned about the future. Utilization will eventually grow beyond the capacity of current mainframes, thus requiring upgrades or replacement.

Selling the system to potential users is another important activity. Users don't grow on trees. They must be convinced by somebody that using the minicomputer will effectively solve their problems. And these users must be soothed over the inevitable downtime incidents.

A successful minicomputer operation needs an advocate. We often find that a small, hard core group of advocates are basically behind most generalized decentral operations. These people are organized in such a way that they have a clearcut goal and are willing to invest time and resources into making a small computer operation work. They often start with one specific application, and bring more applications up as users are sold on the benefits of decentralization.

Minicomputer advocates can be a valuable hidden asset to companies because their motivation and productivity are high. But they can become a liability if they pursue the acquisition of unnecessary or redundant computers. The single most important problem associated with highly motivated computer advocates is termination. When these individuals leave, there is seldom a replacement with the same amount of enthusiasm. The computer center can then turn into a shambles of poor support and sloppy operation.

Turnkey Systems

Turnkey computers are usually installed because a very specific problem needs resolution. Existing computer facilities cannot or will not supply the necessary computing capabilities. Turnkey systems often represent computerization of applications never before touched by computers.

Characteristics that attract the turnkey user are:

- Rather than develop complex software, the user can buy off-the-shelf programs and hardware at a fraction of the price that development would take.
- Users need not be sophisticated in the usage of computers, since most of these systems have been designed to appeal to first time users.
- Staff requirements are usually minimal, because the software/hardware combination is performing one basic task, and this simplicity is quite easy to manage.
- Vendors usually supply software updates and correct problems that users uncover, which relieves the user from systems programming type activity.
- Mature software vendors will often handle hardware maintenance also, giving the user a single source for problem resolution.

Whether or not turnkey systems are successful depends on how carefully they were chosen and how closely they coincide with the solution requirements of the user population.

Well chosen turnkey systems are a very effective way to quickly computerize a solution. Upon delivery, users can literally be producing productive work within days.

But if the system is carelessly chosen and does not meet user requirements, it is as useless as no solution at all.

Chapter 2.4
Distributed Computing

Distributed computing has two basic characteristics:

- Multiple minicomputers are interconnected using telecommunications lines.
- Some form of control software allows each computer to effectively intercommunicate with all other computers in the network.

Each minicomputer that performs a function within the telecommunications network is called a *node.* The term node has a very specific meaning. Each node is remotely located, like a terminal. But, unlike terminals, each node has sufficient hardware to give it standalone processing capability. Node hardware can perform processing for local users, can share in processing needs within the network, and can transmit data to other nodes when needed. Nodes are powerful minicomputers, but are subservient to the larger network of nodes. Depending on the network design, each node can be equal in responsibility to all other nodes, or some nodes can be more important than other nodes.

Telecommunications is vital to distributed computing. Because there is so much communicating between nodes, a high degree of standardization is necessary. The computer hardware generally must be of the same brand and must conform to tight specifications set up by network designers.

COMMUNICATIONS REQUIREMENTS

The basic architecture of computing is fairly well understood by most people. Minicomputer components are similar in function to those of large computers. Only size, capacity, and speed are different.

Within a distributed computing network, individual nodes are expected to process like conventional computers. This may amount to data collection, interactive query support, or batch processing. The node performs as a typical computer for local users.

Where distributed computing departs from conventional processing is in its use of telecommunications. Distributed nodes are expected to intercommunicate heavily, either by sharing data or by participating in network wide data processing.

This computer to computer interaction is carried out using a set of *communications protocols.* There are numerous levels of protocols, and they perform functions such as:

- Carrying out internode message switching.
- Providing a means for retransmission if a message is not acknowledged by the potential receiver.
- Providing for a specific data format with recognizable characteristics. In this way, large volumes of unrelated messages can be efficiently transmitted over a single data line, then stripped out and sent to various destination nodes.
- Providing for error detection and correction techniques.

Protocols are essentially rules that help control the transmission of data. There are many levels of protocols. Some are offered by minicomputer vendors as proprietary software. Every major minicomputer manufacturer has come out with operating system options that perform certain distributed functions. The word "net" is often attached to the manufacturer's name to signify network protocol software.

Other aspects of distribution, such as sending and receiving large packets of data, are handled by common carriers, like AT&T, Telenet, and Tymenet. Common carrier protocols usually meet standards defined by international telecommunications organizations, thus there is more uniformity here than in any other area of protocol development.

Creating a complete package of communications protocols requires the cooperation of the user, hardware vendors, and common carriers. The coordinating job falls under the basic description of network planning. It is a new, fast changing vocation, requiring a great deal of technical expertise. Practitioners are harder to find than programmers.

BASIC DESIGNS

Both centralized and decentralized modes of computing fall under the basic network design called a *star.* That is, a central CPU radiates channels or data lines out to a number of remote terminals. These terminals have little or no intelligence of their own. They don't really need intelligence because of their direct link with the central computer.

Distributed computing deviates significantly from this pattern. Figure 2-5 shows two typical distributed computing networks. Processing nodes are connected

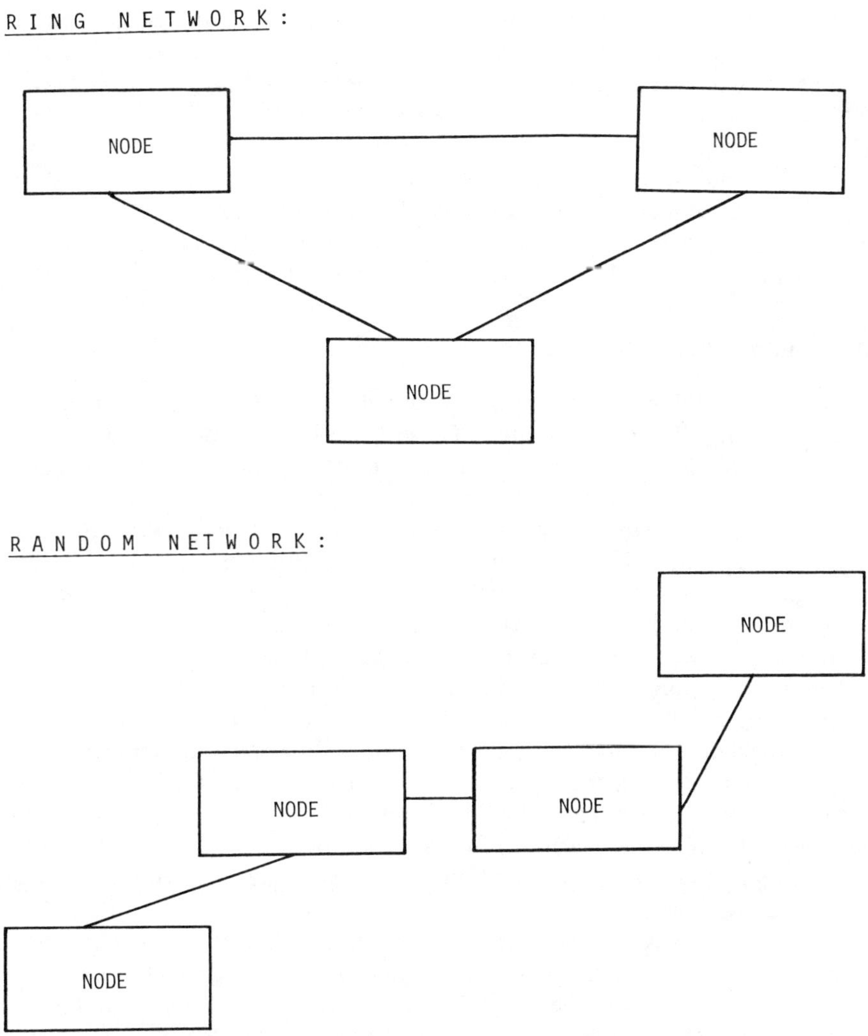

Figure 2-5. Various network options.

by data lines. In the first case, each node is connected to two other nodes, and the design is called a ring. In the second case, nodes are connected in series. The pattern of interconnection probably depends on physical proximity. Nodes close to each other are likely to be interconnected.

The star network used by centralized mainframes implies hierarchy, because more processing power is located at the center than at the periphery. In a star, the remote elements are of less importance than the central element.

Distributed networks are made up of autonomous members that have equal importance. Nodes can stand on their own from a processing standpoint, and merely share data and capabilities with other nodes as equals.

As we shall see later, there are two basic philosophies of DCS (Distributed Computing System) design. One holds that all nodes must be completely autonomous and independent, and the other maintains that a certain amount of hierarchy, or unequalness, is acceptable. The former argument is somewhat purist and academic, and probably not found in the real world very often. In most networks, some nodes are more important than other nodes.

EASE OF IMPLEMENTATION

Because of the unique characteristics of distributed computing, a tremendous amount of planning effort is required to achieve implementation.

User training in a distributed environment is also significant. Not only must each user be proficient at operating the computer for local needs, but he must understand how to transmit and receive data within the network. Each node is a user within a much larger community, thus cooperation is essential.

Bringing a group of diverse users together through networking requires a mastery of telecommunications. The use of data lines to interconnect computers is a relatively new and complex discipline. As we have pointed out, the user, his hardware vendor, and the common carrier all have significant rolls to play in developing distributed computing systems. The user must design the overall system and choose appropriate components, including computer hardware and communications equipment. The common carrier or value added network provides a way to switch packets of data around the defined geographic area in such a way that messages reach their destination efficiently and accurately. And the hardware vendor must provide much of the software to interface between his hardware and the network.

After design, development, and implementation, control of the network becomes another significant task. Since interaction between nodes is usually taking place continuously, the network is a permanent structure, and not just a series of dial-up telephone lines. Monitoring network usage, calculating efficiency, and correcting failures can keep highly trained technicians constantly busy. Because of this, a relatively large staff of professionals is needed to keep the network running. The size of this staff depends on the complexity of the network. On a proportional basis, distributed computing requires more communications technicians than either decentralized or centralized computing.

REASONS FOR DISTRIBUTING

The decision to implement a true distributed network can never be reached lightly. As we shall see, from a financial standpoint it is not clear that distribution is always a cost effective approach, particularly if there is no overwhelming need to distribute.

However, many companies have a legitimate need to distribute. Distribution of computing makes sense when the organization is highly decentralized. If the company is made up of many branches, many outlets, or dispersed production plants, then placing distributed nodes at each location is quite logical. Computer power can then be closely matched to the size of each organization site. If additional computing power is needed from time to time, it can be borrowed from other locations. Data can also be circulated from node to node as needed, thus duplication of processing functions is avoided. But if there is little or no day-to-day interaction between basic business units, then it is of little value to tie all of them together with a sophisticated distributed network.

Distributed computing networks are difficult to design, implement, and operate. The costs are high. Expected benefits, therefore, should also be significant.

Part III
Accounting Concepts

Chapter 3.1
An Introduction to Accounting

In this section we turn to the specifies of accounting and examine how computer operations can use financial data. Most computer installations, whether comprised of minicomputers or central mainframes, can benefit from accounting procedures.

Large, centralized computer operations have been around since the late 1950s. Over the years, various methods of accounting for computer costs and charging them to users have evolved. These methods vary in sophistication. There is no common or standardized computer accounting methodology. Very few articles or books have been written on the subject, and the accounting profession has not developed any consistent principles.

Sophisticated computer accounting systems do exist, however. There are literally hundreds of computer service bureaus scattered throughout the country. They sell computer time. Their accounting methods have been refined over the years to the point where most of these installations feel comfortable with their chosen systems. As this book creates an accounting methodology, it will build on several of these advanced systems. There is obviously nothing to be gained by reinventing the wheel.

As we have pointed out, the present world of data processing ranges far beyond centralized machine rooms. Decentralized and distributed processors are becoming a significant presence. But regardless of the mode of computing under consideration, it is important to understand large computer accounting, if for no other reason than decentral or distributed alternatives are generally measured against the existing central facility. And, as we shall see, all modes of computing have the same basic types of cost. From these costs we can devise uniform accounting standards that will provide control over the data processing environment.

ACCOUNTING GOALS

Accounting provides a method of measuring the performance of management. We may talk in terms of capital or net income, but the basic objective behind all balance sheets and income statements is *performance measurement.* Accounting provides historical perspective, and matches it against current achievement. In this way managers, owners, creditors, governments, and the general public can determine how well or how poorly a company is doing. In recent years, we have judged superior performance as the ability to generate increasing amounts of annual net income. Many in the accounting profession feel uncomfortable with this obsession over earnings. A better picture of a company's underlying strengths or weaknesses can be obtained from the balance sheet, where assets are compared with liabilities. Excessive borrowing has caused many companies to seriously reduce their net worth. This can eventually lead to bankruptcy.

Large companies often find it useful to break the total organization down into manageable accounting entities. Basic and uniform accounting rules are applied to each of these smaller groups.

One very natural accounting entity within most corporations is the centralized computer facility. The principal reasons for this are:

- Large amounts of capital and lease expense are tied up in computer equipment.
- A substantial number of people are required to operate and manage the computers. This includes programmers able to modify operating system software, and programmers who can write application programs.
- The computer operation is essentially separate and distinct from other aspects of the business.

In the early days of data processing it was often felt that computerization was simply a given – that those who didn't automate would be at a competitive disadvantage. After many years of hard experience, most of us realize that computerization often costs more than it saves, can be very disruptive to the work patterns of many organizations, and certainly hasn't replaced the masses of workers originally projected. But computers *have* given us more quality and accuracy, have eliminated many boring and repetitive tasks, and have led us into areas of analysis and design that would have otherwise been untouchable.

At this point in our industrial development, it seems appropriate to conclude that computers are no longer simply playthings. Computers have become ubiquitous, and are completely ingrained in the work process.

Computerization for computerization's sake is foolish. Only when computers clearly improve the bottom line should they be considered. Knowing how the bottom line is effected implies that the results of computerization can be quantified. Accounting gives us the quantitative tools needed to establish value and payoff. Accounting can do this for the company in total, and for the central computer facility and satellite operations, in an equally consistent manner.

COMPUTERS AND ACCOUNTING

There are several forms of accounting. Some forms are simple and some tend to be complex. Without doubt, one of the more complex areas of accounting is *standard costing.* But the results of a standard cost accounting system are very useful to the working manager. He finds it meaningful to use information provided by cost accounting as he tries to keep his department productive and efficient. Yet, according to government statistics uncovered by F.P. Kollaritch in his book *Cost Systems for Planning, Decisions, and Controls* (Grid Publishing Inc., Ohio, 1979), only 30% of the largest government contractors in the U.S. were found to use cost accounting techniques. Obviously, even fewer data processing centers practice this form of accounting.

It is the contention of this book that all mature data processing centers, regardless of size, should have reasonably sophisticated cost accounting systems. Data processing lends itself well to cost accounting because there is such a high degree of automation. Cost categories are easily definable and an identifiable benefit is received by the user community. The ingredients are there for good cost accounting.

Before exploring the complex methodology of cost accounting, we will look at the more common area of general accounting. Data processing centers need to begin with the foundation of general accounting before a cost accounting system can be developed. As it turns out, the information provided by general accounting is also invaluable to computer managers.

General accounting and cost accounting provide a sound basis for the management of computer resources. If we have good accounting, then we can proceed to believable cost analysis and justification. Although the final equipment or personnel decisions may be based on more than just accounting information, the accountant provides a believable quantitative framework. Without this financial information, no manager could honestly say that he or she has made a professional decision.

Chapter 3.2
General Accounting

All managers know, at least intuitively, that no business organization of any size could exist without accounting. Conducting business without some form of financial record keeping would be virtually impossible, and, because of government requirements, illegal. As long as we exist in a competitive environment, accounting will be necessary to keep a record of past events, measure current performance, and help make projections into the future.

Nobody can, or should, claim that accounting is of premier importance. Obviously, there is more to any organization than just accounting. The cycle within all for-profit enterprises begins with the sale of a product or service. But second in importance to the sale is the determination of whether or not that sale is ultimately profitable and will increase the equity of the company's owners. These determinations are made using accounting.

Accounting principles filter down through all parts of the organization. At the lowest job level, individual workers fill out timecards or punch timeclocks, which generate accounting records. At the highest level, consolidated income statements measure the company's overall profitability and the balance sheet determines capital.

The network of accounting principles assures that all parts of the organization are accountable. This accountability is what holds an organization together, so that specific goals and objectives can be pursued with a uniform purpose.

It is the accountant's job to systematize the collection of financial data, then record it, and finally store it in an orderly and logical fashion. Numbers must then be synthesized into concise, meaningful reports.

The accountant's first objective is to serve company management. Then information can be provided to company stockholders and creditors. And, finally, data is supplied to govenmental agencies and the general public.

Collection and synthesis of financial transactions takes place within an organization usually referred to as the Accounting Department (it may consist of many interrelated departments). All companies of any size have an accounting department. It has a certain amount of independence from the rest of the company, which is intentional. Accounting data must remain objective and unifluenced by special interest groups if it is to be useful.

Accounting departments abide by a set of rules that are referred to as Generally Accepted Accounting Practices (GAAP). These accounting practices have been highly refined over many years of experience. Attempting to change these practices is not something that is done casually. Changes must be agreed to by a majority of the accounting profession. Most companies make no attempt to modify these rules in any significant way. To do so would risk censure from the public accounting firm that, by law, annually audits the books of all major corporations.

Types of Accounting

As pointed out in the last chapter, we can break accounting into two basic activities: general accounting and cost accounting. Figure 3-1 shows the interrelationship of these two activities.

General accounting is normally under the complete control of the accounting department. Cost accounting can also be controlled by the accounting department, but it is a much more specialized tool and many of its functions can be

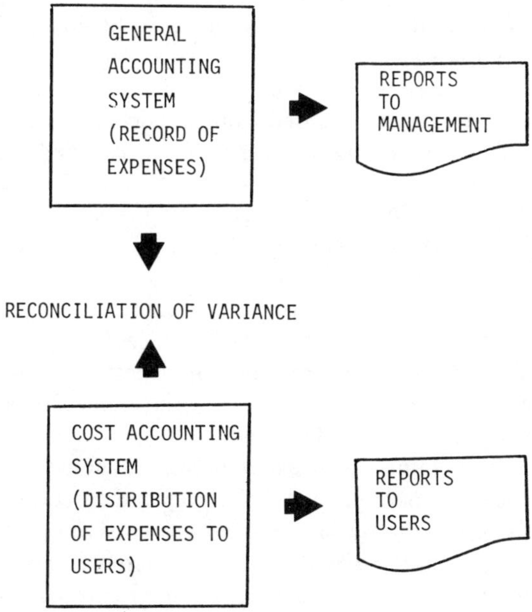

Figure 3-1. Overview of accounting.

delegated to local organizations within the company. A well run data processing organization, for example, can usually perform its own cost accounting functions. Specialized organizations benefit from performing cost accounting activities because they are forced into a better understanding of their own costs. Also, they tend to be outside of the mainstream activity of the parent company, which means that standard corporate cost techniques might not be very applicable to the special organization. An automobile manufacturer, for example, would have cost practices quite unrelated to the accounting needs of the in-house computer organization. CPU cycles and body frames don't mix very well.

In the remainder of this chapter we will examine general accounting and describe how it can be used by data processing organizations. The following chapter will discuss cost accounting.

WHAT IS GENERAL ACCOUNTING?

The basic form of general accounting has developed over thousands of years. It had its beginnings when the first tangible item was traded in return for some form of currency. Whenever currency, or money, exists, accounting becomes necessary. If value is not recorded on paper, then it can be too easily lost or misplaced.

General accounting is the process of keeping a historical record of what has been bought and sold, what is owed, and what is forthcoming. And it provides a means of controlling assets.

Liquid assets such as cash and accounts receivable require careful, day-to-day control. They must literally be guarded from fraudelent activity. Other assets such as equipment, buildings, and supplies are not as liquid thus require less stringent control.

From its simplest beginnings, general accounting evolved into the form that we know today. It is performed through the use of double entry to accounts, and defined as *accrual accounting.*

The double entry nature of accounting is a reference to bookkeeping aspects, and is of little concern to us. The term accrual accounting, however, is very important to understand. It separates the sophisticated form of accounting practiced by most businesses from the simple form, known as cash accounting, that many of us practice as private individuals.

In practicing cash accounting, all expenditures of money, and all revenues, are recorded as incurred or received. This gives cash accounting immediacy. When we, as consumers, write out a check for groceries purchased at the supermarket, we are recognizing the expenditure immediately as an expense because we deduct the amount from the cash balance in our checkbook. The transaction has an immediate effect on cash, and, once it is recorded, no further action is necessary. Likewise, when we receive our paycheck, we count that immediately as income or revenue. Once it is deposited in the bank, the cash balance is increased.

Cash accounting is very crude because it makes no attempt to match revenue with the appropriate expenses that helped to generate that revenue. On the small, personal scale, the margin of error is insignificant. But for large companies, where millions or billions of dollars are transacted annually, the error caused by improper matching can be materially significant.

Under accrual accounting, expenses and revenues aren't necessarily recognized immediately. A business may, under certain circumstances, choose to recognize revenue or expense before they actually occur as the result of a sale or expenditure. Or, the business may postpone an expense or revenue until some future period, even though money has actually been paid out or received.

This unique behavior can be summed up by the classic accounting phrase: "matching current period revenues with current period expenses."

If the revenue or expense is not considered as occurring in the current period, then it is set aside until the appropriate period arrives (a period is generally assumed to be one month). And if the revenue or expense should be recognized but has not yet occurred, then it is literally made up, and entered into the books of account. Setting aside revenue and expense until a future period is called a *deferral.* Making up a revenue or expense for the current period is called an *accrual.*

The physical receipt or payment of cash, then, is kept separate from the things we call revenue and expense. In the cash accounting system, cash is of supreme importance because everything revolves around it. In accrual accounting, cash, although important, is not a significant measurement of business activity or performance. The intent of the situation is more important. The resulting revenues and expense are the only acceptable measurements of how a business is doing.

Instead of dwelling on the activity of the cash account, accrual accounting starts with total revenue generated or estimated by the business, and subtracts an itemized listing of expenses, and the whole process ends with net income. Because of the nature of accruals and deferrals, that net income is not necessarily money in the bank. But it is an accurate estimate of current performance.

It is important that managers accept the concepts of accrual accounting. In addition to accruals and deferrals, other noncash adjustments are made that do not necessarily coincide with the way we would handle our personal finances. These adjustments, which will be discussed in more detail later, are created by asset depreciation and inventory valuation.

There are reasons for the unique adjustments made by accountants, and they have to do with creating a fair representation of the business in an ever changing world. Whether or not the individual manager chooses to accept these practices as reasonable is immaterial. The techniques are universal within the business world and must be used to the best advantage possible.

THE GENERAL LEDGER

Figure 3-2 shows the organization structure of a typical accounting department. A department like this could be found in nearly any large company.

When a sale is consummated, an invoice is prepared and the buyer either tenders cash or a promise to pay. This type of transaction flows through the receivables portion of accounting.

Whatever the company buys is paid for either with cash or a promise to pay, and this type of transaction flows through the payables portion of accounting.

Since all companies primarily buy and sell, these two functions handle the majority of accounting transactions.

All transactions, from both receivables and payables, are recorded in the central *general ledger.* The general ledger is the premier accounting document. All other accounting activities and records are secondary in importance to the general ledger, and must reconcile to it. Accountants put incredible amounts of effort into keeping the general ledger as accurate as possible.

The general ledger is a collection of many different categories of value called *accounts.* Like individual bank accounts, each of these groupings record increases and decreases in money. Understanding what is in these accounts, and how to use them, is the key to building a usable accounting system.

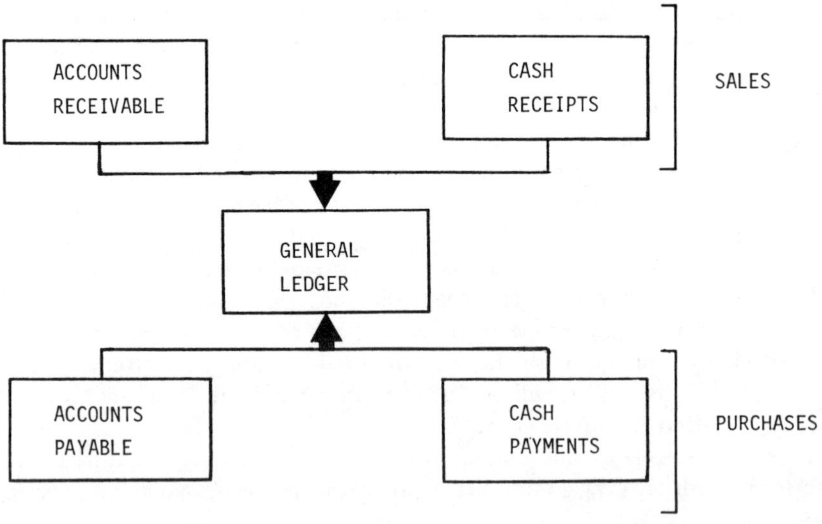

Figure 3-2. Principal divisions of an accounting system.

Every transaction that a business incurs, no matter how small or large, can be recorded in a particular account. The value of a purchased building, for example, can be placed in an account called *Building.* Cash received from a sale can be recorded in an account called *Cash.* The value of a supplier's invoice is placed in the account called *Accounts Payable.*

The general ledger divides all accounts into five basic categories: assets, liabilities, capital, revenue, and expense. As we discussed in the prior section, revenue and expense are used to calculate net income. The assets, liabilities, and capital are called balance sheet accounts. Balance sheet accounts are primarily used by the parent corporation, and are of little value to lower entities, such as the data processing organization. The one exception to this are plant assets such as computer hardware. Such equipment is usually controlled by the data processing organization.

Every company is free to choose the number of accounts it wants. As more accounts are used, greater cost visibility is obtained, which can lead to the possibility of more precise control.

As an example, a company might choose to place all telephone communications expenses into one account. In fact, many companies that have not examined the rapid growth in telecommunications probably still use just one account, probably titled Telephone Expense.

A more progressive company might decide that telecommunications costs are quite significant and need closer control. Instead of one account, the second company could set up the following:

Voice lines – local expense
Voice lines – long distance expense
Data lines – local expense
Data lines – long distance expense
Value added network expense
Microwave facility expense

In the latter case, the company has recognized the difference between voice and data transmission, and wants to keep those costs separated. It also wishes to isolate value added network costs, as well as the capital investment in interplant microwave facilities. The company now has the ability to monitor each cost category closely and presumably take corrective action if any area exceeds what is considered to be a normal expense level. As new and significant forms of communication arise, additional accounts can be added.

THE GENERAL LEDGER AND THE DATA PROCESSING CENTER

In the early days of computing, most companies consolidated their data processing operations under the financial subdivision. It was common to see the director of the DP facility reporting to the company controller or vice president of finance. This made sense because the financial organization was usually the largest user of computer services, running applications like payroll, general ledger, receivables, and payables.

Accounting departments are a part of overhead. Because they are not directly involved in producing the company's product, they do not require very many accounts for their own cost control. Consequently, the costs of computing tended to get buried within the same nebulous accounts. Computer expenses were often hidden. Of course, in those days, nobody realized just how large data processing would eventually become.

As computer costs grew, specific accounts were often set up to handle the most significant items. Hardware lease payments were usually the first big item to be given their own expense account identity. Most early computers were leased or rented.

By the early 1970s, many companies recognized obvious trends and set up additional accounts for such major items as computer software, computer supplies, and hardware depreciation. Each of these areas had become large enough to warrant attention.

This slow isolation of data processing costs, often occurring over many decades, shows both the flexibility of accounting and its shortcomings.

The special accounts that were actually set up indicate that accounting can adapt quite well as totally new forms of work appear within the corporation. Accounting is a flexible tool.

However, accountants never treated data processing as a unique, standalone entity. Accounts were established haphazardly. It was very unlikely that accountants, working on their own, would have the experience or background to set up a comprehensive and meaningful set of expense accounts in the general ledger for the data processing operation.

Accountants, like most people, are primarily interested in what they feel are the mainline aspects of the company. Data processing is seldom a mainline activity. As a result, the principal products of the company are treated lavishly with an intricate account structure, while organizations like data processing are treated almost as an afterthought.

This leads to a very incomplete set of expense accounts for data processing organizations. Some major costs are isolated, but there is no comprehensive picture. Many other costs are buried within generalized corporate accounts and become invisible.

For example, although computer hardware costs are quite easy to identify, because only one or two major vendors are usually involved, communications costs are not so straightforward. When the general accountant sees costs for items like modems, multiplexors, and data concentrators, he has a hard time determining exactly what they are. Without some kind of expert help, he will probably put them in with data processing hardware costs, or throw them into some miscellaneous account with little meaning. The future ability to control these costs is seriously hindered by either action. If costs are not visible, they cannot be controlled.

This basic neglect of data processing is not so much the fault of accountants as of the management of the computer center. Accountants are reasonable people, and will set up new accounts whenever a need can be shown. Data processing experts are the only people with a clear understanding of specific accounts that could be used for control purposes. Computer specialists must therefore approach accountants and work with them to set up a comprehensive account structure that accurately reflects the scope of current computing operations.

THE GENERAL LEDGER REPORTING SYSTEM

Within the general ledger, the only accounts that are useful to the DP department are those classified as assets and expenses. Balance sheet accounts classified as liabilities and equity are generally only meaningful at the corporate level. And the revenue account represents income, which is meaningless to most DP operations because computing services are normally charged out to other segments of the company at cost. This means that the DP operation is a cost center.

Some companies have actually tried to turn their computing operations into profit centers. In this approach, the cost of data processing services is marked up by some fixed amount so that recovery is greater than actual cost. The difference is profit. It is assumed that, somehow, this profit will incentivise DP managers into doing a better job. But the profit is meaningless because it has no relationship to earnings generated by the parent company. And in recent years such an approach has actually become dangerous. The reason is that central computer factilities are being challenged by minicomputers. If the center inflates its costs with a fictitious profit, then it is showing an unfavorable cost to potential minicomputer users. On the one hand we have an inexpensive minicomputer, and on the other we have a fully burdened computer center that has overlaid its costs with a profit. In such cases the minicomputer looks very attractive, financially. The profit center approach is a meaningless and dangerous exercise in today's world of alternative computers.

Important Accounts

The general ledger accounts of greatest interest to the data processing center are listed in Figure 3-3. These are all classified as *expense* accounts. They are representative of what most modern centralized data centers should use. Many of these accounts are also applicable to decentral and distributed computer

LABOR AND RELATED
- Salaries Wages
- Fringe Benefits

DATA PROCESSING EQUIPMENT
- DPE Depreciation Expense
- DPE Owned Maintenance
- DPE Lease Expense
- DPE Taxes
- DPE Installation
- DPE Freight-In
- DPE Expendable Equipment

DATA COMMUNICATIONS EQUIPMENT
- DCE Depreciation Expense
- DCE Owned Maintenance
- DCE Lease Expense
- DCE Taxes
- DCE Installation
- DCE Freight-In
- DCE Expendable Equipment

TELECOMMUNICATIONS EXPENSE
- Voice Line Expense
- Data Line Expense
- Value Added Network Expense

SOFTWARE
- Software License Expense
- Software Amortization

DATA PROCESSING SUPPLIES
- Card Stock Expense
- Paper Stock Expense
- Custom Forms Expense
- Magnetic Tape Expense
- Ribbons Expense
- Minicomputer Support Expense

OCCUPANCY AND RELATED
- Office Equipment Expense
- Utilities Expense
- Amortized Facility Expense
- Rearrangement Expense

OTHER EXPENSES
- Travel/Entertainment Expense
- Outside Training Expense
- Books/Subscriptions Expense
- Postage Expense
- Miscellaneous Taxes Expense
- Employee Recruiting Expense
- Employee Relocation Expense
- Insurance Expense
- Repro Equipment Expense
- Registration Fee Expense

ALLOCATIONS
- Transfers from Corporate
- Interdepartmental Transfers

Figure 3-3. Typical data processing expense accounts.

operations. But to keep our discussion straightforward, we will confine it to centralized computing. From that beginning, we will apply the concepts to other forms of data processing.

These accounts are obviously used to accumulate expenses. As each expenditure occurs, such as a lease payment on hardware, or a charge for supplies delivered, or the purchase of a modem, the value of that expenditure is recorded in the appropriate account.

Accounts are sometimes referred to as *expense buckets.* They group expenses into logical, controllable categories.

Expense Designation Problems

The assignment of costs to the appropriate expense account does not occur automatically. Somebody must make a determination of the account to be charged as each expenditure materializes. An invoice for supplies is received, for example. A clerk checks to insure that the supplies were actually delivered, and signs the invoice to approve it for payment. An accountant then attempts to assign the actual expense to an account. There is no guarantee that the accountant will be an expert and put the expense in the proper account. Does the charge go to Office Supplies Expense, or Data Processing Supplies Expense? Judgement is necessary, and misassignments are easy to make.

As we mentioned before, the general accounting department is primarily interested in the mainline aspects of the company, which are associated with the company's principal product or service. Data processing is a tangential activity. Yet, if accounts are properly set up as shown in Figure 3-3, they can be quite complex. Subtleties between account can be missed by the average accounting clerk who has not been exposed to the terminology of computing. The cost of a high-speed channel switch can easily be mischarged to Communications Expense because a channel can be misinterpreted as a communications device. Actually, the channel switch is part of data processing hardware. This is something only a technical expert would know.

Therefore, once the data processing department has helped to set up a meaningful chart of expense accounts, it must take steps to insure that expenses are charged to the proper accounts. The underlying assumption is that the accounting department is not qualified to properly assign data processing expenses.

If a data processing organization is reasonably large, it is almost mandatory that a dedicated accounting department be set up within the DP group. This special department can rely on the parent accounting department for many services, thus it can remain relatively small and specialized. Two or three people can easily handle the paperwork associated with a $100 million data processing operation, provided the people are conscientious professionals and not just clerks.

This special accounting group forms a central control point for handling the problems that are outlined below. The group's principal function would be to identify the proper home account for each expense, and then turn the paperwork over to the larger accounting organization for invoice payment and posting to the official general ledger and appropriate subsidiary ledgers and registers.

Issues that the DP accounting group would deal with separate into two major categories: noncash related problems and cash related problems.

By understanding what accountants are trying to accomplish in each of these areas, the DP organization can step in and help, thus insuring accuracy in the general ledger and all of its derivative reports, such as the important income statement.

The beneficiary of all this work will be the data processing center and its management. Accurate accounting information leads to better financial data and better overall control.

NONCASH EXPENSE PROBLEMS

Noncash expenses are caused by what accountants call *adjustments.* Nothing physical occurs to create this type of expense. But since the accountant knows that a legitimate expense really exists, he literally makes it up through an adjustment to the general ledger. Figure 3-4 lists the three types of noncash expenses and gives a few examples. It also shows that these expenses coexist with the more frequent physical transactions. Physical transactions always involve the transfer of money.

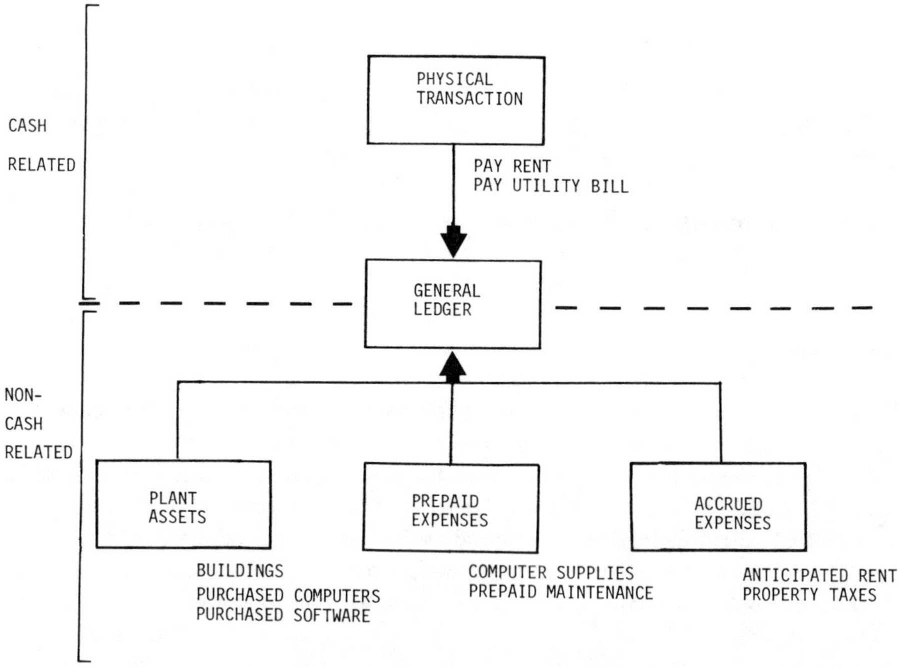

Figure 3-4. Noncash expenditures.

Plant Assets

Plant assets are defined as any tangible item that is purchased and has a useful life greater than one year. Usually, there is also some minimum purchase value, such as $1000. Any item purchased for more than this minimum value becomes a plant asset, and any item worth less becomes a period expense or a physical transaction.

Most purchased computers are plant assets. Only the very smallest microcomputers could be considered expense items. Many purchased software packages are also assets, assuming that they are used for more than one year.

In the early days of computing, DP centers did not have many assets to worry about. Most hardware was leased, and software was bundled into the lease price.

Computer manufacturers eventually modified their pricing structures to the point where hardware purchases often became economical. This was especially true if the hardware was acquired early in its life cycle. At the same time, many peripheral devices such as terminals, remote job entry stations, and minicomputers began appearing. In most cases, purchase was the only alternative for these small devices.

When hardware or software is considered large enough in value to be an asset, it is capitalized. This means that the item is entered onto the books at its purchased price, and a depreciation schedule is created. Depreciation is the method of charging a specific and predictable portion of the asset value to expense each month. The relationship between depreciation expense, which appears on the income statement, and the total asset value, which is on the balance sheet, is shown in Figure 3-5. If the income statement represents a monthly value, then the entire value of the computer ($100,000) would be charged to expense after 100 months, since the monthly expense is $1000.

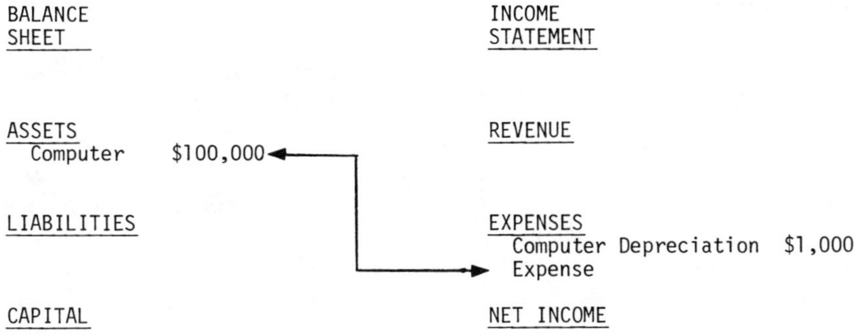

Figure 3-5. Asset and expense relationship.

The time period over which depreciation occurs is called *useful life.* Our example showed 100 months, or about 9 years, which is not normally considered reasonable for computers. Most computers are written off over 5 years. Even shorter write offs may be necessary if the computer is acquired late in its product life cycle (note that the useful life assigned for accounting purposes has nothing to do with the write-off period allowed for income tax purposes). Setting useful lives for computers is an important contribution of the data processing experts, who are in a better position to assess such things than are accountants.

The most critical time period in the life of a computer asset is when the hardware or software is first acquired. At that time it must be placed in the proper asset account. The four major choices are:

- Data processing hardware
- Communications hardware
- Data processing software
- Communications software

The total value of the asset – the purchased price – is placed into the appropriate account. Each month a predetermined amount of depreciation is subtracted from the asset account and moved to a correlated expense account, where it becomes a period expense. The four related expense accounts are:

- Data processing hardware expense
- Communications hardware expense
- Data processing software expense
- Communications software expense

Obviously, if the equipment costs are not assigned to the right asset accounts to begin with, their costs will not flow to the proper expense account through periodic depreciation.

In most cases, the accounting department simply does not have the technical expertise to determine where each purchased piece of computer equipment or software belongs.

For example, in one case a minicomputer may be used as a communications concentrator, thus assigned to a communications hardware account. In another instance, the same type of minicomputer might be used for processing application programs, and should be charged to a data processing hardware expense account.

Sorting out these hardware and software complexities must be left to accounting experts within the data processing organization. As each new computer asset is acquired, the DP group must indicate the proper account to be charged. The exact procedures for communicating this information between data processing and the parent accounting department can be worked out by individuals within each organization. Mutual cooperation will benefit both groups.

There is a possibility that clear-cut distinctions between data processing expense and communications expense will eventually disappear. Various types of front end processors are already handling communications *and* classical DP functions. As this trend matures, separate accounts will probably disappear. Technological changes like these provide even more justification for the involvement of data processing people in the creation and assignment of plant asset accounts.

Prepaid Expenses

Any tangible good purchased in quantity, held in an inventory, and used up over a time period greater than one month, qualifies as a prepaid expense. Intangible items such as prepaid maintenance and property taxes paid in advance are also considered prepaid expenses.

Prepaid expenses represent items that will be consumed by somebody – in our case the data center. There are two things that are important to consider:

- Who is it that purchased the items?
- Who will use the items?

One of the most common and representative prepaid expenses for a data processing center is computer supplies. Items in this expense category include printer paper, card stock, magnetic tape, disk packs, diskettes, printer elements, and ribbons. This is very specialized material, and many companies have found that it is best to let the data processing department directly order and stock it. When the DP department consumes everything that it purchases, there is no problem, since supply costs can be built into the total center cost pool. But as small computers proliferate throughout the company, most data processing supply organizations find that they are purchasing signficant amounts of material for noncenter organizations that have minicomputers.

This becomes an expense allocation problem. A scheme must be worked out to charge decentral users for the supplies that they consume.

How this is done depends on the accounting structure of the company. But most companies work on a *voucher system*. Under this method, a special voucher is prepared by the individual requesting supplies. The requester identifies who he is on the voucher and indicates the items that he needs from stock. The data processing organization must then assign a cost value to the requisitioned supplies, and indicate this cost on the voucher. The voucher is then sent to the parent company accounting department where an intraledger transfer of costs is accomplished. The cost of these supplies is subtracted from the data processing department and added to the requesting department account.

Supplies are a cost that is representative of prepaid expenses. Unless somebody takes the time to set up cost transfer procedures, the total cost of all such items will be charged to the data processing department. Cost transfer requires a voucher system, and somebody with the knowledge to assign costs to the material released. Costing requires specialized data that can only be developed by individuals close to the situation. Perhaps average unit rates can be created, and updated as needed.

Again, this is a case where the special accounting group within the computer organization can be used to control vouchers and set up price structures.

The point to be made about prepaid expenses is that unless somebody actively attempts to assign these costs to the benefitting user, the costs will not be properly allocated, and the central data processing organization will absorb more than its fair share of costs.

Accrued Expense Problems

We discussed the concept of accruals earlier when we developed some basic definitions of accounting. Accruals are a very common type of transaction and are caused by the fact that many vendors and suppliers do not bill for equipment and services within the time period up to the monthly close of the general ledger.

The general ledger close is a significant event in accounting, indicating that the month's activities are complete. The end result of the close is the publication of final reports such as the income statement and the balance sheet.

If, for example, a major supplier of computer components has not yet billed the company for leased equipment, and the month is about to close, then steps must be taken to estimate the cost and get it into the general ledger. This activity is called "accruing expenses."

Most accounting systems provide for automatic accruals each month. If an invoice has not yet been received and processed, the automated system takes an average of the last several months of expense and books that amount. Appropriate adjustments are made later so that when the actual invoice is received it is not double counted.

Because most accruals are automatic, they can usually be handled by the parent accounting department. The DP accounting group should monitor accruals, however, to insure that they are reasonable, timely, and comprehensive.

A specific problem occurs with accruals when equipment is released or discontinued. Hardware removals, particularly of smaller items such as terminals and communications hardware, can easily be overlooked by the parent accounting group. If these items are canceled but remain on the books, cost will continue to accrue indefinitely. Carelessness here can lead to significant amounts of cost being accumulated for equipment that doesn't actually exist.

Fixed asset control is the solution. The DP accounting group must compile records of all fixed assets. As equipment is acquired, it is added to the inventory list. As hardware is released, it is deleted, and a special notification is sent to the accounting department, to insure that the equipment is eliminated from the official system.

Timely removal of hardware from the asset inventory system insures that the costs which make up data processing are accurate and trustworthy.

CASH RELATED PROBLEMS

Cash expenditures that effect computing are created by a group within the central accounting department called *accounts payable.* During the course of accepting invoices from vendors and approving them for payment, the value of the invoice must be assigned to a proper account. We have already introduced a list of appropriate accounts. It is lengthy and quite complex.

The people who approve invoices for payment are usually called accounts payable clerks. They are not highly paid and they are not expected to do a great deal of thinking. Their principal task is to take each invoice and match it with an authorizing document such as a purchase order or contract. The purchase order has information on it that will verify terms, conditions, and quantity. If everything matches, the clerk approves the invoice and sends it on to the cashier for payment.

The accounts payable clerk must also decide which account will get charged with the expense. Identifying the proper account or accounts is an individual activity, very dependent upon the clerk's experience and desire to do a good job. Shoddy work means that the wrong accounts will be booked with the expense.

Not only are data processing costs quite different in nature from costs generated by the rest of the company, but they are ever changing. Technology is moving so fast that new types of hardware costs appear frequently. Communications hardware looks like data processing equipment. Expendable supplies such as diskettes can be misconstrued as equipment. An untrained accounts payable clerk simply cannot be expected to accurately charge data processing costs to each account.

An even greater problem is the tendency to "dump" costs into the largest account whenever there is confusion. In a typical DP operation, the largest expense account will be Data Processing Hardware Lease. It is not uncommon for 30% of the operation's costs to be accumulated in this one account. Thus when the accounts payable clerk is confronted with a confusing invoice, and the purchase order doesn't give clear account visibility, the clerk may end up charging the invoice to the large hardware lease account, using the assumption that the account is so large that a small error will be undetected. But small errors have a way of multiplying until major distortions occur.

The most accurate and time tested method of handling invoices is to appoint individuals as official invoice approvers. These people must be within data processing, where the expertise is. To make the system work, these people should be given complete authority to approve or disapprove invoices for payment. Their second responsibility is to assign proper account numbers.

A typical system could work like this: The accounts payable department forwards all DP related bills, upon receipt, to the special accounting group formed within DP. If the invoice is straightforward, like the unchanging monthly lease cost on a piece of hardware, the DP accounting group assigns the appropriate account number to the invoice, approves it for payment, and sends it back to accounts payable, where it is eventually paid.

If the invoice is unusual or nonstandard, it is sent to one of the special approval individuals.

The authorized approvers are senior people who have been around long enough to have a fairly good idea of what is going on in their area. They should also have a vested interest in making sure that costs get charged to the right account number. This can be accomplished by giving them budget responsibility. That is, part of their performance should be measured by how closely they match actual expenditures to planned values. These people could then have a very strong incentive to insure that proper costs got charged to the accounts they controlled.

Invoice approval individuals would check each invoice for accuracy, assign an account number, and send the paperwork back to the accounting group where it would continue through the normal processing cycle.

Using professionals (which it is assumed the invoice approvers would be) to approve invoices is expensive. But the validity and trustworthyness that is given to the accounting system is worth the investment. A useful byproduct is that budgetary control of various accounts is established.

USE OF GENERAL ACCOUNTING INFORMATION

Why do we go to all the trouble and expense outlined above to insure that costs are correctly gathered and charged to accounts within the general ledger? We do it so that management will be provided with accurate cost information that can be used to control the data processing operation.

General ledger information is eventually synthesized into reports. There are many different reports, but the most useful one to data processing is called the *statement of operations.* It is not a report normally prepared by the parent accounting department, so provisions must be made to create it within the data processing organization.

Preparing the Statement

After accountants officially close the general ledger each month a tremendous amount of information is available for those who want it. The parent company probably provides a few standard departmental reports that are quite generalized and of little use to specialized organizations like data processing.

Sometimes, modern general ledgers can be accessed in an on-line mode to extract summarized data using special report writers. If this is the case, the data processing department can immediately generate useful reports with very little effort.

The more conventional situation is that general ledger information is locked up on a disk or tape file somewhere. Within these files is much more information than the DP organization could possibly need. Special arrangements must be made with the accounting department so that summarized cost information can be stripped off the file and made available for post processing.

The objective is to obtain a listing of all accounts that are chargeable to data processing, along with monthly and year to date money charges.

The special accounting group within data processing can then take this information, rearrange it, and produce the statement of operations, shown in Figure 3-6.

Examination of Figure 3-6 will show that it closely resembles a conventional income statement. The only thing missing is revenue. And the expenses are more detailed than in most statements, because this report is specifically tailored for data processing management.

Expenses are broken down into two basic categories: direct controlled and indirect controlled.

Direct Controlled Expense. These expenses can, to some extent, be managed by DP executives. This is because the expenses tend to be related to the volume of activity being handled by the shop. And, in most cases, the source documents authorizing these expenditures, such as timecards and invoices, have been approved by individuals within the DP organization.

The degree to which these expenses can be controlled is sometimes questionable. If demand for computer services consistently exceeds the current configuration, for example, then management has little alternative but to acquire additional capacity. Forced increases in capacity can make it very difficult to actually control what we have listed as Direct Controlled Expenses. That is why a cost accounting system must ultimately be developed, to complement the Statement of Operations. Cost accounting takes equipment utilization changes into account when measuring performance.

Management, looking for excuses, can always come up with reasons why expenses cannot be controlled. These excuses should generally be discounted. An expense qualifies as directly controllable when management can actually influence that expense. Outside events can always cause problems, but good management should be able to anticipate most of them.

Indirect Contolled Expense. These are allocations to the data processing organization made by the parent company. These expenses are sometimes classified

DATA PROCESSING DEPARTMENT
STATEMENT OF OPERATIONS

Month Ending ______________

Item	Monthly Budget	Monthly Actual	Year-to-Date Budget	Year-to-Date Actual
DIRECT CONTROLLED EXPENSES				
Salaries and Wages				
Fringe Benefits				
DP Equipment – Leased				
DP Equipment – Owned				
Data Communications Equipment – Leased				
Data Communications Equipment – Owned				
Software				
Data Lines				
Operating Supplies				
Travel				
Purchased Services – Outside				
Other Operating Expenses				
SUBTOTAL				
INDIRECT CONTROLLED EXPENSES				
Occupancy Allocations				
General Services Allocations				
Corporate G&A				
Other O/H				
SUBTOTAL				
TOTAL EXPENSES				

Figure 3-6. Sample Statement of Operations.

as overhead, or burden. They are often allocated to data processing based on total direct dollars, or headcount, or occupied square footage. The allocation methodology is generally quite arbitrary, but the costs are nonetheless real and must be dealt with when a total cost picture is desired.

Collecting these indirect costs is a sign of accounting maturity. In many cases these costs are overlooked by people when justifying computers. Many data processing organizations operate under the assumption that they have no indirect costs. Such assumptions are misleading and dangerous. All organizations, large and small, incur indirect costs. In future chapters, we will, therefore, spend a great deal of time identifying and discussing indirect costs for all modes of computing.

Budgets

Along with the actual costs, the statement also contains budget information. Budgets are developed through a process which occurs once each year. Most companies have a formal budget cycle, and the DP organization generally participates in it. Budget data generated by the central computer organization will be used by the parent company for consolidation purposes. Data processing budgeted costs are usually buried within a much larger cost framework. But the budget data should be incorporated into the DP statement of operations, where it will stand out as useful to computing management.

USE OF THE STATEMENT

Financial reports like the statement of operations have little value unless used by management. The top managers of any data processing operation need accounting information just as much as officers of the parent corporation. The information must be presented in an understandable form, and it must be believeable. Techniques to improve believability were discussed in the prior section.

Computer centers tend to be run by technically oriented managers. These people are generally more comfortable directing the operations of computer hardware than they are with analyzing and interpreting financial statements. Because of this, management must literally be forced to periodically review financial results.

The small DP accounting group that we have mentioned a number of times can now prepare each monthly operating statement using summary data out of the general ledger. This is a logical extension of their work on invoice approval, and the coordination of noncash expense problems.

Along with preparing periodic financial reports, the accounting group should be in a position to analyze variations from normal trends. This analysis will isolate two areas:

- Problems caused by accounting anomalies that can be corrected through changes to the general ledger.
- True operating problems that require the attention and action of management.

The latter area is of greatest concern. Suppose, for example, that communications hardware is running 30% over plan. This could be an indication that communications planners are not doing a good job in designing networks. Or, it could mean that a lot more people want communications services than was originally anticipated. The first situation is serious, the second indicates an inadequate forecast. In either case management should be concerned, and should analyze the problem and ask the appropriate people some hard questions.

Figure 3-7 shows a sample statement that could be typical of a moderately large central machine room with a complement of systems programmers and applications programmers. The annual budget, at the total cost level, is 70 million dollars. At the bottom line, the center appears to be tracking reasonably close to budget, with actuals only 0.4% over plan. But a closer examination reveals a rather substantial overrun in ADPE Hardware Lease (50%), and Data Communications Lease (33.3%). These overruns are being offset by a number of underruns in other areas.

The important question to ask is: Why are hardware expenses exceeding budget by such a large amount?

Examination of actual accounting records, and comparison with planned events made at the beginning of the year, will eventually resolve the problem. In this case the answer could be as simple as excessive demand for processing capability by the parent corporation. Perhaps an additional large scale computer and related hardware had to be installed to meet extra demand. But

STATEMENT OF OPERATIONS
12 MONTHS ENDED DECEMBER 31
($000)

	YTD Budget	YTD Actuals	Variance	
DIRECT CONTROLLED EXPENSE				
Payroll	28,000	25,000	3,000	10.7%
Fringe	11,200	10,000	1,200	10.7%
DP Equipment – Leased	10,000	15,000	(5,000)	50.0%
DP Equipment – Owned	11,500	10,000	1,500	13.0%
Data Communications – Leased	3,000	4,000	(1,000)	33.3%
Software	700	700	–	–
Data Lines	500	500	–	–
Operating Supplies	950	900	50	5.0%
SUBTOTAL	65,850	66,100	250	.4%
INDIRECT CONTROLLED EXPENSE				
Occupancy Allocation	1,300	1,300		
General Services	1,000	1,000		
Corporate G&A	2,000	2,000		
SUBTOTAL	4,300	4,300		
TOTAL	70,150	70,400	250	.4%

Figure 3-7. Abbreviated statement of operations.

investigation could also uncover that there was no increase in demand, and cost overruns were due instead to poor management, with reasons like:

- Leasing equipment instead of buying it.
- Leasing at month-to-month instead of longer term rates.
- Acquiring more hardware than demand justifies.

Good managers can learn from financial statements. Admitedly, accounting data isn't the entire picture. Other considerations such as level of service, and technology offerings, may be more important to the company than keeping within arbitrarily established budget levels. The point is not to immediately criticize for negative variances from budget, but to analyze the data and understand completely why the situation is like it is. This kind of analysis gives management a valuable overall view of the organization. By force-feeding managers with financial facts, those managers come out ahead, since they develop a better understanding of the organization that they manage.

Because of the importance of financial data, it should be reviewed with top DP management monthly. It is essential that this meeting be held, without exception, on a regularly scheduled basis. The meeting – a financial review – provides a forum for the discussion of fiscal matters, and gives top management a consistantly unfolding indication of their overall performance.

Accounting information is historical in nature. It takes time for trends to appear. It also usually takes much time for managerial actions to show up as fiscal results. Using financial data is not going to magically change things overnight.

Consistent use of accounting data makes a business out of data processing. It also helps the centralized data center prepare for the challenges it faces from the many new and different modes of computing that are becoming available.

GENERAL ACCOUNTING CONCLUSIONS

Data processing organizations are made up of people who are technical in nature. Most of the top managers have come either from programming or from machine operations. There is seldom any significant financial orientation with these types of technicians.

Without doubt, computer managers need a financial understanding to survive in this complex environment. As a first step in bringing financial regimentation to any large data processing operation, DP must work closely with the parent accounting department. The existing general ledger must be examined to determine if an adequate set of accounts exist to fairly represent data processing. Accounts should be added as necessary to give clear and meaningful financial visibility. Computer operations have very unique account needs which usually differ substantially from those used by the rest of the company. The DP organization has to recognize this fact and participate in the creation of accounts.

To accomplish a review of the general ledger, and to perform the necessary tasks which will assure that accounting data is accurate and meaningful, a special accounting group should be set up within the DP organization. The group need not be large, but it should be competent.

Problems in accounting data occur in two different areas: Noncash problems are caused by prepaid expenses, plant assets, and accruals. Prepaid expenses, which are basically inventories, must be monitored closely to insure that: 1) the proper types of consumables are being charged to the inventory, and 2) outside users of inventory items pay for what they withdraw from stock. Plant assets, representing purchased hardware, must be monitored carefully to insure that each acquisition is charged to the proper account, and each discontinued item is promptly removed from the general ledger, so that it does not continue to build up expense after its discontinuance. Accruals are estimates of future expenditures and must be constantly monitored to insure that proper accounts are being charged.

Cash related problems occur at the time the invoice is approved for payment. The invoice represents an expense, and this expense must be charged to an account. Choosing the right account can be a difficult process, especially when dealing with technical data processing items. Experts within the data processing organization must therefore become involved in the analysis of complex invoices. These specialists can be given authority to approve invoices for their area of expertise, and can assign the correct account number to each bill. In this way, accounting data accuracy is insured.

Information from the general ledger is extracted each month and summarized into a statement of operations. The statement shows direct controlled and indirect controlled expenses, and compares them against budget.

The statement of operations is reviewed with top center management monthly in a formal financial review. Analysis of accounting data is provided in these reviews and the basic financial health of the DP organization is discussed.

Chapter 3.3
Cost Accounting

The previous chapter looked at the general ledger and two of its principal segments – expense accounts and fixed assets.

Expense accounts can be used to represent the essential financial status of any data processing center, regardless of size. To make this financial representation as accurate as possible, a broad range of accounts is needed. Constant vigilance is necessary to insure that costs are properly charged to these accounts. If everything is done right, a meaningful set of reports is produced that forms a bridge between the world of accountants and the world of managers.

Comparing actual expenses with budgeted expenses at the account level is a useful first step in financial control. The analyses of cost trends, variances from budget, and expenditure patterns develop excellent sources of financial information for DP management. But this data is so specialized that it has no value to the user of computer services, nor does it help DP management measure computer utilization. As the previous chapter pointed out, legitimate cost overruns can occur when computer users demand higher than normal levels of support. If a company wins an unanticipated contract, for example, the demand on computer services may quickly exceed existing capacity. If a new mainframe is brought in, budget levels will quickly be exceeded, assuming the computer was not anticipated. But this is an acceptable situation, since more revenue is being generated by the parent company. Nobody would ever deny the acquisition of additional computer hardware if business conditions were favorable. Under such circumstances, budget overruns are meaningless. Budgets must be changed to recognize the improved level of business.

In most corporations, the population of computer users is large and diverse. Yet this group of users must be measured and understood. The objective of cost accounting is to collect expenses associated with computer usage, and charge them out in some logical and consistent way to the user population. Data processing services are provided for a fee.

By associating costs with each job, the computer user can determine the most cost effective use of computer services. Using cost accounting data, each user is able to realistically plan for computing needs, assess trade-offs between various methods of operation, and follow up to insure that projected savings are actually being realized. Through the mechanism of standard rates, cost accounting provides a common denominator similar to the function that price performs on the open marketplace.

The need for computer cost accounting generally arises under the following circumstances:

- The data processing operation has costs that are considered significant.
- There is more than one user of the processing services.
- The use of data processing services is growing within the company, and there are alternative solutions to many DP problems, such as outside service bureaus, turnkey systems, and general purpose minicomputers.
- Cost accounting is practiced throughout the company, thus people are generally familiar with the concepts.

The federal government recognizes the importance of cost accounting. For many years, it has required all major contractors to practice some form of it. This is particularly true if the company has a mix of government and non-government work. Obviously, under such circumstances the government wants to insure that it pays only its fair share of costs.

The federal government has standardized its perception of cost accounting and has issued a uniform set of principles that all major contractors are required to meet. The rule setting body, the Cost Accounting Standards Board, was disbanded in 1980, but the principles that the board created will remain in effect indefinitely.

Although the federal government's cost accounting standards are useful from a total corporate standpoint, they do not adequately meet the needs of specialized organizations such as data processing.

As we shall see, one of the characteristics of cost accounting is that there are very few practical standards. Particularly when used for specialized organizations such as data processing, cost techniques must be customized.

COST ACCOUNTING ADVANTAGES

The most outstanding advantage of cost accounting is that it gives user organizations *better control* of their expenditures. Control is achieved through the consistent dissemination of cost charges to all users of computer services.

Cost accounting also gives valuable information to managers of data processing centers. Cost rates can be used to measure the productivity of the center. If rates continually rise, then productivity may be slipping. If cost rates are declining, then productivity is probably improving.

From the DP manager's viewpoint, cost accounting is an excellent complement to general accounting. General accounting creates a financial foundation by outlining expenses by account. Cost accounting shows why these costs are being incurred through chargeout to ultimate users.

Finally, cost accounting brings a level of professionalism to computer services that no other mechanism can achieve. When users must pay for the services they demand, the data processing organization is brought into the real world of competition. It is not necessarily a comfortable world, particularly when irate users demand better services for the costs they are paying. But the regimentation forced upon the center benefits both the center and the entire company.

There is no longer any one best way to provide computer capabilities. There are a broad range of hardware alternatives. Cost accounting helps to prove exactly which mode of computing is right for the company or for individual applications.

THE COST ACCOUNTING RESPONSIBILITY CENTER

The term *cost accounting* can very easily become misleading, particularly to non-accountants. To some people there is a certain glamor to the term. To others, it represents an exercise in the needlessly complex manipulation of numbers.

Many companies, some of them quite large, do not feel that cost accounting is necessary. While the fundamentals of general accounting must be practiced by all companies if they wish to be held publicly, cost accounting is certainly not mandatory. Only companies that need to know what it is really costing them to do business tend to adopt the principles of cost accounting.

It can be generally stated that as an industry becomes more competitive, cost accounting tends to become more prevalent. Companies with little or no competition have no real incentive to adopt expensive cost accounting systems. It is only when other economic entities are competing against a company in the marketplace that it adopts cost accounting techniques to assure itself that it is producing its products or services for the lowest possible cost.

COST ACCOUNTING DEFINED

The fundamental principles of cost accounting are not particularly complicated. The problem is that there are as many variations to the basics of cost accounting as there are different companies. Each company does things a little bit differently, and this effects the cost accounting structure. Cost accounting is closely aligned with the production and manufacturing functions within the company.

There are three basic aspects to cost accounting that will be useful to review. They are:

- Choosing the cost object – examples are products, processes, and departments.

- Choosing and accumulating the costs that relate to the cost object – material, labor, and overhead.
- Choosing the allocation base.

This section discusses the first aspect, or the cost object. The other two aspects of cost accounting will be developed more fully in later chapters.

The cost object can be defined as the activity that produces a product or performs a service within the company. The performing entity is the key to further development of cost accounting, and we call it the *responsibility center.*

All companies of any size have many logical responsibility centers. The easiest way to identify these centers is to start with the organization chart. At its lower levels, this chart identifies many responsibility centers.

Let's assume that a particular company has an organization like that depicted in Figure 3-8. Each of the six vice presidents oversees numerous responsibilities. At the next level down, actual responsibility centers begin to emerge. The manufacturing vice-president has four functions reporting to him: production, quality control, material inventories, and internal transportation. Each of these functions has a defined set of work to perform.

Figure 3-9 shows a function breakdown for the production activity. Raw materials come in, they are fabricated, and finished goods leave. The fabrication function forms a basic responsibility center. All of the activities associated with producing a finished part can be grouped into this accounting entity.

If the manufacturing process is very complex, then it may be reasonable to subdivide the total function into several responsibility centers. In some cases,

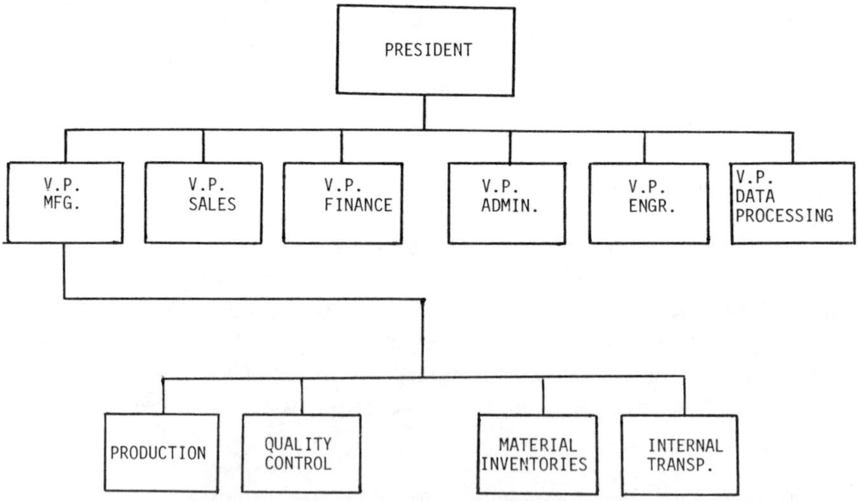

Figure 3-8. Typical organization structure.

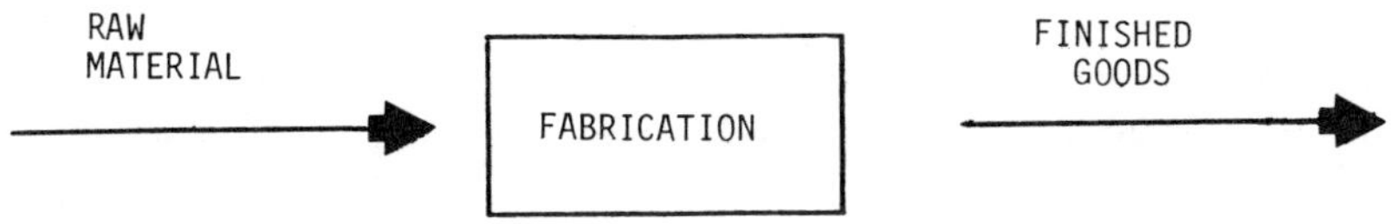

Figure 3-9. Production functional activities.

then, the third level on an organization chart can represent responsibility centers. In nearly all other cases, the forth level down can be identified with specific responsibility centers.

Flexibility is necessary when choosing responsibility centers. Some levels of management have very broad areas of control that can quite naturally be divided into multiple responsibility centers. In establishing these centers, the level of management is sought that has direct control over people, equipment, and facilities. The responsibility center must produce an identifiable product or service.

The concept of direct control over the responsibility center is an important one, because as we develop accounting techniques, they will be created with the assumption that somebody can directly influence the outcome, particularly if problems are surfaced. Cost accounting would be a waste of time if its results were not reported to an individual having sufficient authority to modify or influence future trends, and future costs.

Managers who run the responsibility center have the ability to control direct costs, and accept the responsibility for absorbing indirect costs. All of these expenses are incurred while producing something. Because these costs have obvious relationships to production, they can be controlled just as the production process can be controlled.

If local management has no direct control over its costs, then the proposed responsibility center is at a level that is too low to be effective. Many levels of management perform activities that cannot be directly related to costs, thus their ability to control their expenses is very limited.

The supervisor of a computer supply stockroom, for example, manages people and inventory. But he has very limited control over his costs, since he is basically in a position where he must respond to the demand made on the items that he carries in his inventory. Although he can seek the lowest priced supplier of products, he has little additional leverage. To report back to him on a monthly basis the cost of his electrical consumption or heating would be a meaningless exercise. He cannot do anything about these, and many other costs, except practice a reasonable amount of conservation.

The manager of the entire data processing operation, of which the stockroom is one small part, has a much broader perspective than the stockroom supervisor. Although the top manager may be demand driven, he can meet his overall demand with much more flexibility because he can substitute various activities to achieve the lowest cost possible. He can force users onto CRTs and away from impact printing, thus lowering his supply costs. Or he can acquire more energy efficient hardware, which will lower his electrical charges. And he is better able to understand various company allocations, such as those for personnel services, security, and accounting.

In summary, a responsibility center manager must be in a position where he can control the number of people assembled to perform the task, the amount of equipment installed, and the ancillary services necessary to keep the people and equipment performing. This broad perspective helps him to understand the value of the numerous allocations that the parent company charges him.

Each responsibility center is actually a small company within the larger corporation. The responsibility center must have the means of developing consistent and understandable methods of measuring its output. It must also develop uniform ways of collecting its cost – labor cost, equipment cost, supply cost, etc. When output can be measured and total costs are known, then it is a simple arithmetic exercise to divide cost by output utilization and come up with *cost rates.* These costs rates are then used to charge other responsibility centers within the company when they benefit from the product or service. If the company has a number of responsibility centers, they are constantly charging each other for services or products rendered. The computer organization, for example, will charge the accounting organization each time the general ledger is processed. The accounting department will in turn charge computing each time a special extract of the general ledger is run just for the benefit of the DP department.

The corporation's total cost accounting system, if it is highly developed, consists of a constant flow of costs between various responsibility centers. The corporation develops aspects of a free market economy.

The advantages to the corporation of individual responsibility centers are twofold:

- The corporation is divided up into units that are effectively working to maximize profit and small enough to be managed effectively.
- Performance can be measured by cost rate, thus top management doesn't have to become involved in basic details of each operation.

Good cost accounting systems are found in mature organizations – corporations that are characterized by sound planning, stable hierarchy, and industry leadership.

Just as there are people who have difficulty keeping their personal finances under control, there are many corporations with little desire to carefully control costs. In a competitive environment, however, poor cost control ultimately leads to company failure. A company that does not understand its costs cannot accurately price its product. Bad prices will either cause market share to be lost, if they are too high, or will eliminate profit, if they are too low in relationship to actual cost. In either case the final outcome is disastrous, since company survival is questionable.

Cost control is not established by grandstanding with special cost cutting programs, or by using whatever the current "B school" trend is. Cost control starts and ends with small details. Cost control is hard work. It means that every responsibility center must continuously assess the cost of its production and work to keep that cost as low as possible. Costs are controlled by constantly shaving or eliminating the small, nickel and dime, items. Better utilization of terminals, or fewer custom forms, or a cheaper copying process, represents the level of detail necessary to achieve true cost control.

When responsibility centers each work to lower their individual costs, the entire company can be considered a well managed, efficient producer, and will undoubtedly be successful in the marketplace, provided it has a salable produce or service.

SERVICE ORGANIZATIONS AND COST FLOW

All cost accounting systems make certain assumptions about how costs flow through an organization. Cost accountant's have devised two general methods of explaining costs flow. They are: *job cost* and *process cost* methodologies.

Job costing is used by companies that produce products or services in customized groups or batches. A construction company must use job costing. Each project is handled as an individual unit, and each job has an identifiable beginning and end. Jobs tend to be nonrepetitive. Costs can therefore be grouped together on a job by job basis. Costs are assigned to each project based on resource consumption, such as the use of labor hours or material used.

Process cost methodology applies to manufacturers who develop products continuously. An automobile production line is a good example. Although there may be changes to the product design from time to time, the production rate tends to be continuous. Costs must therefore be collected and apportioned out to each unit of production on some kind of pro rata basis.

The problem with both of these methodologies is that they were developed for manufacturers. Very little attention has been given by cost accountants to service organizations, or to the unique situation of data processing.

Of the two accounting methodologies, data processing comes closest to process cost accounting.

A classic process cost system is displayed in Figure 3-10. The manufacturer assembles various types of raw material and stocks them in warehouses. They are called raw material inventories. The value assigned to each inventory is the

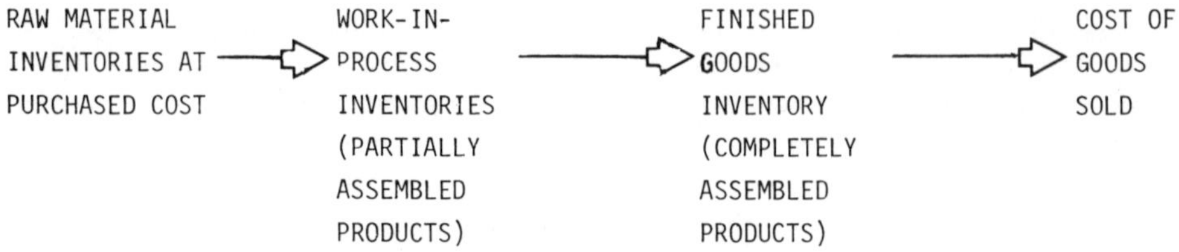

Figure 3-10. Process cost system.

sum of unit purchased prices. From these inventories the raw material slowly filters into the plant, where it is fabricated into products.

There are usually many stages in the production process. At each stage the product develops more value, partially because more of the raw material components have been brought together, and partially because more labor and fabrication machinery have been invested in the assembly. The value of the parts increases until the manufacturing cycle is completed. At that point, the total of all values becomes the final product cost.

The process cost cycle must be modified before it can fairly represent what goes on in a data processing operation. Data Processing provides a service, rather than a tangible product.

Cost Accounting and Services

Classic service organizations within a company are those that support but do not directly participate in the production of the company's product. Examples of services are janitors, maintenance, company cafeteria, advertising, legal, contracts, pricing, and accounting.

Data processing is a hybrid. It performs classic service functions, such as producing the payroll. But it can also participate directly in the production cycle. Computers are used by engineers to design and develop products. Computers can schedule the production line, control machine tools, and help perform much of the direct work on the production line. From an accounting standpoint, computers participate in both direct *and* indirect activities.

Figure 3-11 is a modification of the previous figure. It shows the cost flow of a typical data processing center. Instead of raw material, the cycle is started with an inventory consisting of computers, labor, support equipment, and supplies. We choose to call these *service inventories* to distinguish them from raw material inventories. The computer represents an inventory of processing CPU cycles, ready to be used by those who need solutions.

The inventory of computer resources is not nearly as controllable as a true production inventory. Raw material inventories can be increased or decreased, depending on the production rate. Future deliveries of material can be canceled

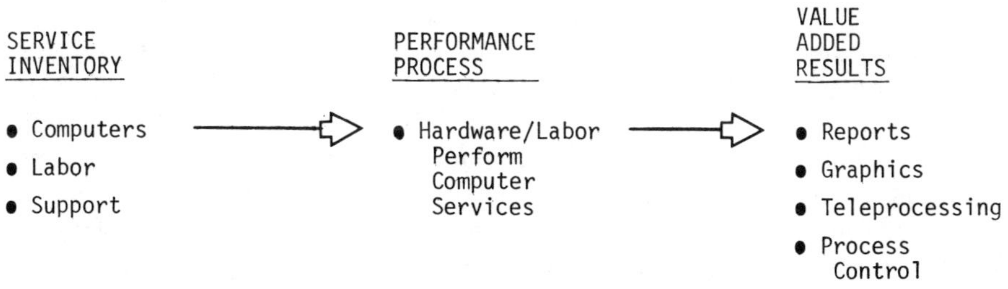

Figure 3-11. Cost flow of data processing activities.

if business is bad. But computers must be configured for peak demand, thus they are subjected to periods of gross underutilization. A critical mass of computers must be maintained regardless of what happens to short-term utilization. This means that the typical DP shop has less control over its costs than most manufacturing cost centers.

The service inventory of computers performs a kind of work-in-process as it executes program instructions. Data manipulation results in the creation of value added information, produced in the form of reports, on-line data bases, raw solutions, and control of manufacturing type operations.

A cost accounting system applies value to the solutions that are produced. If the solutions are used during actual product development or production, then costs flow directly into the company's Cost of Goods Sold account. If solutions are used by other indirect activities, such as accounting or facilities, then DP costs become a part of indirect company overhead.

One of the most important results of a good computer cost accounting system is that a substantial amount of data processing value is charged directly against the company's products. Computers are not simply a part of overhead, but are directly involved with the production of goods and services. This is a realistic way to handle computers, and proves to management that computers are very valuable in the production of the company's product.

STANDARD COSTING

The final step in the cost accounting process is to develop a set of cost rates and use them to charge out services performed by the responsibility center. Rates can be developed using historical trends. Or, they can be derived by making future projections of resource consumption.

The responsibility center is a large entity, and must be broken down into *cost pools.* There are usually a number of different cost pools, representing the various services performed by the center. Within the DP operation, cost pools consist of the numerous computer services, such as batch processing, teleprocessing, and data base systems. The granularity of cost pools depends on how precise management wants to measure its services. An example of how a data center might break itself up into pools is shown in Figure 3-12. This particular shop has three major pools of hardware – IBM, CDC, and DEC – along with a group of application and system programmers. There are also pools providing microfilm services, and data entry. These various pools represent the major services provided by this sample data center. The pools are logical and straightforward. Most modern centralized data centers would look very similar.

The Nature of Cost Pools

The costs that are collected in each pool fall into three major categories. Figure 3-13 displays these costs in the form of a pyramid. Direct costs, which are usually the largest in dollar value, form the foundation. These include costs such as hardward rental, operator labor, software, and supplies. The nature of such costs is that they can be directly attributed to a pool. There is no question about what these costs support, or which pool they represent. The rental costs on an IBM mainframe obviously belong in the IBM pool, for example.

The middle layer of costs, called indirect, are then allocated over direct costs. As their name implies, indirect costs cannot be attributed easily to a specific pool. But they are still required in a general way to keep the data center operating. Representative costs include utilities, facility maintenance, computer room management, and clerical support.

At the top of the pyramid are other overheads. These costs, which are usually relatively small in value, are parent company overheads which are pro-

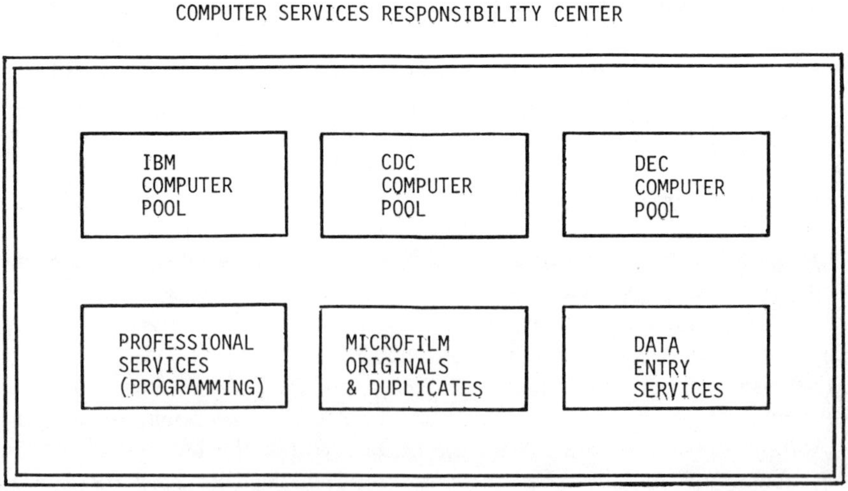

Figure 3-12. A cost accounting system.

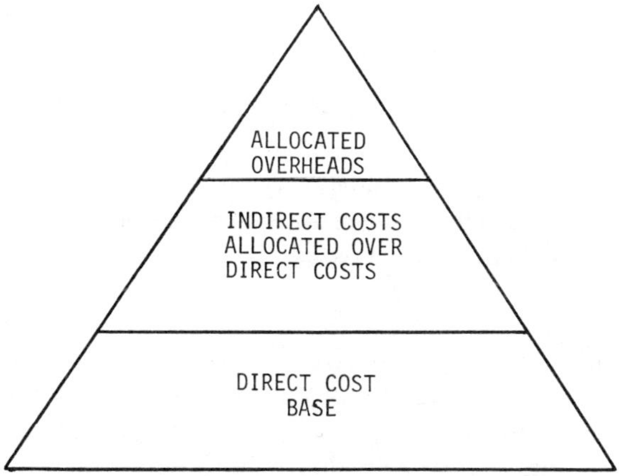

Figure 3-13. Cost pool makeup.

portioned over all direct activities within the company. Representative costs include advertising, legal, insurance, various taxes, and other corporate G&A type charges. These costs have no relationship to the work performed. Because of this they must be allocated to direct work in some arbitrary manner.

One or more utilization measurements must be developed for each pool. These measurements should be carefully chosen to represent the most causal factors within the cost pool. Utilization measurements must be:

- Equitable
- Easy to understand
- Representative of work performed

We will discuss many types of utilization in the following chapters. We will find that there is an inverse relationship between equitability and understandability. If we pursue equitability too forcibly, we create measurements that are incomprehensible to most people. The choice of utilization is therefore a compromise. It is our contention that the compromise should be made in favor of the user because understandability is more important than perfect equitability.

Rate Development

Developing cost rates is as simple as accumulating a total cost pool, and dividing it by some form of projected utilization. In many cases, one pool may have several utilizations. Under these circumstances, the pool must be further allocated into subpools before rates can be developed.

If costs and utilization are based on past events, the rates are said to be historical. Historical rates are subject to fluctuation since actual cost and actual utilization are always changing. This variability is annoying and misleading to the user population, thus the concept of standard costing has gained wide acceptance.

To develop standard cost rates on a prospective basis, the responsibility center *forecasts* its cost and utilization over a projected period of time, such as one year. The forecasts are based on history but can be modified by anticipated future events. Sophisticated statistical analysis such as least squares curve fitting may help to choose believable levels of usage. Computer costs must also be forecast over the future period, and then standard rates can be calculated.

The use of standard rates creates a certain stability for the DP center. This helps users when they try to forecast their future computer expenditures. If rates stay stable over a one year period, forecasting becomes a relatively simple task. We have all learned the frustration of trying to plan financial events, even those of a personal nature, during periods of high inflation. Prices rise so quickly that it becomes difficult to budget our income. The computer user is in the same position. He needs stable computer cost rates so that he can plan his computer expenditures with confidence.

Variances

Standard rates can never be completely accurate. There will always be differences between forecasted values and actual costs. All standard cost systems therefore develop variances.

Each month, after the close of the accounting cycle, standard costs are compared with actual costs. Standard costs are based on forecasts. Actual costs are based on dollar values taken from the general ledger. If actual costs exceed standard costs, the pool is said to be *underapplied* because less cost has been distributed than has actually been incurred. If standard costs exceed actual costs, the pool is *overapplied* because distributed costs exceed actuals. These variances are usually passed on to the parent accounting system, where they are posted to special variance accounts. The theory is that in the long run, overapplied costs will offset underapplied costs and the net will be close to zero.

If the standard rates were carefully chosen, and if the responsibility center matches its resources with demand for services concientiously, then variances should be very small. Variances should rarely exceed 5% of the total cost pool. If, however, cost or utilization has been erratic, large variances can occur. If the variances persist, then rates must be adjusted up or down, depending on the direction of the variance. A well-tuned cost accounting system should not have rate changes more than once or twice each year. As mentioned before, frequent rate changes upset the user community, and make it difficult for people to plan future expenditures.

Data processing organizations that use standard rates have a very high financial visibility within the corporation. As rates change, those who use large computers see what is happening. In most companies, the user community is literally the whole corporation. Every time the computer center changes its rates, everybody knows and everybody makes judgements based on the change. This high visibility alone is reason enough to adopt a computer cost accounting system. A DP organization that is not under reasonable control can develop some very embarrassing cost rate trends and variances. It is hard to hide inefficiency when the entire company can see what is going on.

Paying for the Cost Accounting System

There is always a price that must be paid for good information. As information becomes more meaningful and useful it is usually increasingly difficult to obtain and maintain. A good cost accounting system requires the following:

- Computers must automatically account for their activities.
- Operators and programmers must record their time in a timekeeping system, and that system must be automated.
- Knowledgeable accountants must develop standard rates, monitor those rates constantly, and develop variances periodically.
- DP management must work under the constraints of a publically disseminated set of standard cost rates, and live with the consequences of change.

Data processing centers, regardless of size, lend themselves quite well to standard costing. All computers, from large centralized machines down to minicomputers, account for themselves automatically. Most hardware vendors supply machine accounting utilities as part of the basic operating system software. So utilization is always available. And cost pools are usually obvious, as Figure 3-11 pointed out. If the accounting data is processed off shift, when utilization at most centers is quite low, then critical resources won't be required, which can lower costs somewhat.

Standard cost systems are not inexpensive to implement, nor to run. But there is simply no better way to monitor the productivity of a highly technical computer center. Nothing else can quantify computing like a good cost accounting system.

Chapter 3.4
Reporting Cost Data

The whole point behind going to all the trouble of accumulating responsibility center costs, calculating standard rates, and collecting equipment utilization, is so meaningful financial data can be reported back to interested people. Cost data should be disseminated to data processing managers and to those who use computers. DP managers are concerned with rates and how much they vary from standard. Users are concerned with overall job or system cost. These two needs differ from each other.

COMPUTER CENTER FINANCIAL NEEDS

From a cost accounting standpoint, data processing managers are primarily concerned with cost variance. Significant variance implies a problem. Managers must therefore periodically review cost data to determine if a rate change is necessary.

When you ask an accountant about how to handle variances from standard, he will explain that rate change rules should be established so that the whole process becomes automatic. If, for example, a variance of three percent in either direction occurs, then standard rates might automatically be adjusted to offset the variance. As long as the variance remains under three percent, no changing would be necessary.

Standard rates can become a very political issue, however, and straightforward accounting rules may not work. When DP managers know that their rates are being watched by many segments of the corporation, they may be very reluctant to make drastic changes. Their concerns are over such things as continuity, believably, and credibility. Rates that fluctuate a great deal are generally perceived as representing poorly managed operations. The incentive, then, is to restrain rate changes for as long as possible.

Such a situation inevitably leads to strain between accountants, who desire rate accuracy, and managers, who want rate stability.

This is an adversary relationship, and is actually quite healthy. The accountants' pressure keeps DP managers aware of cost and financial performance. The manager's concern keeps the accountant on the lookout for ways to keep costs in line with the plan, through early warning of potential cost problems. The end result is a cost conscious computer operation.

USER REPORTING REQUIREMENTS

As we have pointed out, sophisticated data processing users are concerned with what it costs to run their jobs. From a broader perspective, they want to know what the overall value of solutions is. The computer center must provide this cost information, using a formal reporting system.

Normally, cost accounting data flows between the computer operation and the parent company accounting department. During each accounting month, various users submit jobs to the computer using manual or electronic inputs. Computers process the jobs, generate some form of utilization measurement, and pass the utilization on to the cost accounting system. The cost accounting system multiplies utilization by rate to determine job cost. At the end of the accounting period, or month, the job costs are accumulated against some form of user identification number. These numbers, sometimes called cost charge numbers, or accounting control numbers, are established by the parent accounting system. Charge numbers identify such things as user, contract, or production segment.

In addition to passing costs on to the parent cost system, the DP department may generate custom cost reports that can be helpful to individual users. Whether or not special reporting is required depends on the flexibility and usefulness of the parent cost accounting system. However, since most cost systems are there to support mainline business segments, the chances are very good that the specialized needs of data processing cannot be satisfactorily met.

If they are needed, data processing cost reports should show such things as user ID number, resources consumed during the period and year to date, and extended cost values. Cost information should be easy to understand and be useful to the individual who actually created the cost. Cost accounting data is worthless unless individuals understand it and can do something to influence future outcomes.

Beginning with the lowest levels of cost reporting – the job level – a hierarchical set of reports can be developed that summarize cost data at higher and higher levels. The structure of these reports should follow the structure of the organization. A typical series of reports could be as follows:

- Report by Job Number or Program Number
- Report by Cost Charge Number

- Report by Department
- Report by Directorate
- Report by Division

The higher level reports would be quite summarized, without detailed usage data. Information at higher levels is used for trend analysis, while lower level reports are used to judge the efficiency of programmers and programs.

Using Reports

The rule of thumb is that there can never be enough information for users, particularly when they become sophisticated. It is nearly impossible to anticipate the convoluted ways that users will want to see their data processing costs displayed.

Since the DP organization cannot satisfy everyone, it must aim for satisfying the average user. This is only a partial solution, however, because 50% of the user population will probably be unsatisfied with the information provided. The best thing to do is spin off a constantly updated accounting information data set, either on tape or disk. This information can then be provided to interested users, who can process against it to satisfy their specialized needs.

What do users do with all of this cost information? Many, particularly at the lower programming levels, do nothing. After all, if there is a specific job to do, it will get done regardless of the cost. When this attitude pervails, cost data can be easily discounted into oblivion.

But most users manage their data processing expenditures to some extent. If the company has budgetary control, then each department is given a data processing budget, and actuals are tracked against that budget. How closely these budgets are controlled depends on the accounting and financial philosphy of each company. If the company is at all serious about cost control, then DP accounting data can be very important.

In the long run, cost information can be used to justify new software systems, discontinue ineffective programs, or encourage moves to new forms of automation, such as distributed and decentral computing. Part five of this book looks more closely at the uses of cost accounting information.

The data processing organization has a very important interest in the utilization patterns of its user population. Long-range utilization trends determine whether the data center will grow or decline. To a DP manager, there should be nothing more important than that.

Chapter 3.5
Accounting Overview

The two forms of accounting – general accounting and cost accounting – are both extremely important to service operations such as computer centers.

General accounting provides information for overall control. Since most DP centers are not required to make a profit because their only customers are within the corporation, only expense accounts are applicable. Revenue is meaningless.

With the aid of the parent accounting department, the DP center can set up a broad range of expense accounts that control the important aspects of computing. As actual expenses occur and are reported against accounts, management gains insight into the fundamental costs of doing business.

The DP department can help to improve accounting accuracy by participating in the approval and collection of cost data. The computing organization can also arrange this accounting data into meaningful reports, which can be presented to management on a periodic basis. These reports would summarize the financial performance of the center.

Cost accounting provides a means of charging out to the users of DP services the expenses collected by the general accounting system. This is done through the establishment of cost pools, utilization measurements, standard rates, and various reports that accumulate costs each month and display them to users.

By implementing the concept of standard cost rates, a powerful management control tool becomes available. Standard costs are compared with actual costs to develop variances. These variances measure how effectively management is matching resources with demand. Large variances in either direction from standard will inevitably require management action, since they indicate that the operation is not completely under control.

Figure 3-14 summarizes a complete data processing general and cost accounting system.

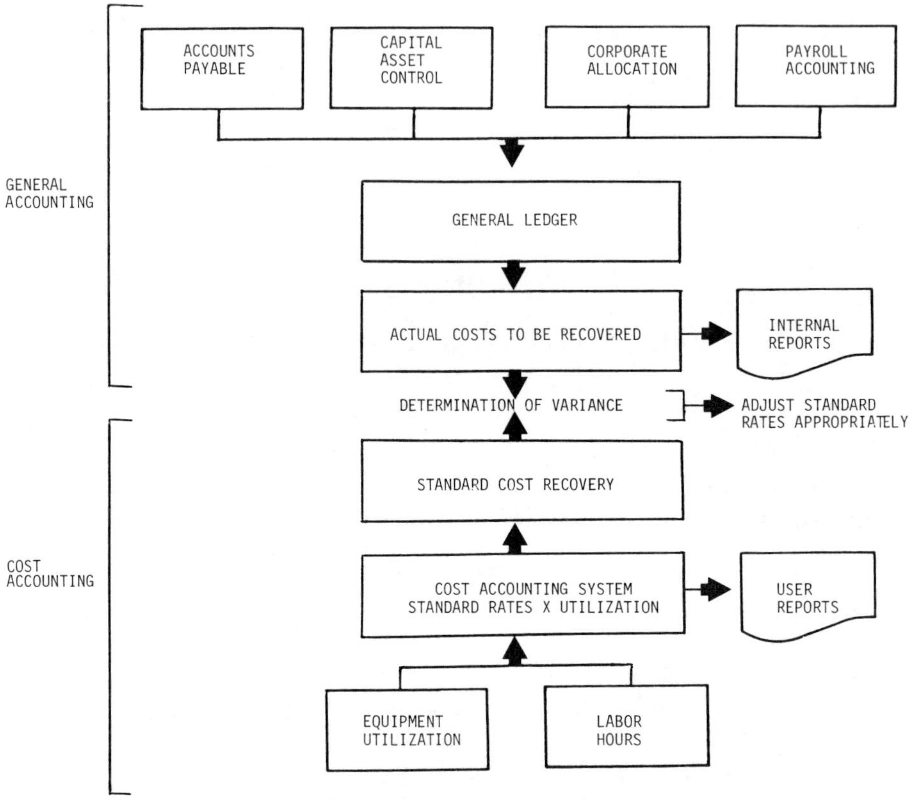

Figure 3-14. Complete DP accounting system.

Part IV
Cost Accounting for Centralized Computers

Chapter 4.1
Introduction

The last section explored a number of basic accounting concepts, and related them to centralized computing. Centralized computing has been around long enough for reasonably sophisticated accounting to have evolved.

This section will examine central DP cost accounting in detail. The basic accounting methodologies developed will then be used for decentralized and distributed computing in the following two sections.

HISTORICAL PERSPECTIVE

In the early 1960s, large, centralized computer centers began to develop around second generation computers such as IBM 7094s and Univac 1108s. Although these computers were fast, they were serial processors, which meant that only one job at a time could be handled through the central processing unit.

With these machines, the concept of *economies of scale* became quite popular. The feeling was that computer cost was proportional to computer productivity. If the investment in mainframes went up 100%, for example, productivity would increase by 150%. Based on this concept, many companies assembled numerous huge computers in central machine rooms.

Because of the nature of early computing, these large computer centers were very labor intensive. Large staffs of operators handled each CPU and its peripherals. Much of the processing was card oriented, and people constantly rushed about with trays or boxes of punched cards, because they were the principal form of input. A good operator was extremely valuable. He could keep the computer working productivity and efficiently by minimizing the setup time between jobs. There was an art to operating a computer well.

Along with operators and card carriers and tape hangers and people transporting heavy boxes of paper around, programmers usually roamed the machine room, nursing their jobs through the CPU. If a large program failed, the programmer could often change the necessary instructions right in the machine room, restart his job, and get a successful completion. Development programmers not lucky enough to get into the machine room, or have an operator friend, usually had to be content with one or two job executions each *week*. Programming was a frustrating, time consuming occupation of very low productivity.

In general, the machine room was an exciting, busy place. Even the local managers tended to be charismatic, hard driving, outspoken pioneers, doing the best job they could under difficult circumstances. New ground was being broken in unexplored territory. The emphasis was on operating machines, and the programmed output was almost an afterthought.

Today's machine room is quite different. There are very few operators. And certainly no applications programmers are allowed near the machines. There is not much human activity. Just the low hum of electronics. The atmosphere is cool and subdued. If there are multiple CPUs, most of the consoles blink away unattended. Only at some central station are CRT screens banked, with a few operators standing around, quietly monitoring the progression of jobs being processed. Disk drive units are hermetically sealed, and seldom touched. Even the labor intensive tape units are beginning to be replaced by mass storage units, which mechanically mount cylinders of tape as needed. There are no decks of cards. Jobs enter the closed off machine rooms over telephone lines, and output is transmitted back to various remote printers Programmers carry on their work over terminals scattered throughout the company. They now have instantaneous access to the computer, and the concept of job turnaround is meaningless. Presumably, these programmers are immeasurably more productive than their earlier counterparts.

The massive CPUs that once dominated the machine room have been replaced by smaller boxes filled with semiconductor chips. The most dominant hardware within the room is disk storage. There is a never ending need for more and more on-line storage space, to the point where most machine rooms devote at least 50% of their space to disks. The earliest 2314 type disks held 50 million bytes of information on a single pack. The newest disks hold 25 to 30 times that amount of data, and take up less floor space. But still the disk units continue to multiply.

Technology has made the CPUs incredibly fast, and enhancements double these speeds every few years. Large scale integration has produced memory chips that are so cheap and plentiful that memory is no longer a restraining factor, nor even a concern at all.

There are some new additions to the modern machine room that did not exist in even the most advanced second generation centers. These are communications devices, represented by modems and control units. They are hooked to data communications telephone lines. Hundreds of incoming calls are handled by the computer with no human intervention in the machine room.

Since nearly all processing jobs are submitted over telephone lines, the communications equipment is an extremely important and growing area. New organizations within the DP department have been created to specialize in data transmission.

As remote devices have evolved from relatively straightforward batch oriented card readers/printers into terminals, CRTs, and graphics devices, the dependency on data communication has increased significantly. Intelligence has been built into the network. And technology has allowed higher and higher data transmission speeds to be achieved.

With the exception of major hardware failures, which occur less and less frequently, the machine room is a quiet, even boring, place. The excitement and human activity of earlier machine rooms has gone. Hardware has replaced the human element.

But excitement and a pioneering spirit are still around.

Excitement is with a mechanical engineer at a graphics CRT, designing a part using a light pencil against the screen. The distant computer does all of the mathematical calculating, and draws appropriate lines for the engineer. He needs no slide rule, no paper or pencil, and no drafting board. His design becomes a set of digital coordinates which, when complete, can be directly transferred to numerical control machines that actually fabricate the part. The engineer is relieved of tedious calculations and can concentrate on creative design. There are virtually no limits to the possibilities open to him.

The excitement is with an accounts payable clerk, who now views the status of all outstanding invoice payables on a CRT. The computer automatically calls up each invoice when due, matches it with the appropriate purchase order and receiver, prints out a check, stuffs it into an envelope, and prints an address label. The clerk now has the time to look into problem areas, where invoices do not match purchase orders, or where payment is improperly authorized. Perhaps he can save the company tens of thousands of dollars each month through proper cash management. And, because his job requires thought, he is not stuck with the dull, repetitive work associated with manually approving invoice payments.

Excitement is with the product support professional, monitoring a CRT and watching a customer, perhaps in a foreign country, place an order for spare parts using a remote terminal. No frustrating paperwork or half understood phone calls taken by harried clerks. Just one-on-one, customer to computer. The order is placed and the computer sends out precise shipping instructions to the stockroom where the part is boxed and mailed within minutes. And accounting data is automatically and accurately updated. Electronic signals have replaced a bottleneck of paperwork.

Excitement is with a management accountant, who sits at a terminal. He has large amounts of data that must be arithmetically manipulated and sorted into a finished report for anxious executives. Using a simple, high level language, he interacts directly with the computer, creating a program in the English language. He designs the report format, inputs the data, and tells the computer how he wants the information processed. In seconds, a clean, well formatted report is printed out before him. The single hour of interaction at the terminal has saved him a week of tedious clerical work, and several days of final typing. Now he has time to analyze the data, and prepare a more in-depth interpretation of it for his management.

In all of these cases, the power and flexibility of computers has been brought to the nonprogrammer. Tedious, repetitive, boring work has been automated, so that people can look at their finished data in new ways, perhaps gaining a better insight into the nature of their jobs.

THE MEANING OF COMPUTING

Computers have brought a massive change to the way many people work. Engineers, accountants, office workers, bank tellers, grocery checkers, airline reservation clerks, and many others have had their capabilities expanded with computers.

As data processing has developed over the years, we have learned that there is one basic thing that people want from computers. That is: *solutions.* People no longer care how computers run, nor who runs them, nor who programs them. People simply want automated solutions to the daily problems that face them.

If the central computer can't supply solutions adequately, perhaps because of work overload, or repeated hardware failures, or poor management, then the engineer or clerk or office worker will seek solutions elsewhere. He may go to an outside service bureau, or he may obtain a minicomputer.

In the 1960s, the central machine room had a monopoly on automated solutions. In the technologically advanced 1980s, nobody has a monopoly on solutions. Computational power can be easily obtained in a variety of ways.

This inevitable spread of various types of computers is not going to stop. Accounting systems must be developed based on this fact. Computer accounting should be flexible so that it can equitably handle many different modes of processing. And accounting must be related firmly to solutions. If it is not, then nobody will pay any attention to it.

Most computer accounting used today was derived from principles created in the late 1960s. But just as surely as the machine room has changed since then, accounting will have to change. Accounting will have to adjust to the new modes of computational power, and to the sophisticated desires of the user population.

Chapter 4.2
Computer Utilization—A Background

Before we can develop any kind of cost accounting system, we need a means of measuring work perfomred on the computer. Measurement tells us how much work has been done, and assigns a relative resource consumption value to each job.

The measurement of computer utilization evolved very slowly. Because large, centralized computers have been around so long, they were first to develop accounting measurements.

It is interesting to note that equipment suppliers such as IBM, CDC, and UNIVAC have tended to hinder the development of computer accounting. Vendors quite logically try to sell as many mainframes as they can within each company that they have penetrated. Good computer accounting can hinder that proliferation of mainframes because users have a better understanding of actual workloads and potential capacities. They are not as likely to be panicked into obtaining another CPU on the advice of a smooth talking salesman. And accounting allows users to share the computer since each customer pays for his share of the resources based on usage. Vendors, of course, would rather see many individual groups within each company get their own mainframes, rather than share.

It is the sharing of computers that created the need for accounting. As diverse user groups began using the same central processors, allocation of costs became a major issue. Nobody likes to pay for somebody else's consumption.

Many studies have shown that most companies placed the cost of their first centralized processors into overhead, generally within the financial subdivision. As the use of computers grew, the costs also expanded. Most companies eventually split computer operations off into separate subdivisions, and the concern for computer accounting rose to a visible level. Standalone computer organizations must account for utilization, because the user population is diverse and spread throughout the company.

With second generation computers, utilization accounting was quite simple. Since only one job could be processed on the CPU at any given moment, elapsed wallclock time was a very reasonable way of charging usage. One of the more efficient methods was to place a timeclock at each processor console. The lead card accompanying each job was actually a timecard. The operator punched this card into the timeclock as the job began, and repunched the card when the job terminated. These accounting cards were then fed into a program where elapsed time was calculated and assigned to the job identity on the card. This elapsed time formed the basis of the cost accounting system, in sophisticated companies, or was used as a measurement tool to judge the productivity of various jobs in other companies.

Utilization measurements became much more complex and difficult to implement with the introduction of third generation computers. The concept of multiprogramming was introduced, with software products such as IBM's MFT (Multiprogramming with a Fixed Number of Tasks) and MVT (Multiprogramming with a Variable Number of Tasks). Multiple jobs were resident in core memory at one time, and the CPU would give slices of time to each job, based on a complex system of priorities. Jobs of higher priority could force jobs of lower priority to wait in a nonprocessing mode for long periods of time. A job's elapsed time on the mainframe therefore had no relationship to actual processing time. In addition, many peripherals such as disk and drum were introduced. A job could relinquish control of the CPU to perform some peripheral activity, and then come back to the CPU for more processing. Peripheral utilization therefore became another factor to consider in usage schemes.

Companies like IBM were again reluctant to supply much help in accounting for this new generation of computers. By the late 1960s, various users began developing their own approaches to computer accounting. To this day, most accounting is the result of developments created by users or third party software houses, and not by computer manufacturers.

Although user involvement has worked well in the past, there is increasing concern that relatively unsophisticated users will be unable to keep up with the incredible pace of CPU technology. Computers are beginning to process jobs in random fashion, very much depending on workload conditions. A job may make use of special high speed memory in one pass, and conventional lower speed memory during another run. This leads to nonrepeatability, which current accounting systems simply cannot handle.

COMPONENTS OF THIRD GENERATION UTILIZATION MEASUREMENTS

First, accurate job timings on the CPU had to be developed, and this was a significant task. Third generation CPU speeds were dramatically increased over second generation equipment. Interval timers had to be developed that gave reasonably repeatable and believable CPU timings. Systems programmers created special software hooks to capture this data and store it for future use.

As sophisticated installations learned more about their equipment, additional accounting measurements were developed. From this point, two different approaches were taken to utilization measurement. One approach was known as resource accounting, and the second was called machine unit accounting. A third method, developed much later, was called transaction accounting.

Resource Accounting

Resource accounting measures all relevant aspects of the job. Each of these measurements becomes an independent form of utilization. A typical job will generate the following resources:

- CPU time (in minutes or seconds)
- Memory occupied during the job step
- I/O activity (usually based on I/O seeks)
- Cards read and punched

Resource accounting is workable and used by many major computer installations up the present time. Its principal drawback, however, is the bulk of accounting data that must be gathered, priced, and reported. Even a moderately sized DP installation can process several thousand jobs each day, thus the volume of accounting data can become overwhelming. Whether or not users appreciate all of the detail offered by resource accounting depends on individual personalities. Some people enjoy detail and some do not. If, however, any user has even a moderate amount of processing activity, the volume of accounting data becomes difficult to deal with.

A second problem is determining how to handle all of the variables in the cost accounting system. A cost rate must be developed for each resource, and the variances must eventually be determined. The various resources may not move in consistent patterns. Memory occupancy utilization may increase, for example, while lines of print decrease. Without predictable relationships, developing meaningful rates and keeping them meaningful becomes a very difficult task for the computer installation. Resource accounting does not meet the criteria of simplicity although it does tend to be reasonably understandable.

Machine Unit Accounting

The second machine accounting technique requires the development of an *accounting algorithm.* This is a more elegant approach to the problem of utilization measurement, and has a wide acceptance within the computer industry.

This method takes the same values measured by resource accounting and uses them as variables in a formula, or algorithm. Special constants in the formula are used to give relative weights to each resource. In the algorithm's earliest form, these constants were used as an attempt to bring the total value of all resource usage back to an equivalent of wall clock time. In fact, the driving force behind creating algorithms was a desire to emulate elapsed time, just as it was used on second generation equipment. This goal was never achieved.

Each I/O seek to disk, for example, was charged with a coefficient that was an approximation of the rotational speed delay of a 2314 disk drive, using the assumption that rotational delay was roughly how long the seek took. By counting the number of I/O seeks and multiplying by the constant, I/O time was derived, in a sense.

One of the earliest algorithms used, developed by R.E. Lawrence (under the auspices of McAuto, a subsidiary of McDonnell Douglas Corporation) for an IBM 360/65, was introduced to the IBM user organization called SHARE in 1967. It is shown in Figure 4-1.

The algorithm starts with an overhead factor of 1, using the assumption that there is a certain amount of system overhead that is expended before the job even begins to process. The number of tape data sets is factored by 0.075, and the number of disk data sets is multiplied by 0.05. Region size is factored in a quadratic equation so that the charge for memory increases exponentially as region size increases. In those early days of computing memory was a precious resource and was very limited, thus a heavy penalty charge was applied to discourage excessive consumption.

The sum of all these charges was then multiplied by CPU time in minutes. Because so many constants were arbitrarily chosen, and because large memory usage was penalized, the algorithm approach did not produce a measurement anywhere close to elapsed time, regardless of what its creators wanted. Instead, the algorithm generated a relative value for each job processed. The resulting utilization measurement was usually called a *unit* and had no meaning except in comparison to units generated by other jobs on the same machine. The

$$\text{MU} = (1.0 + .075T + .050D + (2.5 \times 10^{-3} + 5 \times 10^{-6} R)\, R)\, t$$

t is the chargeable step time in minutes.

D is the number of direct access data sets.

R is the region size in 1K units.

T is the number of tape data sets.

NOTE: Quadratic terms meant to penalize large core users.

Figure 4.1 An IBM computer accounting algorithm.

industry never developed any algorithm standards and to this day it is impossible to draw comparisons in the usage generated by different computer centers.

Algorithms have been refined over the years. Accounting algorithms are offered by a number of different software companies. These programs are compatible with standard operating systems. A detailed description of everything available can be obtained from an organization called AGT, noted in the bibliography.

Accounting algorithms are easy to implement and maintain. As computer mainframe architecture changes, the algorithm can be modified to recognize different values for hardware and software. The algorithm introduced in Figure 4-1 would not be appropriate today, since the cost of memory has been reduced so dramatically. In the late 1960s, half a million bytes of memory was all that could be placed on an IBM mainframe, such as a 360/65. Today, real memory can exceed 30 million bytes. With virtual capabilities (using disk space to substitute for real memory), the amount can be increased tenfold. Memory is therefore not a constraining factor. It is no longer necessary to penalize users when large amounts are needed for processing. It can even be argued that a charge for memory usage is meaningless.

Because accounting algorithms are abstract, they are hard to understand and visualize. As with resource accounting, it is not really completely obvious that programmers or other computer users understand the accounting concept well enough to use it as was originally intended. The interaction of the various factors produces an incomprehensible product. This complexity probably leads to neglect and disinterest by most users. Because of this rather negative conclusion, methods that vastly simplify computer accounting will be introduced in the next chapter.

Transaction Accounting

In recent years an attempt to simplify computer accounting has led to conceptual discussions concerning transaction utilization.

The proposal is to charge back users in units of measurement that they completely understand. These units would specifically relate to program or job output. A payroll program, for example, would generate usage based on the number of payroll checks printed. Program development would be charged based on the number of edit statements executed.

The concept is appealing because of its simplicity and understandability, particularly by the user. Unfortunately, there are major obstacles to implementing such an approach, and that is primarily why discussions have been kept at the conceptual level to date. Very few computer organizations have actually implemented universal transaction accounting. The exception to this is single service computers. When the output consists entirely of one or two transactions, such as processing checks, or reserving airline seats, then transaction accounting is relatively easy to implement. But if the DP organization is general purpose, there is difficulty.

The problems begin with the computer operating system. All other methods of accounting use data actually produced by the basic operating system. IBM, for example, calls the accounting module SMF (System Management Facility), and it is part of all currently available operating systems. Transaction accounting, however, requires data that cannot be supplied by the operating system, because utilization must come from the application program.

Since each major program would have its own unique set of transaction measurements, accounting would have to be generated by the application program itself. Adopting transaction accounting would require that all existing application programs be modified to include accounting subroutines. This would be a considerable task for most installations, and would squander precious programmer resources.

Determining the transaction or transactions that most fairly represent each application would probably require a committee consisting of user and data center people. Each program would need careful review to determine a representative measurement. And there would be many applications, particularly in the scientific area, where transactions would be hard to determine. What, for example, are the transactions for an interactive graphic design system, or a structural analysis program, or a loft job? The effort required to analyze all of the jobs processed through an installation to come up with meaningful transaction measurements hardly seems worthwhile.

Cost chargeback would be another problem. When overall cost accounting variances occurred, it would be very difficult to know how to adjust each type of transaction so that the variances could be recovered and future rates would be representative. There is not necessarily a linear relationship between transaction volume and cost. As transactions increase, program overhead functions such as table overflows, data base expansion, and string manipulations increase processing time at more than proportional levels. Monitoring application program activity would be extremely difficult in a large installation.

Those who advocate transaction accounting methodology have recognized a legitimate user problem and have tried to solve it using techniques that are common in the consumer marketplace. But the complexities that would be created for the cost accountant, and for the data center trying to administer a vast array of transactions, more than offset any user benefits. Measuring and charging for transactions would become so unwieldy that the data center would eventually lose control of its cost accounting system. Such a condition would be worse than having no accounting system at all.

We therefore conclude that transaction accounting is nice in theory, but impossible to implement for most general purpose data processing centers.

Chapter 4.3
Centralized Computer Cost Accounting

The modern large scale computer is powerful, but expensive. A top of the line IBM processor, for example, with a full complement of peripherals, costs about $6.5 million. Roughly one half of that cost is for central processor/memory, and the other half is for peripherals and related hardware.

The cost of central processor equipment has risen with inflation over the years. But significant improvements in technology have increased the power of modern CPUs 60 fold since the mid 1960s. An IBM 7094 was rated at about 0.2 MIPS (Millions of Instructions per Second), and the newest popular machines are running at about 10 to 15 MIPS. The growth rate of processing power per dollar of hardware has stayed significantly ahead of the inflation rate.

Even with the incredible growth in CPU power, many companies find themselves in a constant cycle of upgrading to newer machines of greater power. There seems to be an insatiable demand for more computer resources. Thus DP budgets continually increase as more and more capability is provided. Although economies of scale may be a fact, nobody could prove such a theory by looking at actual computer expenditures made by most companies. Investments in hardware continuously spiral upward, at a rate so fast that nobody can actually analyze the situation.

HARDWARE COST RELATIONSHIPS

Figure 4-2 graphically displays the cost makeup of a typical large-scale mainframe. CPU costs represent about 65% of total hardware costs. Peripherals of various types make up the balance.

The relationship between CPU and peripherals has been changing slowly over the years, with CPU costs decreasing while peripherals such as disk devices have increased in number and in total cost. Mechanical devices, such as printers and tape drives, have not benefited much from the semiconductor revolution, and thus have become significantly more expensive over the years.

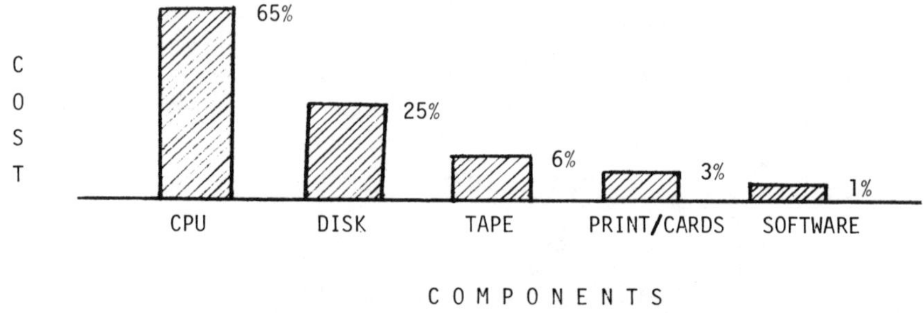

Figure 4-2. Relative value of hardware components.

Disk storage is probably the most volatile peripheral device. The capacity of this hardware has increased tremendously, and the cost per unit of storage has steadily decreased. But the actual quantity of devices installed on each CPU has tended to grow geometrically. This is partially caused by the introduction of virtual operating systems, which require more disk space. But the biggest cause of growth has been the ever-increasing demand for data storage made by typical users. Large, constantly growing data bases have become reality for most modern data centers.

While costs for peripherals have been growing, the CPU has had some interesting changes in its cost structure over the years. The cost of random access memory within the CPU has declined dramatically. In 1970, IBM charged $170,000 for a half million bytes of core storage. Today, 4 million bytes of memory can be added for an incremental cost of $150,000. Cost per megabyte of memory has therefore been reduced by a factor of nearly 10.

The significant decrease in memory has obviously been caused by semiconductor technology. Memory can now be manufactured using automated techniques, while in 1970 it was produced by complex manual operations.

It is not difficult to predict, then, that the relative cost of central processors will decline. The largest technological improvements have their greatest impact on CPUs, and a lesser influence on peripherals.

This change in relative values will influence the way in which we account for computers. It is senseless to spend inordinate amounts of time and money accounting for something that is becoming less and less valuable.

MODERN CPU ALGORITHMS

The prior chapter pointed out that although a number of machine accounting alternatives exist, algorithm accounting is by far the most popular method.

Older algorithms had to take into account the fact that resources like core storage were expensive and precious. These algorithms therefore attempted to encourage efficiency while being equitable to the general user. However, the speed and size of modern computers, as well as the decline in relative value of CPU/memory, are things that were not even contemplated in 1965 when fundamental algorithm techniques were being formulated.

Most computer algorithms today are actually holdovers from those earliest formulas. Consequently, they have the following characteristics:

- An extremely fine measurement granularity. Events such as CPU time are often measured in microseconds (thousandths of a second).
- A stiff charge for memory occupancy.
- A charge for I/O events, usually in the form of EXCP counts(Execute Channel Program counts) multiplied by a coefficient representing microseconds.

Because of the sheer power of modern computers, most of these accounting details are no longer meaningful, or have very marginal value. Cost relationships have changed yet many of the concepts used in accounting algorithms are more than two decades old.

In place of these older accounting techniques, we must substitute an algorithm with the following characteristics:

- Simplicity
- Repeatability
- Imperviousness to changes in computer technology
- Understandability

To achieve such an algorithm, we must change several preconceptions about computer accounting.

A NEW APPROACH

Is there any value in timing components of each job step down to the microsecond? Not really. The accuracy of such timings is questionable and very nonrepeatable.

One of the real reasons why so many algorithms still measure in microseconds is that computer manufacturers supply microsecond timers. There is no more logic to measuring events in microseconds than there is in asking the grocery clerk to count out change in pennys, instead of nickels, dimes, and quarters. Microsecond accounting is something that a technician would come up with, perhaps as a way of displaying technical competence. Such logic has little value in the hard world of accounting.

As a first step in simplifying accounting, therefore, the internal clock should be modified to increment in whole seconds. Any job step processed on the computer would be rounded off in whole seconds to avoid fractional charges.

The charge for memory is another archaic holdover in many accounting routines. With the introduction of semiconductor memory, and of virtual storage techniques, the whole concept of memory occupancy tends to become less important. Because of the significant reduction in memory cost, as pointed out before, we can conclude that there isn't any reason to continue charging for memory occupancy. It's term can be dropped from the accounting algorithm.

Charging for I/O is another activity that is hard to justify. Is the measurement of EXCPs, for example, tracking some critical resource? Most EXCPs are generated as programs access data on disk. This is a secondary activity that ultimately generates more CPU time, since the additional data must be processed. Counting EXCPs is therefore a redundant activity, adding complexity to the accounting process, with benefits that are hard to identify.

There is one minor exception to the concept of eliminating EXCPs. I/O seeks made to setup devices such as tape represent a definite cost increase to any data processing operation. A seek to tape requires that the tape must be physically acquired from a library, carted to the drive, and placed on the drive by an operator. This is labor intensive activity, which is expensive. EXCPs created while accessing setup devices should be charged by the accounting algorithm.

A modern accounting algorithm can therefore be presented as follows:

$$\text{units} = A \times \text{CPU time (seconds)} + \text{tape and disk setup EXCPs}/500$$

The coefficient A is used as a speed balancing factor. If the original factor is 10, for example, and a new CPU with a speed 25% faster than the original machine is introduced into the processing complex, the coefficient can be raised to 12.5 on the new computer. This provides a balance between the different computers, so that no single machine has a speed advantage over any other machine.

Note that CPU time is recorded in whole seconds, as previously discussed. There is also a one second minimum charge. This minimum can be interpreted as step overhead, since it is known that several hundred thousand instructions are processed by the operating system before any job step even begins executing.

EXCP counts are recorded in units of 500, to cut down on their physical quantity.

Many modern installations are phasing out setup type devices because they are so labor intensive. There is a real possibility that at some point in the future charging for setup EXCPs will no longer be necessary. At that point, the term could be dropped from the algorithm.

SIMPLIFYING UNIT ACCOUNTING

As mentioned before, an accounting algorithm is abstract because it does not relate directly to time. Even our simplified algorithm contains abstract elements, caused by I/O counting.

There is a possible solution to this problem. The advantages of accounting algorithms are retained but simplified so that the group of users most likely to be confused by abstractions is offered a very fundamental accounting measurement. This user group consists of people who submit relatively small jobs to the computer.

The graphs in Figure 4-3 show the job profile of a typical large, centralized processing center. This profile is based on a limited, in depth study of several installations. Although the sample base is small, the results seem to be intuitively correct, since they are based on the theory of a normal distribution of jobs. Readers are advised to study their own computer job profiles to verify these findings.

The top graph shows that 80% to 90% of all job steps generally execute in less than two CPU seconds. Most of the remaining job steps are quite large, in the ten second and above range (note that these findings are obviously dependent on the actual speed of the CPU, and timings are relative – a slower main-

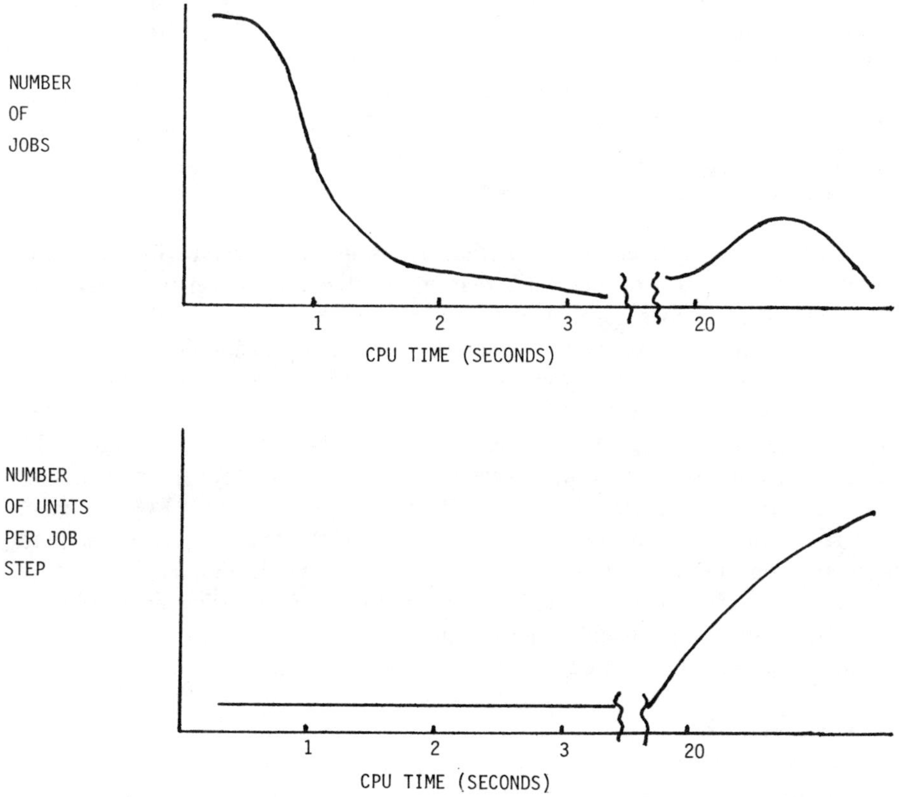

Figure 4-3. Job times and utilization.

frame would display the same characteristics, except that 80% of all jobs would process in less than, say, three seconds).

This profile illustrates that there are a large group of users submitting jobs that use relatively trivial amounts of CPU time (of course, at 6 to 10 million instructions processed per second, these jobs are doing considerable amounts of processing).

There is a second class of jobs, usually large business applications such as payroll, receivables, manufacturing control, etc., that have big data bases and consume significant quantities of CPU time.

In other words, there are two distinct classes of users in most large processing centers.

Cost recovery is inversely proportional to job step profile, as shown in the bottom graph of Figure 4-3. That is, most of the total utilization is generated by the large job steps. Nearly 80% of the total utilization is caused by a group of job steps that make up as little as 10% of the actual number of jobs. These large users are the ones who really justify the computers. The small users are merely going along for the ride, and do not have a significant impact on configuration designs.

Job profiles such as this are obviously dependent on the makeup of each data center, and the ranges can vary somewhat. But the point is that most of the computer cycles are being consumed by a relatively small group of users.

Job Class Accounting

Basic accounting data can be simplified by using insight gained from the previous discussion. If we determine that most utilization is generated by very large jobs, then it does not make a lot of sense to spend a great deal of time and effort accounting for very small jobs. Neither the utilization nor the eventual cost recovery generated by these small jobs is significant. For most data centers, these small jobs are almost a nuisance.

Although accounting for small jobs can't be eliminated, it certainly can be simplified. Suppose, for example, we created the straightforward rule that all job steps that ran in less than two CPU seconds would cost $1.00 per step. The remaining job steps, making up about 20% of the total, would continue to generate conventional algorithm usage. Doing this would dramatically reduce the accounting workload associated with small jobs. Such a chargeback scheme would be easy to explain and easy to comprehend.

In summary, a flat charge for small jobs would be:

- Simple
- Easy to understand
- Repeatable

These characteristics are important aspects of a good accounting system.

Because of the intricate nature of most large jobs, the full accounting algorithm is a reasonably good measure of work performance. Large users are in a better position to accept complex accounting because they are relatively sophisticated and can take the time to analyze accounting data and develop a fuller understanding.

The segmenting of processing users into two categories simplifies accounting for the computer center, and presents a clear and understandable methodology to the end user.

Small users tend to be vocal. They complain when they feel they are being treated unfairly, or when service is poor, or when they can't understand accounting. Because there are so many small users, the data center has a difficult time effectively communicating with them and defending its position. Accounting must be simplified for these people to the point where it is not an issue worth complaining about.

Large users are not very numerous and tend to be more tolerant of the data center because they are very dependent on computers. The center can deal directly with these people to explain the principles of the accounting system and the complexities of the algorithm.

It therefore makes a great deal of sense to simplify accounting as much as possible for the large mass of small users, and keep reasonably complex accounting for the few large users. By reducing the level of complaints, the data center's image is improved, and accounting system and the complexities of the algorithm.

It therefore makes a great deal of sense to simplify accounting as much as possible for the large mass of small users, and keep reasonably complex accounting for the few large users. By reducing the level of complaints, the data center's image is improved, and accounting is removed as an issue of complaint.

Dual accounting also helps to simplify record keeping because up to 80% of the user population is flat charged. The flat charging eliminates complex accounting calculations, and reduces the size of customer utilization data bases.

Chapter 4.4
Using Accounting Algorithms

The fundamental accounting algorithm discussed in the last chapter, along with the dual accounting treatment, is generally applicable to between 60% and 70% of the work performed by a typical centralized computer operation. What is left falls into the category of non-CPU resource usage, such as printing, tape handling, and data storage. Before discussing peripheral resource accounting, we will look at some of the differences between batch and interactive processing.

BATCH AND INTERACTIVE PROCESSING

The accounting characteristics of centralized processing fall into two broad categories, known as batch processing and interactive processing.

- Batch processing is computer processing characterized by the fact that all computer resources required are known and defined at the time the job begins execution. Resource requirements are listed as a set of stored instructions executed before the job actually begins.
- Interactive processing is computer processing characterized by the fact that machine resources required are determined as the job session advances. The user interacts directly with the computer using some form of terminal.

Batch processing is a very formal method of data processing, and is used by large, scheduled, business-type applications. Batch processing can be performed against interactively generated data files, and can be used for updating and consolidating files that were created by interactive, on-line systems.

Interactive processing tends to be informal. This type of processing is generally performed by individuals, sitting at terminals, carrying on a dialogue with the computer.

Both modes of computing use the CPU. There is no fundamental difference in the way that the CPU is used, so the basic algorithm developed in the last chapter is applicable to each form of processing.

Interactive processing generates a large number of jobs with very small CPU usage. A dual mode of accounting is therefore as appropriate for interactive computing as it is for batch processing.

In the interactive mode there is no job step, but the equivalent is referred to as a job session. This is the elapsed time from log-on to log-off. Once again, an arbitrary cost, such as $1.00, can be applied to all interactive sessions that use less than two seconds of CPU time per hour of session connect time. Sessions exceeding the arbitrary limit should be considered large, and should be charged using the conventional accounting algorithm.

It is important to stress that the CPU time cutoff, which separates small jobs from large jobs, depends entirely on the speed of the computers used. We have found through observation that job volumes tend to have a normal distribution, with a mean of less than one CPU second, using computers in the 5 MIPS class. It was further observed that a range of two standard deviations above the mean captured about 70% of all jobs processed, and none of these jobs exceeded two seconds in CPU duration.

But all data centers don't use the same kinds of equipment. Even the internal speeds of identical computers can vary between computer centers because the operating systems have been modified in different ways.

Each data center should analyze its job mix and gather CPU usage statistics. It should calculate a mean CPU time per job, and then determine the CPU value that is two standard deviations above the mean. This should become the upper limit for flat charging. Roughly 30% of all jobs will be above this limit and should be charged using conventional accounting. As Figure 4-3 in the preceding chapter indicated, there is usually a large gap between small jobs and large jobs. All this means is that large jobs are very large, and consume substantial amounts of CPU time. Small jobs tend to be homogenous and clustered tightly around their average CPU time.

DATA BASE SYSTEMS

There is a distinction between interactive systems and data base systems. The data base system makes use of interactive techniques, but the interaction is very well defined. Only prescribed interactive transactions can occur, such as data base queries and data base updates. Data base systems are characterized by software like IMS, CICS, and TOTAL. Conventional accounting techniques are not appropriate for these types of software.

Data base systems consist of various interactive terminals supported by the CPU in an on-line mode. The data base system is a never ending task, from the central processor's standpoint. Because of this it can consume large amounts of CPU resources. Machine unit accounting, using a conventional algorithm, would not be an equitable measurement of resources consumed by the users of data base systems. The CPU, locked up in its never ending task, would generate enough machine units to dwarf all other utilization created by batch and interactive jobs.

Data base systems use their own special software to handle incoming transactions. IBM, for example, calls their software Data Language I. This software provides its own utilization measurement, in the form of I/O counts caused by each incoming transaction. This is a reasonable measure of central processor usage; thus it is usually adopted as the accounting measurement. More complex algorithms can be established, but the increased equitability achieved by such formulas is marginal.

With data base systems, the important achievement is to insure that the total costs of maintaining the entire system are recovered. Whether or not these costs are charged back with complete equitability to each user is of less importance, because none of these users is demand driven. Costs will not change the way users operate. The typical user invokes transactions during the day as outside events occur, such as customer orders, maintenance calls, etc. The user has no choice but to interact with the computer, regardless of what the cost is.

The level at which data base system costs become important is, of course, at the top. The overall system manager is interested in costs per transaction. If costs become too high, the manager may change the way the system operates.

To summarize, then, the CPU can be measured in three different ways. Small jobs, running as either batch or interactive, can be flat charged some arbitrary amount, such as $1.00 per job step or job session. Batch and interactive jobs exceeding a predefined level, such as two CPU seconds, should be charged using conventional accounting algorithm techniques. Data base systems should be charged based on I/O activity, which is measured by counting input and output transactions.

PERIPHERAL ACTIVITY

All users of centralized computers, whether batch, interactive, or data base, make use of peripheral devices. By standardizing utilization measurements, a great deal of confusion can be eliminated, and the accounting process can be kept simple.

Peripheral activities break down into the following categories:

- Transmission over data lines
- Storage
- Output services

First, we will discuss data transmission, then storage, and finally output activities.

Data Transmission

In addition to the data line, special hardware such as modems, multiplexors, and control units are needed before data transmission can be accomplished.

Local transmission costs, particularly intraplant, can be reduced in the short term. For example, it is now economically feasible for plants within a reasonable distance from each other to install low cost microwave stations on top of their buildings to carry all interplant communications, including voice and data. Microwave stations represent a one-time cost, which can often break even with conventional land lines in less than two years.

Transmission costs associated with points outside the company's immediate plant area are less controllable. These costs have generally kept up with or exceeded inflation, and this is because so many of the services are offered by monopolies. Value added networks and specialized carriers are beginning to provide competition to telephone companies, but there have not been any significant reductions to cost, particularly for the transmission of high-speed data. There is some speculation that when very large satellites are placed in orbit, point to point communications without the use of land lines will be possible. However, the pricing structure of satellite usage is still not clear.

Figure 4-4 shows to basic communications links. Each must be accounted for in a different way.

The top diagram represents an in-plant, or company controlled communications setup. That is, the DP department or its communications group controls all aspects of the network. Communications is supplied by telephone company

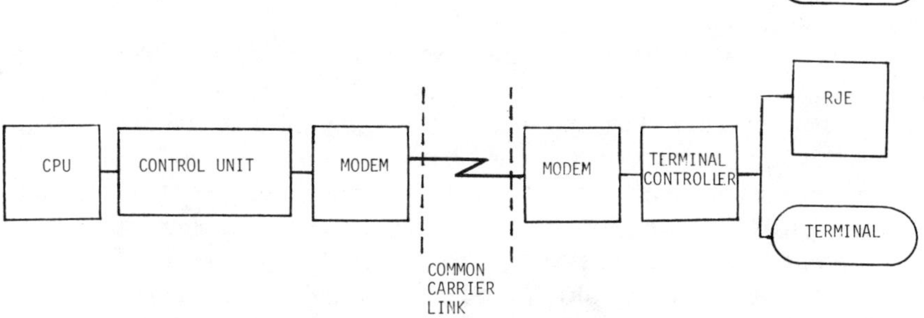

Figure 4-4. Data communication components.

twisted pairs, company installed coaxial cable, or by company owned microwave stations.

An in-plant communications network can be considered a relatively fixed resource, just like electrical wiring, plumbing, and air conditioning ducts. Most of the components of the network are, therefore, purchased, and amortized over a period of time. Corporations fortunate enough to construct new buildings usually design communications facilities into the actual structure.

The fixed pool of communications costs should be allocated to users in a straightforward manner.

The only variable for most in-plant communications setups is line speed. As line speed increases, certain hardware costs increase, primarily to handle the greater volumes of traffic.

We can divide utilization into three basic categories, patterned after three line speed groupings. They are:

- Low-speed (30 cps to 7600 cps)
- High-speed (9600 cps)
- Wideband (above 9600 cps) (cps = characters per second)

Connection to any of these categories can be designated as a *port.* A separate price can be established for low, high, and wideband ports. The port should be considered a flat monthly fee.

A user with a small typewriterlike terminal connected to an interactive service would generate one low speed port each month. A CRT connected to a data base system such as IMS would most likely generate one high speed port each month. And a Remote Job Entry station would require a wideband port, since the transmission rate would be significant.

This type of network utilization and chargeback methodology is simple to implement, simple to maintain, and easy to understand.

Figure 4-4 also shows a second network option. In this case the company transmits data beyond its area of control, and must make use of common carriers or value added data lines.

The cost of this type of data transmission is dominated by data line costs charged by the common carrier. These costs are quite variable, and depend on transmission distance, line speed, length of transmission, and time of day. Because of this complexity, there is no good rule of thumb that can establish the average cost of a data transmission. It is therefore necessary to charge actual common carrier invoiced costs back to each user of the outside network. Any user coming in through outside telephone lines would be charged back for a basic port unit, which would cover hardware and in-plant communications, and he would receive a monthly bill for the invoiced common carrier charges.

Unfortunately, direct chargeback of data lines is time consuming to administer. An extensive communications network can use many different common carriers, and the various costs must be matched back to appropriate terminals. The task is difficult and error prone. But as long as common carrier data line costs are significant, there does not seem to be any alternative. As the competition sorts itself out, the high-speed transmission of data may become very standardized, from a cost standpoint. Other transportation industries such as trucking, airlines, shipping, and postal services have been able to come up with common, industry-wide billing methods. When data transmission vendors achieve this level of consistency, more straightforward standard costing could be used by customers.

Storage Devices

We have already pointed out that storage of data, particularly on-line storage, is the fastest growing service that most data centers offer. While the space requirements of central processing units are declining because of more compact components, occupancy demands of storage devices are increasing. Storage of big data bases may be one of the most important services offered by centralized computer centers. Large computer rooms have the space needed to maintain large numbers of disk drives, tape units, and reels of tape.

On-line Storage. There is no doubt that the premier form of mass storage is *disk.* There have been significant improvements in the cost per unit of on-line storage over the years. Packing densities have increased, and the reliability of electromechanical devices has improved significantly. Although disk is being constantly challenged by devices such as solid state semiconductors and bubble memories, the cost per bit of information stored is still overwhelmingly in favor of disk.

In anticipation of future technological advances, it is purdent to develop a storage utilization measurement that is device independent. Measuring the *quantity* of stored data is a reasonable choice. A useful increment of measurement is *millions of bytes*, or megabytes, of storage.

There are a number of software packages on the market that determine the quantity of storage, in megabytes, on a daily, weekly, or monthly basis.

An effective scheme is to measure the high-water mark of storage for each user on a weekly basis, and use that as the chargeout mechanism. Megabyte weeks is the utilization term that can be used.

Tape Storage. For the user, tape has the disadvantage of difficult access, since it is an off-line medium, but the advantage of nonvolatility, safety, and inexpensiveness. A tape can also store massive quantities of data. It is unfortunate that most users only fill up the first few feet of a 2400 foot reel.

Tape presents many disadvantages to the data processing center. It must be stored in a secure, environmentally controlled vault; it must be retrieved and mounted on drives by human operators; and it must be accurately filed back in the vault for future use. Tapes break easily and are prone to read/write errors, particularly if mishandled. Tape makes a heavy demand on data center resources, such as hardware, space, and labor.

The CPU accounting algorithm introduced earlier made a point of charging for tape usage, through the use of the setup I/O factor. But to cover the additional costs of storage, handling, and the tapes themselves, a flat monthly charge, per reel, should be developed. Such a charge should be high enough to discourage users from keeping needless or useless tapes in the library.

Output Services

The most common peripherals produce output. This is an area of declining importance because so many forms of output are now being handled directly by the user, in his own area. The importance of paper and cards is declining as CRTs become more user oriented. After all, it makes much more sense to get only the information needed on a CRT screen, than to leaf through a 500 page report to obtain the same data.

Most large batch oriented users have their own remote job entry stations (RJEs), which perform all input and output activities at the user's location.

Output activity remaining in the machine room generally consists of the following items:

- Printing
- Card punching
- Microfilm/microfiche
- Plotting on paper

Because of the distribution of so many input/output activities, the largest portion of output is transmitted over communications lines. It is assumed that remote users pay for their own hardware and supplies, thus no further chargeback is necessary.

Local peripheral activities can be charged by using another algorithm. A typical formula follows:

peripheral units = lines printed + cards punched + microfilm frames + plots drawn

The peripheral resource unit is a measure of output in the most fundamental measure available from each resource. It might be advisable to divide lines of print by 1000, if a smaller unit is desired.

The one problem associated with peripheral resource charging is that multipart paper cannot be measured. This type of information is usually embedded in the application program JCL, and is not available to the accounting system. Six part paper is obviously more valuable than one part paper. However, most users will not use more than four part paper because legibility on the fifth and sixth copies is very poor. Four part paper is probably the standard in most data centers, thus the actual inequity is much less than it could be. New technology devices, such as laser printers, eliminate this problem since one part paper is the only option available. Multiple passes must be made to generate additional copies.

Front-end Processors

Semiconductor technology has allowed computer vendors to develop some extremely powerful small computers. This class of computers falls somewhere between the average minicomputer and a centralized mainframe.

Centralized computer installations often use these smaller machines as front ends to larger processors. Relatively trivial transactions can be handled by the front end, freeing the central machine for more important processing.

A common situation would be to provide simple interactive processing on the front end equipment, for such activities as editing and word processing. Many program development tasks could be handled on the front end, while the central machine processed production programs and big number crunchers.

Front end computers are evolving into the support of two categories of interactive users: low volume and high volume.

The low volume user will tend to be a word processor. He or she will be doing editing, report preparation, statistical analysis, and typing. Many of these activities are similar to those handled on conventional word processors.

Because of the similarity to word processing, utilization should be compatible. We will cover word processing concepts in detail later, but the basic utilization is called a monthly subscription unit. That is, a low volume user would incur a single monthly unit regardless of how much work was performed.

High volume users would also generate a subscription unit, but it would be specially identified so that the cost accounting system could apply a higher rate.

The subscription fee concept recognizes two basic facts about small computers:

- Accounting on small machines can consume more than a reasonable amount of resources and leave little room for productive work.
- Because these computers have limited capabilities, users tend to be homogeneous, that is, they are all basically doing the same things.

We have no choice but to make accounting simple. And there is nothing simpler than a subscription unit. Each user represents one unit (users are often called terminal IDs).

The important option that the machine room has is its ability to add additional front ends. If the workload on one front end computer becomes inhomogeneous, with a few users making larger than normal usage of the machine, then a second mini can be obtained for those atypical users. They will then become homogeneous users on the second machine, and subscription units will once again be an equitable measurement.

This entire concept is explored in much greater depth when we cover decentralized computing.

Chapter 4.5
Accounting Summary

At this point we have developed a complete accounting methodology for centralized computing system. Before we continue, it will be useful to review all of the resources.

CENTRAL COMPUTER USAGE

Central computer usage can be broken down into batch, interactive, and data base systems.

Batch and interactive processing can be measured using CPU time. Most jobs execute in a very short amount of processor time. If we calculate the average CPU time, and measure two standard deviations above it, we generally find that at least 70% of the jobs are processing in less than two CPU seconds (on a 5 MIPS class computer). All jobs processing in less time than this arbitrary point should be flat rated. That is, a uniform charge can be assigned to these jobs, and no further accounting is necessary.

When the job times are significant and exceed the point of two standard deviations above the mean, they should be charged using a standard accounting algorithm.

Data base systems are generally measured on a transaction basis. The most straightforward method is count the input and output transactions. This transaction count becomes the basic utilization.

PERIPHERAL USAGE

The three basic categories of peripheral usage are data transmission, storage, and special peripherals.

Data that is transmitted over local lines, which are either owned by the company or rented for a very small fee from common carriers, can be identified with a fixed utilization per month, with the only variable being line speed. Three basic categories of line usage are:

- Low-speed port (30 cps to 7600 cps)
- High-speed port (9600 cps)
- Wideband port (above 9600 cps)

If data transmission occurs over long distances, then significant common carrier costs will be incurred. Under these conditions, it is best to charge each user directly for the telephone expenses incurred. This is quite easily done using the monthly invoice provided by the common carriers.

There are two basic types of storage: direct access and tape.

Direct access storage devices such as high-speed disk are charged out based on amount of storage, as measured in millions of bytes (megabytes), and duration. A common method would be to charge for disk in megabytes per week, using the high-water mark of storage during each weekly period.

Tape storage can be charged based on the number of reels stored each month.

Special peripherals are made up of devices that perform input and output functions in the local computer area. Services include printing, card punching, microfilm, microfiche, and plotting. All of these resources are grouped together in an algorithm. The basic unit of measurement is lines of output, or frames, in the case of microfilm and plotting.

FRONT END PROCESSORS

Minicomputers attached to the central hardware are called front end processors. They can support low volume and high volume users.

Low volume users perform word processing type activities, such as editing. These users can be charged a flat monthly unit per terminal ID or connect. This is called subscription fee charging.

High volume users perform activities such as graphic and program executions. These users can also be charged a flat monthly fee, but the fee is set higher to compensate for the greater hardware usage.

Chapter 4.6
Cost Pooling

OVERVIEW

Cost accounting begins with the development of standard rates. These standard rates are then put into a cost distribution system, where they are multiplied against utilization. The resulting distributed cost is then passed on to the computer user. The user presumably uses this cost to help control his own computer activity.

The data center must create rates prospectively. That is, utilization and costs are unknown and must be projected. Forecasts never completely materialize, thus variances occur. Variances are generally passed on to users at the close of the accounting period. If variances are large, they are an indication that rates must be changed.

Because so much forecasted data is used – both utilization and cost – the creation of standard rates is closely tied to planning. Most companies have an annual planning cycle, and it is during this time that the computer center should build standard rates for the coming fiscal year.

The rate building process uses costs derived from the general ledger. These costs are rearranged into cost pools. Cost pools are directly related to utilization measurements; thus a simple division of utilization into pool dollars will yield standard rates.

As we go through the rate building process, it will become apparent that success depends on how well costs are segregated in the general ledger, and how accurate the actual costs are. If the data processing department has taken the time to create a meaningful set of general ledger accounts, as suggested in Part 3, then the rate building process will go very smoothly. A believable general ledger is necessary before standard costing can work.

THE NATURE OF COSTS

A cost pool is any meaningful collection of costs. The term *meaningful* has to do with understanding, particularly by the outside world. It is not good enough that computer technicians understand what goes into the cost pool. The average user, who's bill is based on the cost pool, must also understand what the pool is measuring.

Data processing management often thinks in terms of the components of a CPU, such as processor, channels, and switches. Understanding of these items is obviously necessary when building a configuration, but they have little meaning to the user community. Cost pools must translate computer complexity into understandability.

A typical data center is made up of many costs. They fall into four basic categories:

- Payroll/related
- Hardware/related
- Other partially controlled costs
- Allocations

Payroll/Related

Payroll costs consist of salaries and wages payed to all employees within the data processing responsibility center. This includes computer operators, tape librarians, management, systems programming, and applications programming. In addition to direct pay, fringe benefits are usually included. Fringe benefits include items such as the employer's portion of FICA, paid vacations and holidays, company paid insurance, and other company reimbursed benefits. Fringes are a significant cost item, often adding as much as 40% to basic payroll costs (fringe benefits continually increased during the 1960s and 1970s, peaking around 1978, and have slowly declined since then).

Hardware/Related

The largest segment of a typical data processing operation's costs are usually tied up in computer hardware and associated costs. These costs include rental, lease, and depreciation for computers, communications, data lines, operating system software, computer supplies, and expendable equipment. Other related costs include transportation, taxes, maintenance, and installation.

Partially Controllable

These costs are often allocated to the data processing department by the parent company. If the DP organization is large enough, it may incur and pay these expenses itself. Costs include occupancy (heat, lighting, electricity, janitorial services, building maintenance), general services (personnel, accounting, plant security), and other operating (office furniture, employee travel, postage, facility lease/amortization).

Allocations

This is a basic charge for what is often called G&A (General and Administrative expense), which is usually made up of headquarters costs allocated equally over the entire company. Costs may include imputed interest, reserves for contingent liabilities, taxes, and executive staff.

The important distinction between all of these costs is that some are controllable and some are not. The data center can do something about costs such as hardware rent and operator labor. The center can authorize the installation of hardware, for example, or cancel unneeded equipment. The same kind of control can be exercised over labor because people can be hired and fired. Costs that are allocated to the data center are not as controllable, however. These costs are incurred by other responsibility centers and arbitrarily charged to the data center.

Most controllable costs can be directly associated with a task. Computer hardware, for example, is used to process programs. And labor costs are expended in operating the machines. These types of costs are formally referred to as *direct costs.*

Uncontrollable costs cannot be easily associated with the performance of work. They materialize as allocations, or burdens. They are formally referred to as *indirect costs.*

FROM PLAN TO COST POOL

Forecasting the values of various expense items is an activity that has been touched on before. Planning is a combination of studying past trends and projecting them into the future. This activity must be performed for all categories of cost and utilization. The actual tasks of planning and budgeting are beyond the scope of this book. It should be pointed out that the greatest value of planning is that it brings to those managers who do it a much greater understanding of the entire computer operation.

Creating cost pools can be a difficult process without some logical approach. The use of a device called a *cost planning matrix* is a logical and effective way to approach this task. A matrix, prepared for a centralized computer operation, is shown in Figure 4-5.

The value of the matrix is that is provides a financial summary of the data processing center. The matrix lists all general ledger expense accounts that are charged to the data center across the top. In some cases, accounts have been expanded, and in some cases they have been consolidated. The goal is to keep things understandable.

COST PLANNING MATRIX
THOUSANDS OF DOLLARS

COST POOL / GENERAL LEDGER ACCOUNT	BILLABLE LABOR	ALLOCATED LABOR	ADPE RENT	ADPE DEPRE-CIATION	COMMU-NICATIONS RENT	COMMU-NICATIONS DEPRE-CIATION	DATA LINES	SOFT-WARE	SUPPLIES	GENERAL SERVICES	OCCU-PANCY	OTHER OPERATIONS	G&A	TOTAL
DIRECT COSTS														
LABOR														
PROGRAMMING – APPLICATIONS	5000													5,000
SYSTEMS PROGRAMMING		3000												3,000
OPERATORS		4000												4,000
TOTAL LABOR	5000	7000												12,000
EQUIPMENT														
CPU/MEMORY			2000	3000				300						5,300
TRANSMISSION														
LOW-SPEED PORTS					200	50	200							450
MEDIUM-SPEED PORTS					220	60	275							555
HIGH-SPEED PORTS					250	65	320							635
DASD STORAGE			1500	1000										2,500
PERIPHERAL I/O			300	250					450					1,000
SUBTOTAL			3800	4250	670	175	795	300	450					10,440
DEDICATED EQUIPMENT			500	100	250	400		50	100					1,400
DEDICATED DATA LINES							750							750
TOTAL EQUIPMENT			4300	4350	920	575	1545	350	550					12,590
INDIRECT COSTS														
MANAGEMENT/STAFF	750													750
INTERNAL CHARGES	100													100
OTHER OVERHEAD										1500	2000	1000		4,500
G&A													2000	2,000
TOTAL OVERHEAD	850									1500	2000	1000	2000	7,350
TOTAL	5850	7000	4300	4350	920	575	1545	350	550	1500	2000	1000	2000	31,940

1M72118

Figure 4-5. Central computer cost planning matrix.

Labor, for example, has been expanded into billable and allocated categories. The reason for this will be covered later. But the actual split can be accomplished by dividing the head count up between those who bill their time out and those who allocate to pools, and prorating dollars appropriately.

Consolidating occurs in the general services/occupancy/other operating expense sections. There are a number of general ledger accounts that fit into these areas, but since they all allocate out over the same direct cost base, there is no advantage in showing the detail. Detail can be kept on backup displays.

The rows listed along the left side of the matrix are the DP center's cost pools. There is a row for each utilization measurement, and additional lines for items that will be allocated.

Note also that the matrix is divided into a section containing direct costs, and a section containing indirect costs. The direct costs will be used in the rate building process, and indirect costs will form the overhead, or burden, pool.

The actual number of rows and columns, and their titles, will vary from center to center, depending on local conventions and the degree of detail desired. Each DP operation has its own unique blend of hardware and labor resources. Centers will have different types of hardware, and each type will have its own distinct set of cost pool categories. Some centers include applications programmers, and some do not. The matrix in 4-5 is offered for discussion purposes only. The dollar values placed within the matrix are also examples, and are not intended for comparison with actual operations. An attempt was made, however, to make the relationships between values as realistic as possible.

The matrix in Figure 4-5 represents a computer operation with annual costs of about 32 million dollars. The center has a staff of machine operators, systems programmers, and applications programmers. The center has one major processing pool that offers batch and interactive processing. Further offerings would obviously be possible but were not considered in our example so that the situation would remain relatively simple. The center is also allocated a full range of indirect costs from the parent company.

WHY A COST PLANNING MATRIX?

One of the contentions of this book is that a cost planning matrix is applicable to every form of computing, and every significant computer installation. The matrix will be referred to a number of times in future chapters, so it should be useful to discuss the theory behind this planning document.

The most fundamental problem faced by data processing financial managers is the need to translate general ledger cost information into a structure that can be meaningfully charged back to computer users. The structure of the general ledger does not lend itself well to chargeback, nor to cost accounting.

For example, the general ledger tells us the total value of computer hardware expenditures. But total hardware costs mean nothing to the computer user. He thinks of computer needs in terms of CPU usage, DASD, and hours of connect activity.

The question is, how do we get from general ledger accounts to an understandable cost accounting structure?

The simple solution is to rearrange general ledger cost accounts into special groupings called cost pools, as we have already discussed. But the task is not easy. There is usually not a direct correlation between accounts and pools. The hardware account referred to above may be split up among many different pools before equity is achieved.

The cost planning matrix formalizes this whole process to the point where an excellent audit trail is developed. The matrix visually shows how each general ledger account is apportioned to specific cost pools. It doesn't actually do the allocation, but records precisely how each allocation to cost pool was made.

Aside from making the accountant's life simpler, the matrix opens up the financial process to nonaccountants. A potentially complex discipline is simplified to the point where nonfinancial managers can understand it and use it in their day-to-day decision making.

The cost planning matrix, then, formalizes the cost accounting process. And it simplifies the potentially hard to understand world of accounting.

DETAILS OF THE COST PLANNING MATRIX

Following is a narrative description of each cost pool row on the matrix, and details on how they were calculated.

Programming

When the data processing department offers programming services, these services are generally considered billable. That is, programmer time is costed and charged out to the department that requested the work. Offering programming services is important to most data centers, because it promotes use of large computers.

The individual rates of programmers vary widely, depending on length of service and individual ability. To avoid an eventual wide proliferation of labor rates, it is generally wise to group programmers into several broad categories, from which composite rates can be developed. This saves a lot of time, and simplifies the rate structure. A useful grouping might be:

- Junior Programmer
- Programmer
- Senior Programmer
- Consultant Programmer

Various actual job classifications can be arbitrarily assigned to each major grouping. The total salaries, wages, and fringe benefits are then added up for each subpool, placed on the matrix, and used in the actual rate building process.

Standard rates can be developed based on the total projected dollars in each category divided by the average hours billed per year. There is a difference between hours worked and hours billed. The difference is often called *company paid lost time.* There are 2040 hours per person in a standard year of 40 hour workweeks. The average person loses about 200 hours of vacation, holiday, sickness, and miscellaneous activities such as jury duty and military leave. Using 1840 hours per person per year, therefore, an average standard rate can be developed for each classification, as shown in Figure 4-6.

Operators

The operator labor expended in support of computer hardware is usually quite significant. Each new generation of equipment reduced the number of people necessary to keep machines running, but sizable staffs are still required for mounting and storing tapes, monitoring communications loads, and handling emergencies such as hardware failure.

Operators are usually assigned to a specific class of machine. In our example, it can be assumed that all operators support the single hardware pool. If various types of hardware exist, such as IBM, CDC, and Univac, then procedures must be set up to assign people to appropriate pools.

Total labor costs are collected and charged to the machine pool or pools. This is an arithmetic allocation process that will be discussed later. The point is that operator labor costs become part of the machine pool, which is then used to develop processing rates. As with programmers, the costs consist of total wages, salaries, and fringe benefits.

CLASSIFICATION:	Programmer
NUMBER OF EMPLOYEES:	20
TOTAL ANNUAL WAGES:	\$560,000
FRINGE BENEFIT RATE:	35%

$$\frac{\$560{,}000 + (\$560{,}000 \times .35)}{20 \times 1{,}840 \text{ hrs/emp/yr}} = \$20.54/\text{hr}$$

Figure 4-6. Labor rate buildup.

Systems Programming

Systems programmers work on computer operating systems. They implement new operating system releases and make modifications to existing software. Because their activities are so closely associated with hardware, their total costs are collected and assigned to the processing pool, for inclusion in the processing rates.

CPU/Memory

This is the first of the major equipment subpools. There is no need to separate CPU from memory since the accounting algorithm treats them as a single charge. In our matrix, there are three major accounts making up CPU/memory. They are: ADPE rent, ADPE depreciation, and software.

Translating general ledger costs into subpool categories requires the expertise of the data processing accounting department. Pool identity can be assigned at the time actual invoices are paid. When the invoice for the CPU is paid, for example, the cost can be assigned to the CPU/memory pool.

Collecting equipment actuals by cost pool is not something most accounting systems can do automatically. Often, this must be accomplished through manual analysis, perhaps done on a quarterly or semiannual basis. Source documents such as vendor invoices and depreciation records are generally used.

To do a proper cost assignment, other subtle changes must be made to expenses. Although the matrix does not show the actual mechanics, certain costs have been taken out of their pool of origin and placed into the CPU pool. This is because the basic operating system uses hardware from other pools for its own purposes. The most commonly borrowed resources are:

- Disk space
- Printers
- Tape drives

Disk is used to store the actual operating system software and to provide scratch space for processing application programs. The cost of that disk should be transferred to CPU. Printers are used to record various system outputs used for diagnostic purposes.

By including the cost of these specialized devices with the CPU, they will be recovered over CPU utilization.

It is generally recommended that a technical expert, such as a systems programmer, map out the hardware that is required by the operating system. This is not a negotiable situation, since, for example, disk spindles are actually clipped and permanently assigned to the operating system.

Tape drives are setup devices, and the CPU algorithm is structured to recover these types of expense. All costs associated with tape equipment are therefore also included in the CPU.

Just how much cost gets moved around between pools depends on how sophisticated the center wants to get. We recommend that a simple structure be used in the beginning. From this understandable base, more complexity can be implemented as a fuller understanding of the relationship between various types of equipment is grasped. The cost planning matrix is an evolving document, and depends on the sophistication of practitioner users.

Transmission

Transmission costs are made up of fixed and variable expenses. Fixed costs include in-plant data lines and control units attached to the CPU. These costs can be apportioned to the three transmission pools based on the number of ports each pool has. Port counts can be determined by systems programmers.

A sample allocation follows:

Controller costs	$100,000 per year
Other fixed costs	$ 5,000 per year
	$105,000 per year

	Number of Ports	%	Allocations
Low-speed	25	44%	$ 46,200
High-speed	30	53%	$ 55,650
Wideband	2	3%	$ 3,150
	57	100%	$105,000

Costs that are unique to each pool include modems, multiplexors, value added networks/long lines, some types of concentrators, and any other devices needed to control the basic speed of the line. These variable costs are grouped into the appropriate pool, based on actual usage. The initial assignment of costs will probably require analysis and guidance from communications experts.

DASD Storage

On-line storage not used as system space, scratch space, or setup, is included in the DASD cost pool. This kind of storage is sometimes referred to as user library space. Any data that must be stored over a long period of time, but which must be available on-line, is placed here.

It is not necessary to determine the cost of individual disk units. The cost of total DASD storage can be determined and then allocated to the appropriate pool. Figure 4-7 illustrates the allocation technique. Equivalent pack counts are determined for mainframe (system packs, scratch packs, backup packs, and spares), and DASD storage (user controlled data). Equivalent packs must be determined because many installations have several different disk pack vintages that hold varying amounts of data. All disk packs should be brought back to an equivalency with the most common pack size used by the center. From the equivalent pack count, allocation percentages are determined, and used to split costs up, as illustrated in the figure.

Dedicated Equipment

As remote processing took hold and began to grow, most companies recognized that some kind of central control over terminals and decentral processors was necessary. We have chosen to call this class of hardware *dedicated equipment*, using the assumption that it is physically possessed by non-DP departments but under the cost and inventory control of the data processing department.

Originally, most dedicated equipment was connected by communications lines to the central processing complex. Now, dedicated equipment is being obtained that is not connected to the central computer. Standalone minicomputers represent this class of equipment.

By assigning all such equipment to the data processing center, management gains a perspective on the total dollar investment in hardware.

Dedicated Lines

Communication line costs come from common carriers such as telephone companies and value added networks. These costs are very similar to dedicated

	PACK EQUIVALENTS	ALLOCATION FACTOR
SYSTEM PACKS (MAINFRAME)	40	40%
USER PACKS	60	60%

TOTAL DISK COSTS		ALLOCATION FACTOR	
$2,000,000	X	.4	= $ 800,000 TO MAINFRAME
$2,000,000	X	.6	= $1,200,000 TO USER POOL

Figure 4-7. Allocation of disk storage.

equipment. For overall control, they are assigned to the computer organization, but the costs are passed on to each individual user.

Both dedicated lines, and dedicated equipment discussed previously, are sometimes called *passthrough* costs.

Internal Charges

If the data processing center chooses to track its own use of computers and people, this is where the costs go. Activities such as developing an internal accounting system fall into this category. There are arguments for and against charging back internal work, going something like this:

- Pro: Internal work must be tracked and costed because it can become significant. If a center is not careful, it can find that its own people are using computers to the point where they are contending with outside users for processing cycles. Chargeback is the only method of keeping these costs under control.
- Con: Work performed for yourself is a cost of doing business, and will occur whether or not it is costed. It can best be controlled through good management practices, thus it is a waste of money to go through the exercise of chargeback.

On the sample matrix, we have taken a compromise position. We have identified only those *labor* costs expended on internal activities. We have not identified processing costs, using the assumption that they are continuous costs of doing business. Internal computer usage is relatively light. The marginal cost of such time is virtually zero.

Labor costs identified as internal must be deducted from direct labor so that a double count does not occur.

Other Overhead

Everything not already identified, but that the data center pays for directly, is included here. Costs include occupancy (electricity, heating, facility maintenance, etc.), general services (personnel, advertising, security, etc.), and other operating expenses (postage, outside training, travel, etc.).

G&A

These are allocations passed down from the parent company that cannot be specifically identified. These costs are highly dependent on corporate accounting policies and the size of the corporate staff.

MATRIX MECHANICS

We have kept the discussion of cost categories very generalized. There is simply no way to anticipate the variations that each data center can produce. But there are several key points that should be kept in mind:

- Follow the general rule of keeping expense accounts listed across the top and cost pools down the left side. Don't intermingle, or the process will become more confusing than it should be. The matrix is a flexible document, and should be shifted around until it makes good sense to the organization using it. If center management can't understand the matrix, it is too complicated.
- Include *all* costs. Many companies do not actually charge the data processing organization with some costs, such as those we have called indirect. These costs may be consolidated at a level higher than the computer operation. But it is to the data processing organization's benefit to work closely with the parent accounting department to identify any hidden costs and force them onto the DP operation's books. This may require certain convolutions of the existing accounting system, but no professional accountant will ever resist such a move. The point is that a DP operation will *never* reach maturity until it is fully costed.
- Expect that the first cost matrix won't be very accurate or complete. Start simple, so that nonaccountants can understand. As management gains financial expertise, more intricacy can be built into the matrix. A matrix may need iterations over many years before it fully develops.
- Make liberal use of technical expertise in assigning costs to appropriate pools and subpools. But leave the actual distribution mechanics, and the final decisions, in the hands of accountants. Technicians have an incredible ability to convolute procedures and worry about insignificant items. The whole process must be kept simple and straightforward.
- Keep the process flexible. If management is not happy with the way things are turning out, the matrix should be modified. Costs should never be hidden, but they can certainly be rearranged if management feels such an action is necessary. The goal is to satisfy data processing management, so that they feel comfortable with the cost accounting system. Once management feels good about the numbers, they will use them in future decisions.
- Use the matrix to isolate cost problems. Perhaps internal costs are too high, or systems programming is not reasonably proportional to mainframe costs. Use cost relationships to challenge individual managers, and make them justify their expenditures. Good cost control is not something caused by a once-each-year grandstanding effort by top management. Cost control occurs through day-to-day detailed effort. If each first level manager knows that his costs are being monitored and analyzed, he will institute his own system of controls that, ultimately, are the best controls a company can have.

FROM COST POOLS TO STANDARD RATES

A completed cost planning matrix is a financial picture of the next twelve months in the life cycle of a computer operation. All costs are included. There should be no surprises over the next fiscal year. The matrix grand total, at the bottom right corner of the page, should balance exactly with the DP budget submitted to company planners. The entire center operating plan is therefore summarized on a single sheet of paper.

Building Utilization Forecasts

Forecasting machine utilization is the final step required before standard rates can be calculated. Utilization measurements that would correlate with our simple matrix are as follows:

- Programmer hours
- CPU units
- Low-speed ports
- Medium-speed ports
- High-speed ports
- DASD megabyte weeks
- Peripheral machine units

Utilization forecasting is something of an art. It takes experience to do well. It is a combination of historical actuals weighted by future events. Assuming that a historical baseline of utilization is available, an effective method of forecasting usage follows:

- Using linear regression techniques against historical data, project 12 months of utilization for each major customer, prior to the beginning of the new fiscal year. Linear regression may or may not be appropriate, but at least it provides a statistical baseline.
- Meet with each major user and discuss the forecast. If this is a formalized process, which it should be, the user will have his own utilization projections, or at least have an idea of future major events. Forecasts can be compared and negotiated values should result. The goal is to get agreement between user and DP management on what utilization values will be during the next year.
- If there are classes of users without representation, ballpark estimates should be made by the center. In a mature planning process, all users should be represented by a planning entity.
- Let a few weeks pass, then reassemble to finetune the utilization values. Three or four meetings may be necessary before a truly satisfactory plan emerges for each user.

• Summarize these plans into a consolidated document and publish, so that all interested parties understand what the plan is.

Rate Building

With final utilization values accumulated, the rate building process can begin.

Each rate is composed of several layers of costs such as direct, indirect, and overhead. The three basic categories are as follows:

- Labor rates
- Processing rates
- Pass-through costs

Labor rates are created for all directly billable professional functions. Programmer services are the most common, but other support functions such as terminal operators may also be included. It is to the center's benefit to bill out all labor that it possibly can. For example, communications expertise may be needed by a department that is setting up a distributed computing system. Although the DP center will get no processing benefit from the distributed system, it should willingly provide the expertise, and should bill for it. In this way the center develops important skills, and gets some cost relief it would not otherwise have had.

The calculation of sample programmer labor rates was illustrated earlier. Rates for any other billable category would be determined in a similar way.

Processing rates are built from many different costs shown on the matrix. The major processing pools consist of ADPE rent and depreciation, software, operator labor, and systems programming labor. Other pools also include communications rent and depreciation, data lines, and supplies. The CPU/memory pool, for example, is a combination of ADPE rent, depreciation, and software, and totals $5,300,000.

To the direct hardware costs, operator and systems programming labor must be charged. In most cases, this labor is allocated rather than discretely billed to make it easier on those who must record their time on cards. Prorating labor costs to each pool and then building the final rate is straightforward, and occurs as follows (using figures from the matrix):

Step 1. Prorate labor

CPU/Memory = 50.7% ($5,300,000/$10,450,000)
50.7% × $3,000,000 = $1,520,000 of allocated operator labor
50.7% × $4,000,000 = $2,028,000 of allocated systems programming labor
Total allocated labor to CPU = $3,549,000

Step 2. Build cost pool

Direct equipment	$5,300,000
Allocated labor	$3,549,000
	$8,849,000

Step 3. Calculate rate, using utilization gathered from the forecasting process
$8,849,000 (total cost)/7,500,000 (utilization) = $1.18 per CPU unit

The above procedure can be repeated for each of the equipment pools, using appropriate dollar and utilization values.

The rates established thus far for labor and processing are called *direct rates* because they are composed of pure direct costs.

Passthrough costs were identified on the matrix as dedicated equipment and dedicated data lines. As indicated earlier, these costs usually represent actual invoiced amounts. The center may choose to add a small handling fee onto these costs to cover paperwork and inventory carrying charges. The costs are then passed directly on to those who actually have physical possession of the equipment.

Overhead

Overhead is the final allocation that gets applied to the direct cost base. All of the indirect costs identified in the lower portion of the matrix are considered overhead. These costs are pooled together and allocated over the entire direct base, excluding passthrough costs.

From the matrix, total direct costs are $22,440,000, and total overhead is $8,250,000. The overhead rate is therefore calculated as follows:

$$\frac{\$8{,}250{,}000}{\$22{,}440{,}000} = 36.8\%$$

Calculating final rates, which are sometimes referred to as fully burdened rates, would proceed as follows:

Labor	$21.74 × 1.368 = $29.74 per hour
CPU/Memory	$ 1.18 × 1.369 = $ 1.61 per unit

These final rates would then become part of the user chargeback system.

The overhead rate provides a very useful means of control. Overhead activities are a fact of life for all forms of business. But overhead does not directly contribute to the generation of income. It is therefore an area that should be constantly scrutinized. Overhead can very easily get out of control, particularly during periods of business decline. Because overhead is not related to the production process, it does not decline proportionately as direct costs are cut back. The relationship between direct and indirect, which is shown by the overhead rate, should be closely watched. If direct costs go down, then the overhead rate will increase unless indirect costs also decline. The rule of thumb is that the overhead rate should remain quite constant or go down over the years. An increasing rate should never be tolerated without very good justification.

COST ACCOUNTING AND COMPUTER USERS

Computer utilization is usually very dynamic. Most data processing installations using large computers handle thousands of jobs every week. Workloads like this obviously demand that the various forms of usage must be generated automatically by the operating system. There is no alternative.

Utilization generated by the computer system is often called raw accounting data. This data is too granular to be used by anybody. It is usually fed into a set of postprocessor programs that edit, sort, and collate the data into a more meaningful format. This may include eliminating extraneous data and obvious mistakes. It may also include sorting the data by client identity and summarizing it into a useful time period such as a month. Finally, each of the utilizations is extended by appropriate standard rate to calculate cost for each user.

Utilization and cost data are then consolidated into reports. These reports should be designed with the user in mind, and various levels of summary should be provided. This is because first level programmers have different needs from top levels of management.

Reporting procedures will be discussed in much greater detail in a future section. But it is important to observe that the data center must remain flexible and cooperative with the computer user community when developing reports. A great deal of time and money is invested in developing cost accounting techniques. Much of it would be wasted if reports were unusable or ignored by users.

CALCULATION OF VARIANCE

The final step in the cost accounting cycle is the calculation of variance. This is a function performed by the center for its own information and control. If the variances are large enough, then specific action must be taken. Large variances inevitably point to problems.

Because standard rates are used, as time passes a variation will develop between costs applied at standard, and costs actually incurred and reported through the general ledger. This condition is often referred to as overabsorption and underabsorption. Absorption is the amount of distributed cost.

Variances between actual cost and distributed cost are inevitable. Standard rates are based on forecasted data, and forecasts will never materialize with complete accuracy.

In a well-run center, variances may not be significant over long periods of time. It is advisable, however, to go through the variance calculation process each month.

The variance reconciliation is performed as follows:

- From data supplied by the utilization system, calculate costs applied by each utilization pool, such as cost for CPU/memory, or DASD, or peripherals.
- From data provided by the general ledger, create a cost matrix.
- Compare actual costs by pool, contained in the new matrix, with distributed costs by pool, from the distribution system. Calculate the percentage variance for each pool. Variances should not exceed 5% in either direction.
- If the variance is small, it should be carried over into the next period, and placed in a special account in the general ledger set up for that purpose (a common account title is Prior Period Adjustments). Month-to-month variances tend to offset each other, netting out close to zero in the long run.
- If the variance is significant, it must be passed back to the parent company. In effect, the parent has not been billed the proper amount of cost. Exactly what form the variance chargeback takes to the parent company is negotiable. Some companies close total variances into a single account. Others want departmental visibility, and still others want variances distributed back to individual users on a retroactive rate-change basis. The parent accounting system should be used if special requirements are necessary.
- If the variance is significant, determine the cause. Also, determine the amount of rate adjustment necessary in future periods to eliminate the excessive variance. Increase or decrease rates appropriately.

Changing rates is more art than science. There is obviously no guarantee that past conditions, which created the variance, will continue into the future. In many cases it isn't even clear what has caused the variance, because two independent variables are at work. Utilization can vary over or under anticipated levels. And actual costs can be greater or less than expected. Two items that can vary in two different directions each can produce six possible combinations.

One approach to washing out variances is to make very small adjustments to the standard rates each month, and keep adjusting until an equilibrium is reached. At that point the rates should remain fairly stable for reasonably long periods of time, assuming that the center is not subjected to violent business conditions.

The most common causes of variance are as follows:

- Large personnel turnover.
- Significant reorganization.
- Unplanned acquisition of hardware or related items.
- Sudden, unplanned changes in the parent company's business level.
- Significant hardware performance problems.
- Poor cost control.
- Poor planning.

Most of the items that cause variances have negative connotations. This is because the most serious forms of variance occur when actual costs exceed standard costs. Such a condition requires a rate increase, and nobody likes rate increases. Rate reductions, on the other hand, are usually caused by good cost control or luck.

Like overhead increases, variances can point to managerial problems within the data processing center. Consistently large variances generally indicate a situation that is out of control. A parent company that constantly sees large variances from its data processing operation should probably consider changes in center management.

Chapter 4.7
Observations on Centralized Accounting

Central computer operations have been around for many years. They have had time to mature. Centralized computers are important components of all corporations. Most companies could not meet their payroll nor produce their products without large computers. Corporate America as it exists today depends on centralized computing.

One aspect of maturity is solid cost accounting. Part four has attempted to cover all aspects of cost accounting as they should be practiced by centralized computer operations. Many of the techniques can be used by other modes of computing.

It is important to note that we have stressed the full cost approach. A great effort must be made by the data center to identify all costs associated with operating computers and writing programs. If anything less than the full cost approach is used, then the accounting effort is meaningless and a waste of time. Either you full cost or you don't bother with accounting. There is no middle ground. Partial costing is arbitrary and subject to the whims of managers anxious to make themselves look as good as possible. When you partial cost, then you can pick and choose between which costs you present to the world, and which costs you hide. This kind of situation leads to abuse and even fraud.

Another important reason for full costing is that it sets the DP operation up as a model to be emulated by other data processing installations within the company. If the central facility full costs, then decentral and disturbuted computing installations can also be expected to full cost.

No mode of computing is above the concepts of cost accounting. But the central operation must first set itself up as a believable accounting entity, before other types of computing can be asked to develop good accounting practices.

The most important result of computer cost accounting is the standard rate, or rates. Rates are easy to understand and easy to track over a period of time. If the rate fluctuates significantly, the organization may have problems. If rates stay stable, then it is most likely that the data processing organization is also stable and well managed.

But, as with all accounting, if the final result is to be believed, the techniques that produced that result must be fully understood by the general user population. That is why it is so important to stress simplicity. In cost accounting, the simplest method is the best method.

The cost accounting system that is doing its job is the one that can help in answering the familiar question: Am I getting my money's worth? It is a valid question that many DP organizations have failed to answer for many years. In later chapters we will explore the answer to that question.

Part V
Decentralized Computing

Chapter 5.1
Introduction to Decentralized Computing

We pointed out earlier that there is a tendency to confuse decentralized computing with distributed processing. Both modes of computing use minicomputers. But while distributed computing operations use many small processors that are tied together by some form of communications network, decentralized computing systems consist of standalone machines that are self-contained. Decentralized equipment is used to run specific applications for users who directly control the machine and operate it. The decentral computer does little or no communicating with other computers. In many respects it is a miniaturized copy of the centralized machine room that we examined in the previous section. This commonality means that some of the accounting techniques developed for central operations can be applied to decentralized computers.

Decentral machines may be batch oriented, but they usually make significant use of interactive techniques. Desktop terminals are used as a principal source of input and output. This eliminates the need for a dedicated data preparation group, such as keypunch clerks, and reduces operator requirements.

Decentral computing is a relatively new phenomenon, made possible by the introduction of powerful small computers capable of working in less than ideal environments. A properly configured and programmed minicomputer appears to require much less support than a multiple use centralized mainframe. This is a direct contradiction to the principal of economies of scale. Although this contradiction has not been proven, it appears to be intuitively correct. Decentralized computing allows people to "do it themselves." Because of this, the high overheads associated with full-time computer professionals are eliminated. Just as it is cheaper to repair a broken appliance yourself, it costs less to operate your own computer.

Most companies have been experiencing growth in decentralized computing facilities even when large, centralized computer resources exist. If decentral computers are acquired in addition to central facilities, there is a possibility that the decental computers simply add costs to the corporation without providing any significant increase in computing cabability. This observation is debatable, and will be explored later.

Many decentral operations are started by people who are relatively sophisticated in the use of computers, but who are not associated with the central computer operation. These people have decided that the central computing approach does not fulfill their needs.

A minicomputer is a complex collection of hardware and software. People who are willing to invest the time and effort necessary to start a small computing center must be highly motivated. Operating any computer, regardless of size, is more difficult than hardware vendors claim in their sales pitches. Problems as diverse as erratic power supplies, malfunctioning connectors, fire protection, late delivery of important components, and overheating of disk drives, can make the user very miserable and very preoccupied with areas not associated with the processing of data. The ability to overcome these inevitable problems and develop a workable computing center requires fortitude and endurance. It can drain human resources away from productive jobs. Instead of processing invoices or designing products, for example, individuals find themselves tending computer hardware and dealing with uncooperative vendors who are more interested in selling than maintaining.

Because of these many problems, decentralized computers have no obvious advantages over centralized approaches. The advantages that minicomputers have, such as local control, are offset by the centralized machine's vastly superior speed and diverse collection of hardware and software capabilities.

There appear to be two fundamental reasons for switching to decentralized equipment: 1) dissatisfaction with the central computing facility, and 2) a desire for self control.

Both of these justifications are qualitative and hard to measure. Dissatisfaction with central facilities has been around as long as the facilities themselves have existed. Central facilities should survey their user population extensively to find the reasons for this negative attitude. Perhaps the central operation has to promote itself better within the company, and develop a more service oriented attitude.

The urge for self control, that is apparent with so many minicomputer users, obviously evolves from deep human emotion. Most people, when given a choice, would rather control their own destiny than depend on somebody else. Some people have higher desires for self control than others. Individuals who rise to positions where they can authorize the acquisition of minicomputers are the people most likely to desire self control. Anything that promises fewer problems and more productivity will receive strong consideration from them. Minicomputers have that aura about them.

Unfortunately, subjective feelings and emotions do not automatically lead to greater profits or more productivity or less problems. The fact is that considerable amounts of money must be spent when creating a decentralized computer facility. And the ongoing costs are also large. Justification of decentralized computer facilities should include much more than a manager's gut feel that the concept will be beneficial.

It is important at the outset to identify all costs associated with the decentralized approach, and to report them in a manner identical to that of the centralized computing facility. Standard costing techniques should be used to compare and contrast all modes of computing.

Claims have been made that computer hardware is becoming so inexpensive that accounting for it is an unnecessary activity. This is a misleading attitude. Although semiconductor technology has dramatically reduced the cost of central processors and memory, peripherals such as disk storage and printers have not seen similar price reductions. But more important is the observation that hardware expenses make up a small part of the total cost of a decentralized operation. Capturing these nonhardware costs is an important aspect of computer cost accounting. It can also be an enlightening experience for the practitioner.

The costs of decentralized computing will almost certainly grow. This growth will come regardless of how much cheaper semiconductor chips become. Cost growth will continue because of the nature of most computer users.

Computer users constantly want more. They want faster response, more terminal connects, larger data bases, more software capabilities. There is an insatiable desire for more *solutions*. This has been the principal characteristic of data processing since the 1950s. In the early days of computing, even IBM felt that only about 20 large corporations throughout the country would ever require big computers. That assessment was completely off the mark, as we look at the billions of dollars worth of computer gear that is shipped each year. And many of these new mainframes are larger and have more capacity than even the wildest visionaries could have predicted back in 1950. With all computers there is an ever increasing desire for more automated solutions, and this has driven the industry to constantly expand the capabilities of computers.

Regardless of the speed of small CPUs, people will push them to their natural limits, and then seek upgrades in capacity. So, what starts out as an inexpensive system will inevitably grow larger and larger. Small operations become big operations. It is almost as if there is a law of human nature behind this desire for more computing power. It is something that all computer practitioners must recognize and learn to cope with.

Monitoring the growth of decentralized systems will become an important corporate activity. Unrestrained or poorly justified computer acquisition is obviously not in the best interest of the company. But determining acceptable growth requires cost data. That is why users of decentralized equipment must be forced to provide adequate cost accounting visibility to the parent company management. Cost accounting techniques used by centralized computing facilities can and should be adopted by all but the most insignificant decentralized computing operations. That is the least that a company can ask from this new breed of computer operation.

Chapter 5.2
Decentralized Costs

Based upon the cost accounting methodology developed in part three, each decentralized operation should be set up as an independent responsibility center. Common sense must be used in determining whether or not a particular minicomputer qualifies as important enough to form a responsibility center. If the installation is very small, it may not be worth the trouble to develop accounting. Accountants handle relatively low cost items by expensing them. That is, the value is charged as a period expense, and the item has no further value in future periods.

To help in determining if the computer is significant enough to form a responsibility center, the following points should be considered:

- Is the computer supporting general purpose applications, or is it specifically dedicated to a single application? A minicomputer operating a machine tool or monitoring a production line would generally not qualify as a responsibility center. Nothing would be gained from accounting and chargeback. But a general purpose installation, which performs conventional data processing functions, should qualify as a responsibility center.
- Is there potential for significant growth? Even small systems can experience fast growth and turn into large systems. It depends on the user population and what they perceive as their future requirements. The typical user population will increase its computing expectations as they gain experience with the hardware.
- Is the computer being run by a group of dedicated, highly motivated people? If the computer is forced on unwilling users, then it is unlikely that future growth will occur. But if the users actively acquire the computer themselves and operate it, then it is more likely that the machine configuration will grow into a major operation.

If the computer supports general purpose applications, and if a group of sophisticated individuals acquired and operate the hardware, then there is a strong tendency for significant growth in the furture. To at least monitor, and hopefully control, future growth, a responsibility center must be set up, and cost accounting principles implemented.

COST PLANNING MATRIX

As each responsibility center is created, the accounting department should select a series of general ledger accounts to gather specific costs chargeable to that particular operation. Examples of these accounts are listed across the top of the cost planning matrix shown in Figure 5-1. In this case the accounts are nearly identical to those used by the centralized computer facility discussed in Section 4.

As with large computer facilities, the task is to take costs identified to account numbers and segregate them into cost pools. The cost pools are similar to work functions, and are listed as rows on the matrix in 5-1.

The cost planning matrix in Figure 5-1 represents a moderately sized decentral facility with annual costs of about $380,000. The facility has one full-time applications programmer and two full-time operators. A systems programmer is borrowed on a part-time basis from the central facility, so there is cost associated with this individual. Actual computer equipment (ADPE and communications) is only one sixth of total costs. All equipment, including dedicated terminals, is less than one third of total costs. This single observation justifies the cost accounting approach we will outline in the following sections. The point is that knowing hardware values is only a beginning to creating a total cost picture of decentralized computing.

COST POOL DESCRIPTIONS

The costs shown in the planning matrix are reasonably representative of an actual installation. Each of the cost pools will be discussed in order.

• Application programming labor. Computers must be programmed. Although user friendly languages exist, it is still not practical or productive to let users become directly involved in programming large or sophisticated applications. Users are generally restricted to programming relatively minor activities such as data base inquiries, or special reports. The time and detail necessary to program a major application could overwhelm the average user. And the end result would probably be a set of inefficient, poorly documented programs. On the matrix, we have included the cost of one programmer, who will develop new applications and maintain existing programs.

• Systems programming. Systems programming support is a cost that is often overlooked. Although computer vendors supply some types of system support, for a fee, users inevitably need things like custom utilities, and plotting software. The hardware vendor may not be willing to supply such packages.

COST PLANNING MATRIX

DECENTRALIZED COMPUTER
THOUSANDS OF DOLLARS

COST POOL \ GENERAL LEDGER ACCOUNT	BILLABLE LABOR	ALLOCATED LABOR	ADPE LEASE	ADPE DEPRE-CIATION	COMMU-NICATIONS LEASE	COMMU-NICATIONS DEPRE-CIATION	DATA LINES	VENDOR SUPPORT	SOFT-WARE	SUPPLIES	GENERAL SERVICES	OCCU-PANCY	OTHER OPERATIONS	G&A	TOTAL
DIRECT COSTS															
LABOR															
PROGRAMMING – APPLICATIONS	40														40
SYSTEMS PROGRAMMING		20													20
OPERATIONS/SUPPORT		55													55
TOTAL LABOR	40	80													120
EQUIPMENT															
CPU/MEMORY				35				20	5						60
DASD STORAGE				15						5					20
PERIPHERAL I/O				10						10					20
SUBTOTAL				60				20	5	15					100
DEDICATED EQUIPMENT					5	10	5			2					22
TOTAL EQUIPMENT				60	5	10	5	20	5	17					122
INDIRECT COSTS															
MANAGEMENT/STAFF		50													50
OTHER OVERHEAD											10	12	10		32
G&A														60	60
TOTAL OVERHEAD															142
TOTAL	40	130		60	5	10	5	20	5	17	10	12	10	60	384

1M72117

Figure 5-1. Decentralized computer cost planning matrix.

Systems support is more likely needed by mature installations that have had time to develop a significant collection of programs. The complexity of additional requirements is beyond what the vendor is willing to provide, thus a specialized systems programmer is called in. These people are generall supplied by the central computer facility, and they support decentral operations on a part-time basis. On the matrix, a half man-year of programmer cost has been included.

• Operators/support. One full-time operator and one assistant have been included on the matrix.

Operators are a touchy subject with most decentral installations, particularly when they are new. The people who acquire minicomputers generally feel that they can and should operate the equipment. The concept is that casual, part-time operators drawn from the ranks of professional employees can adequately service the equipment. This is not a satisfactory solution, particularly if there is a large user population. Complex computer hardware responds best to the consistent, dedicated care that a full-time operator can supply. And an operator does many general tasks, such as order supplies, clean disk packs, organize work flow, and perform minor repairs. The support person is necessary for backup, plus administrative duties such as delivery of output, and accounting. If the complexity of the computer grows, or if hours of operation spread over more than one shift, then substantial cost increases will occur in this area because more people will be needed.

Of course, if an installation can continue to operate with casual operator support, this cost category will not exist.

• CPU/memory. These costs are made up of hardware depreciation, software lease/amortization (software that is purchased can generally be amortized over a number of years – the time period depends on what management feels the useful life is), and vendor support. Since most minicomputers are purchased, the principal hardware cost is depreciation, which is a periodic charge to expense based on the purchased price of the asset and its useful life. In this case, we have chosen hardware with a purchased value of $175,000, and have depreciated it over five years. The hardware expense charged each year is $35,000 ($175,000/5 years). Vendor support costs are made up of charges from hardware suppliers for maintenance, special trouble calls, and software support activities. This tends to be a relatively large charge for minicomputer users, thus it was isolated. Software costs are identified because most vendors now charge for all system software, as well as conventional application software.

• DASD storage. DASD includes disk media such as rotational packs, and the smaller diskettes. Tape is not included because it is usually an insignificant cost and can be included with the CPU. As with large computers, DASD is an area that is growing at a considerable pace as users develop large data files.

• Peripheral I/O. Peripherals include printers and card equipment. Supply costs are also included.

• Dedicated equipment. There are many devices that are remotely located from the machine installation but are connected to the CPU. These devices support teleprocessing activities. They include items like terminals, remote work stations, data lines, modems, and concentrators. Supply costs were also included to cover consumables used by terminals. Charging such devices to the minicomputer responsibility center imparts a certain amount of control over them. They are at least identified in one place.

• Management and staff. Because people are involved in operating and programming the computer, management is necessary. One full-time manager is included in the matrix, along with a partial secretary. It is conceivable that quite a few support type professionals could be justified in this area as the decentral operation grows and as outsiders become involved on a part-time basis.

• Occupancy/general services. These are costs associated with the general support of the computer. Costs include electricity, heating, air conditioning, janitorial services, and administrative functions such as personnel, accounting, and security. These costs are usually bundled together by the parent company and allocated out over some uniform base, such as occupied square feet or gross payroll. It would not be practical to break out the actual costs incurred by each minicomputer installation.

• Other overhead. These are easily overlooked costs that are nontheless required to keep any computer installation running. Costs include vendor training, manuals, special documentation, and travel to vendor and user conferences. Smaller items such as periodicals, seminars, and postage are also included. Most of these costs are incurred to keep people current with the state of their art. Computing is a fast paced, changing environment, and much contact with the outside world through training, conferences, and periodicals is necessary to keep up with it.

• G&A. This is an allocation from headquarters to cover various central administrative costs, such as executive management. It has been fully described elsewhere.

Gathering the necessary information to forecast total responsibility center costs is an administrative function that must be performed by somebody within the decentral operation. As we explained in part three, much of the work can be done through a cooperative relationship with the parent accounting department. But experts within the decentralized responsibility center must make the final choice of assigning costs to their appropriate pools on the cost planning matrix.

Such a task is probably best accomplished by the responsibility center manager. On an annual basis corresponding to the parent company's operating plan cycle, the manager should forecast each cost element using past experience and projected trends. An annualized planning matrix should result.

Decentralized operations are relatively small, so the manager probably knows all of his employees by name, and has a fairly good idea of the money he spends on hardware, software, and support activities. And with help from the parent accounting department, the various allocations such as occupancy and general services can be forecasted. Building the cost matrix should not be very difficult nor time consuming.

OBSERVATIONS ON DECENTRAL COSTS

The nature of certain cost categories on the cost planning matrix require more elaboration.

Depreciation

Decentral computers are relatively small and inexpensive. Because of this, they tend to be purchased rather than leased. In fact, many hardware vendors will not lease this type of equipment under any circumstances. And if they do lease, it is usually with very unattractive terms.

Because depreciation is such a significant cost, it justifies further analysis.

Depreciation expense is a function of useful life. As the length of estimated life increases, the annual depreciation cost decreases. As the asset depreciates, its value in the general ledger decreases. At some point in time, the value of the asset will become zero, and at this point it is said to be written off. That is, all of the asset's cost has been charged to expense over the projected lifetime.

The life span of most modern computers is very short. Assigning an accurate useful life can be quite hard, and somewhat risky. Five year useful life is allowable by the IRS, but even shorter useful lives may be appropriate.

Useful life can be variable. It often depends on when in the life cycle of the product line the gear was purchased. Figure 5-2 illustrates the situation. The set of curvilinear plots represent relative values of CPUs over their respective life cycles. Computer A has a reasonably stable value (usually determined by resale price on the open market) until computer B, which is an improved version, is introduced. At that point, the value of computer A begins dropping off quickly. The cycle then repeats itself for computer B when computer C is introduced.

Each of these hypothetical computers probably had many years of physical life left, but technological obsolescence drove their market value down to nothing. Although some users can get along with technologically obsolete equipment, the vast majority are anxious to upgrade to the new equipment just as rapidly as possible. This is why the old equipment's value drops so quickly. Vendors help this movement along by discontinuing or threatening to discontinue support of older equipment. And users, particularly programmers, tend to want the latest equipment so that they can remain stable with the state of their art.

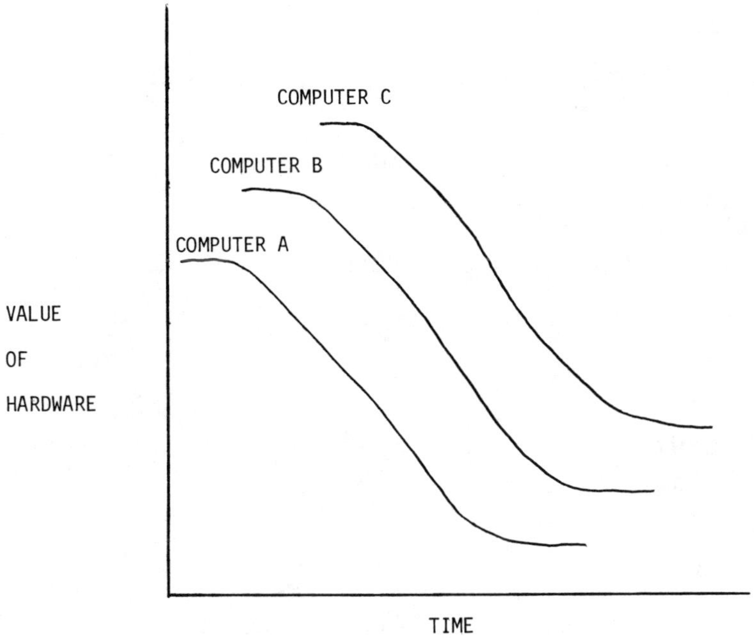

Figure 5-2. Life-cycle CPU cost.

Nobody likes to write programs on a technologically obsolete computer. It does not look good on the job resume.

If gear is acquired early in its life cycle, then a useful life of somewhere between three and five years is reasonable. But if the gear is acquired late in the product's life, management must make some very hard decisions about exactly how long that gear is going to be around.

If useful life is erroneously set for a period longer than actual retention, a large one-time charge to expense will result when the computer is replaced. This one-time adjustment, also called a write-off, charges the undepreciated book value of the asset to computer expense for the current period. Computer costs suddenly jump up. They become distorted and cause variations that are hard to explain.

As the pace of technology increases, computer users must be extremely conservative when estimating useful lives. Figure 5-3 illustrates a possible outcome. In this example, an error to annual depreciation expense in the fourth year of 67% occurred because an asset that was estimated to last five years actually lasted only three years before it was replaced. A large one-time increase in cost like that can confuse management and has the potential of causing significant errors in judgement.

VALUE OF ASSET	$200,000	
ORIGINAL ESTIMATE OF USEFUL LIFE	5 YEARS	
ANNUAL DEPRECIATION	$ 40,000	
ASSET DISPOSED OF AT THE END OF THE THIRD YEAR		
UNDEPRECIATED BOOK VALUE CHARGED TO 4TH YEAR	$ 80,000	
EXPECTED ANNUAL CHARGE IN 4TH YEAR	$ 40,000	
PENALTY FOR EARLY DISPOSAL	$ 40,000	(100%)
TRUE DEPRECIATION RATE PER YEAR	$ 66,667	
ORIGINAL RATE PER YEAR	$ 40,000	
ANNUAL ERROR	$ 26,667	(67%)

Figure 5-3. Effect of overstating useful life.

Think back to how the minicomputer was justified in the first place. If it was justified based on a five year life, what looked like a good, cost saving solution may turn into a loser when costs must be depreciated over three years. When using three year life instead of five years, monthly computer expenses are 65% higher.

Those who approve justifications of computer acquisition should develop a savvy, knowledgeable outlook of the computer marketplace and the pace of technology. Unrealistically lengthy useful lives cannot be accepted.

Vendor Support

Large, central computer facilities can usually justify hiring hardware and software specialists because the critical mass of installed computers is so large. The center can trouble-shoot many of its own equipment problems, and develop unique operating system modifications.

But a small decentral operation has no critical mass, thus support from vendors is often necessary since the equivalent experience cannot be economically hired. The cost matrix has included a special column for this type of cost because it can be relatively significant for a decentralized operation.

This type of cost can become particularly burdensome if several different brands of equipment are included in one responsibility center. Vendor A supplies the CPU, vendor B supplies communications interfaces, vendor C supplies typewriter terminals, and vendor D supplies CRTs. Another vendor built the power supply and still another supplied special plotting equipment.

From a technical and cost standpoint, second sourcing of hardware and software is inevitable. But when unique problems occur, particularly when communications is involved, multiple vendor involvement in problem diagnosis becomes necessary. This increases the cost of problem resolution. It also requires coordination by management. Vendors inevitably begin pointing fingers at each other when an easy solution is not possible. Each supplier blames another. Local management must somehow reconcile these conflicts so that the computer can keep operating. And, of course, this assumes that all vendors cooperate by showing up within reasonable amounts of time after trouble is reported. If the installation is small, vendors may take weeks before responding, even when the trouble is serious.

Labor Costs

The costs of dedicated programmers and operators are easily assigned to the responsibility center, as is the overall manager and his staff. But there are many other people who can become involved in the operation, particularly if it grows into a substantial data center.

Many of these outsiders can be called hobbyists. For their own reasons, they become closely associated with the decentralized data center. They may help operate equipment on a part-time basis or become involved in programming. They may even make it their business to become experts in computer configuration, thus strongly influencing the acquisition of additional hardware and software.

Many of these peripheral hobbyists may play a substantial role in helping the decentral operation succeed. We have pointed out before that a great deal of human comittment is necessary to overcome the inevitable problems associated with a computer operation. Outsiders may play a key role in making the decentral computer succeed.

The dilemma is, what do we do with these types of individuals?

If a person spends a great deal of time associating with the decentralized computer center, then the value of that time should be assigned to the computer responsibility center. The principle to apply here is one of *assigned task.* Everybody within a company has an assigned task which, except for people directly involved with the operation of the computer, has nothing to do with computers. If any of these outsiders cross over the boundery of their assigned task and become substantially involved with the operation, programming, or justification of computers, then a portion of their time should be assigned to the computer responsibility center. Transferring costs can be done using allocation techniques similar to those used for systems programmers. Perhaps 25% of an individual's time, for example, can be subtracted from his own department and transferred to the decentral responsibility center.

Admittedly, this is a hard rule to enforce, and difficult to handle in the accounting system. Computer center management has everything to lose and nothing to gain by increasing its costs through charges coming from outsider activity.

Other segments of the company gain through time charging techniques, however. If an electronics engineer, for example, begins spending 50% of his time operating a computer, that time is actually being taken away from his assigned task. His computer related activities might be beneficial, but his duties as an engineer suffer. The engineer's manager should therefore make sure that costs are transferred to the computing responsibility center.

The casual method of operation used by many decentral computer operations causes the problem just discussed. These machines are usually easily available, and outsiders are encouraged to use excess capacity. There is nothing inherently wrong with this as long as labor costs are properly charged to the benefitting organization. To make this cross-charging work, management commitment is obviously necessary.

Chapter 5.3
Decentralized Computing Utilization

Developing a complete cost picture of each decentral computing operation, as we did in the last chapter, is an activity which makes sense to any company that is concerned about controlling expenses. But developing utilization measurement schemes for minicomputers does not necessarily make sense. These machines are small, thus CPU and memory capacities are limited and must be conserved for productive work. Accounting systems can rob cycles from applications. Using sophisticated accounting algorithms to generate utilization data may not be economical.

We have already pointed out that machine accounting has tended to become too complex on large computers. It would be foolish to repeat this mistake on small systems. Complex accounting algorithms can consume more CPU time than many of the jobs that they measure. This situation cannot be tolerated on minicomputers because it would defeat the purpose of adopting small machines. If any minicomputer utilization is used, it must be simple and undemanding of computer resources.

TYPES OF USERS

The way in which minicomputers are used has a large influence on how the decentralized processor should be measured.

The vast majority of decentral operations today are used interactively. Programs are written on-line. Users input data directly into applications using terminals. Output is either directed back to the remote user, or is held by the CPU for further batch processing and eventual printing or transmission. There is a preponderance of on-line activity, with some background batch processing.

But these remote users differ quite a bit from their large computer counterparts. Because the minicomputer is decentralized, it is close to the user. Although he uses a terminal, he is usually within a few feet of the computer.

Once a computer is installed, and has run for a reasonable period of time, the user population can change. Users may begin to spread throughout the company, and new applications may be developed.

There are three basic ways that a decentral minicomputer can ultimately be used:

- The CPU can be dedicated to one principal user.
- There can be one dominant user and several minor users.
- There can be multiple users, with no single dominant user.

Figure 5-4 shows examples of the three alternatives. The single user option is self-explanatory, and will not be discussed.

The dominant/minor profile suggests that one single user originally justified the computer and is the largest processor. The hardware has been specifically configured for his needs. Other users, usually running light interactive processing, fit in and around the dominant application. These casual users appear because the dominant processor has determined that excess capacity exists, and he makes it available in an attempt to reduce his costs.

In the multiple user situation, various users with individual applications share the CPU. There is no dominant user. Applications are developed independently and are not generally interrelated. Hardware is configured to give all processors a reasonable response time.

The multiple user minicomputer has many aspects of a centralized computer operation. Most aggressively operated computers, regardless of how they start out, will end up being general purpose, unless there is some sort of specific company policy against it.

Creating a general purpose machine is job enriching and ego gratifying to the practitioners who are involved. By bringing in more users, managers can build larger systems than their single application could justify. With big systems, many marginally justifiable peripherals, such as plotters, high speed printers, and color graphics tubes, can be obtained. Besides, operating sophisticated computer systems is fun, and makes practitioners popular among a sophisticated group of users.

UTILIZATION ALTERNATIVES

Based on the specific user population, we can tailor utilization measurements, choosing the most equitable and least expensive alternative.

When the CPU is dedicated to a single user, accounting really is not necessary. Any kind of resource measurement calculation would be a waste of time and processing cycles, because all responsibility center costs are going to be picked up by a single user anyway. Actual costs should be collected accurately and charged to the single user.

In most cases, however, truly dedicated processors do not exist. Other people inevitably find reasons for using the computer. This brings us to our second alternative, where we have one dominant user and a number of casual, or part-time users.

If casual utilization is small and insignificant, it may still be practical to charge all costs to the dominant user. It obviously depends on the attitude of this major user. The rule of thumb is that casual usage must reach a point where the benefits of chargeback exceed accounting costs, before accounting should be contemplated.

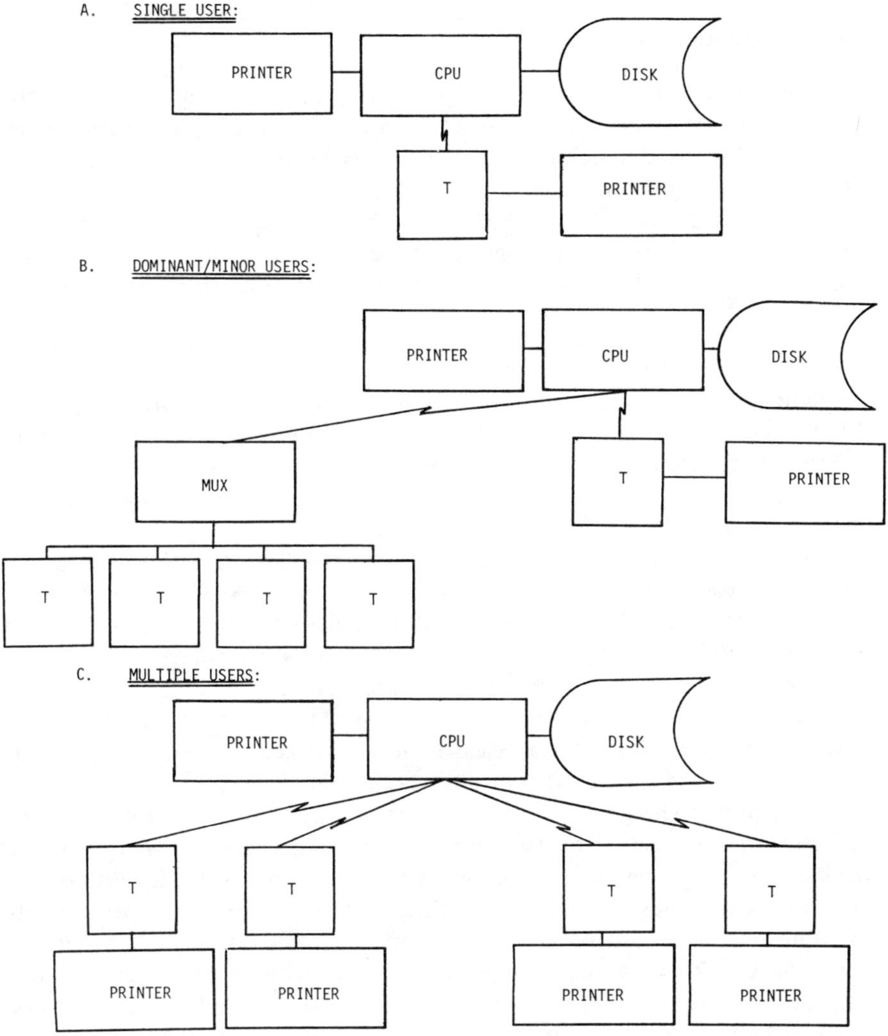

Figure 5-4. User profiles.

At some point the dominant user will perceive that casual usage is getting out of hand. His own response time may be suffering because the CPU is cluttered up with many other users. Or, perhaps, he is forced to acquire more disk storage units because users other than himself are demanding additional capacity. At this point a utilization scheme should be considered.

As with large computers, there are two basic requirements of any measurement scheme. They are:

- Simplicity
- Equitability

There are a number of utilization choices available. Unfortunately, the simplest method, which is to charge all costs to a single user, is not always the most equitable, as our dominant user has already determined. It is almost a truism that as equitablity increases, simplicity decreases. But as simplicity is lost, the costs associated with gathering accounting data inevitably increase. The goal is to draw a reasonable balance between cost, simplicity, and equitability.

In order of increasing complexity, the following utilization alternatives are available:

• Prorate costs based on a predetermined percentage. This method involves negotiation and bargaining. All users get together and determine what percentage of the responsibility center each of them uses. Each user's negotiated share may be based on gut feel, or some measurement of the volume of data processed over a selected period of time. Or, the dominant user may arbitrarily assign shares on a take it or leave it basis.

The expectation is that past utilization profiles will continue into the future. This, of course, is a debatable attitude, since some users will probably grow faster than others, which will cause inequalities to develop. However, the method tends to be self correcting, since any user who feels overcharged will usually come forward and ask for a change in cost allocation.

Once the user percentages have been determined, the decentralized responsibility center divides its costs up each month as agreed, and charges costs out appropriately, using the parent company's accounting system.

• Subscription charging. Once a system has no clear dominant user, then the preceding method tends to fall apart. Negotiating costs among equals is a thankless, never-ending task. Each user views equitability as the lowest possible cost to him, regardless of how much he uses the system. In such cases, the subscription method is much easier to enforce. This method assumes either that each connected terminal makes an equal use of the CPU, or that each terminal's usage is so trivial that user equality is a reasonable assumption. The method therefore works best when the user population tends to be homogeneous. That is, they all make similar demands on the CPU and peripherals.

The number of user connects, or number of users, is totaled using a measurement such as User I.D. code, and the costs are spread equally over the user population. A flat monthly charge results. With a little planning, the subscription fee can be turned into a standard rate that is adjusted infrequently. The important thing is to accurately estimate the number of users who will use the computer in the future.

Surcharges may be added to the basic rate to penalize unusually large or aggressive users. This option will be discussed more fully in a later section.

• Connect hours. Most minicomputer vendors provide accounting packages that collect the elapsed wall clock time during which each terminal is actively connected to the CPU. This is often called log-on to log-off time.

This connect time can be collected for each terminal, and used as the accounting measurement. The assumption with this method is that each terminal makes roughly equivalent usage of resources during the time it is connected. As with subscription chargeback, if the user population is relatively homogeneous, this is probably a good assumption.

Using techniques such as weighted priorities and time slicing, most users can consume only a certain amount of the CPU before they are replaced by another job. As long as the CPU is reasonably busy, the resources made available to each user are limited. Under these conditions, connect time accounting is a good chargeback method. If the CPU is not busy, however, the user has unlimited use of the computer during his connect session. But since there is no contention for the CPU cycles, the user is not hurting anybody else through excessive utilization.

• Resource accounting. When the users are nonhomogeneous and make significantly different demands on the CPU, then full resource accounting may be necessary. As stated before, this is not a desirable method of accounting for small computers.

If the method is necessary, we can borrow techniques from centralized computing, where we learned that CPU time is a reasonably good measurement of user activity.

The computer maker may supply CPU accounting software, or the user might have to use in-house systems programmers to develop the programs. Using the CPU clock, processing time can be associated with each job, and recorded in a file that can later be processed and fed into the accounting system, after cost rates have been applied.

BEST CHARGEBACK SCHEMES

There is no chargeback scheme that can be universally applied to all forms of decentralized processing. It is therefore necessary to discuss several alternatives.

There is no question about accounting methodology when only one user processes on a minicomputer. Obviously, all costs charge back to that single user because the system is dedicated.

Dominant/Casual Users

When one dominant user demands most of the computer resource, but allows others onto the system, then the most workable chargeback method is the negotiated chargeback scheme.

The dominant user who originally justified acquisition of the computer will generally absorb the largest portion of total costs. A small segment of costs, perhaps 10% to 20%, can be spread among other users. The precise charge to each of the smaller users can be nogotiated or dictated. Figure 5-5 gives an example of a negotiated chargeback agreement. In this case the dominant user absorbs three quarters of the total costs. The other three users negotiate among themselves and agree on a 10-10-5 split. These users are free to renegotiate at any time, should any of them feel that current charges are inequitable.

The key here is that the principal user gets some cost relief in recognition of the fact that he is allowing other users onto his system at some sacrifice to his own productivity.

The cost distribution mechanics of this method are quite simple. Once percentages have been determined, total monthly costs for the responsibility center are appropriately divided up. This can be accomplished by the parent accounting department, or by the responsibility center administrator. In all cases, the charges are eventually fed through the parent company's cost accounting system.

Homogeneous User Population

When the user population is diverse, and no single dominant user can be identified, then subscription fee charging is a very good alternative. This method is reasonably equitable and is very inexpensive to administer.

USER A (DOMINANT)	75% OF TOTAL COST
USER B	10% OF TOTAL COST
USER C	10% OF TOTAL COST
USER D	5% OF TOTAL COST
	100%

Figure 5-5. Negotiated chargeback agreement.

The success of subscription chargeback depends on the homogeneity of users. If all users do about the same thing, then equitablity is assured. A flat, equal monthly charge is assessed against each identified user, regardless of what his actual utilization has been.

The value of the subscription charge is set to recover total costs. Rate determination is as simple as taking total responsibility center cost, from the planning matrix, and dividing by the number of users.

This kind of chargeback is extremely appealing to users. They can easily estimate future billings and the method is so simple that anybody can understand it.

Nonhomogeneous User Population

If the user population is very diverse and each member makes different and unpredictable usage of the CPU, then the decentral computer center begins to take on aspects of a centralized operation, with a similar range of problems. Flat monthly subscription charges tend to become inequitable. For example, one user may be processing a sophisticated CRT graphics package, which consumes large amounts of compute power, while another user is doing a simple program edit, which is a trivial user of CPU resources. They use unequal amounts of the computer.

The accounting solution to this is full resource accounting. But the penalties, in terms of CPU cycles consumed, are significant. To save money and CPU power, a modified form of resource accounting can be developed, as follows:

- Determine what a *standard* user should look like in terms of critical resources. This means that the user population must be examined to determine how much CPU time, memory, and DASD space each user consumes, on average, per session. Special analytical programs may have to be written to obtain this kind of data.
- From this information, determine the average amount of CPU time that would be consumed by a typical user during each job session.
- Divide CPU usage hours by connect time and devise a ratio. Plot the user population on a graph similar to Figure 5-6, where number of users are related to their CPU time per connect hour. There should be a normal distribution of ratios. That is, most users will have a CPU to connect hour ratio close to the mean. Calculate the arithmetic mean and the standard deviation. From the leftmost value to the point of plus one standard deviation, 84% of the user population will fall. All users within this range should be considered normal. They should be charged based on subscription fees. Any user ranging above plus one standard deviation should be considered abnormal, and should be charged a penalty. If, however, the shape of the bell curve is extremely narrow with minor tails, a high concentration around the mean is indicated. In such situations, it

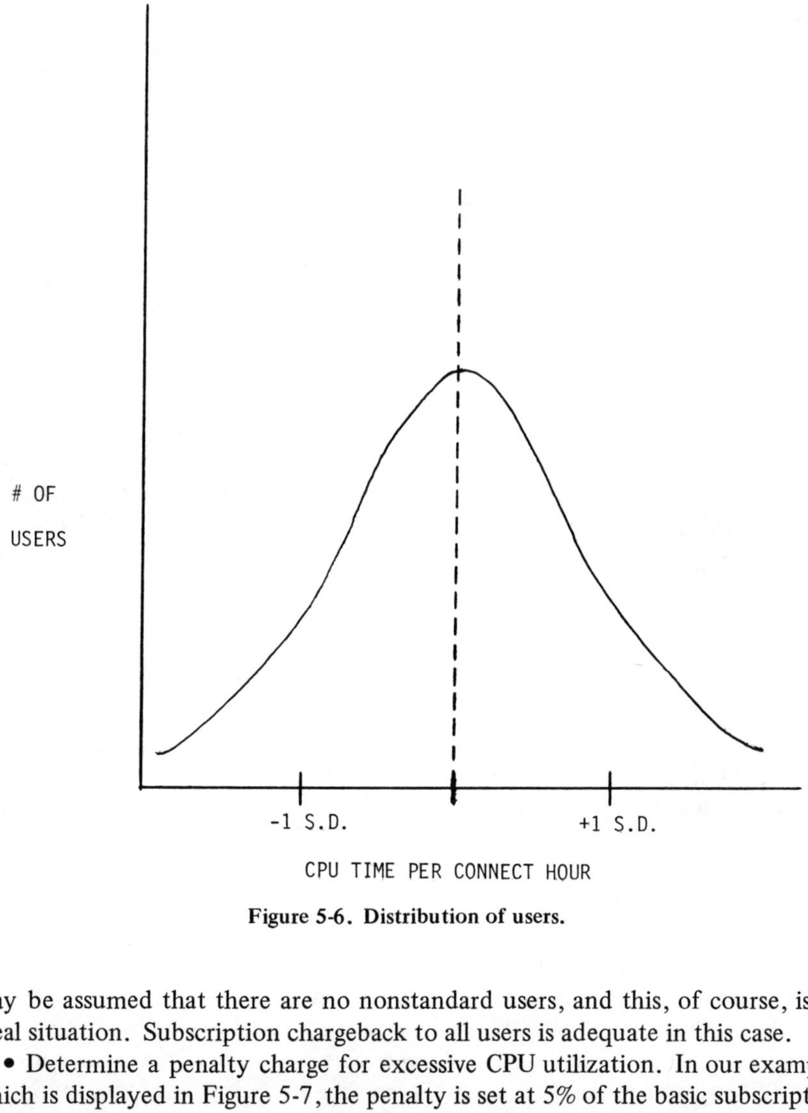

Figure 5-6. Distribution of users.

may be assumed that there are no nonstandard users, and this, of course, is an ideal situation. Subscription chargeback to all users is adequate in this case.

• Determine a penalty charge for excessive CPU utilization. In our example, which is displayed in Figure 5-7, the penalty is set at 5% of the basic subscription fee for each session using excessive CPU time. Exactly how much to charge as a penalty depends on the desires of computer management. If supervision wants to discourage nonstandard users, then a high surcharge can be set, perhaps in the 25% range. The 5% used in our example is a nominal surcharge, and probably wouldn't discourage the nonstandard user.

• Develop a simple analysis program that would match CPU usage to connect hours, using information produced by the vendor's accounting package. This

A. MONTHLY SUBSCRIPTION FEE	$150
B. CPU SURCHARGE (CPU TO CONNECT RATIO)	5% OF SUBSCRIPTION FEE PER SURCHARGED SESSION
C. DISK SURCHARGE (DISK USED PER WEEK IN EXCESS OF 3 MEGABYTES)	$ 2.00/MEGABYTE/WEEK

Figure 5-7. Subscription chargeback scheme.

analysis could be run during off-shift hours, when there was no contention with production work. Based on the analysis, atypical usage could be identified for each accounting period, and surcharges applied.

• Determine a reasonable limit for direct access disk storage. Take total disk capacity available for application programs, and divide by the number of potential users expected to run on the system. This value would become the DASD limit. In our example, three megabytes was determined to be a livable top end for most users. As long as each user stayed under the three meg limit, the subscription fee would cover disk usage. If the user exceeded three megabytes in any week, then a utilization charge would be assessed – in this case $2.00 per megabyte per week.

Disk utilization data could be obtained using vendor supplied utility programs, which could be processed weekly during off-shift. Charging for excessive DASD usage is important. This area is likely to be abused. Users neglect to clean up old files, and data may lie stagnant on disk for indefinite periods. By charging for excessive usage, each client is given the incentive to periodically clean up his file space.

Although the subscription/surcharge accounting scheme seems to add complexity to the accounting process, that complexity is applied to a small minority of users. By using the standard deviation techniques outlined, 80% of the user population will never receive a charge other than the subscription fee each month. This is simple, easy to understand utilization.

The small number of nonstandard users who make excessive demands of the CPU or DASD will incur surcharges that can be calculated using programs run during nonpeak hours, when productive demand of the CPU is low. By automating the entire process, and by using low value compute time, the accounting system can become a very trivial exercise.

We mentioned before that the amount of surcharge applied to those users identified as nonstandard depends on the control philosophies of the responsibility center managers. The key problem to consider is whether or not abnormal processing jobs should be discouraged or encouraged.

Figure 5-8 shows the job mix of two installations. The two user populations have substantially different characteristics.

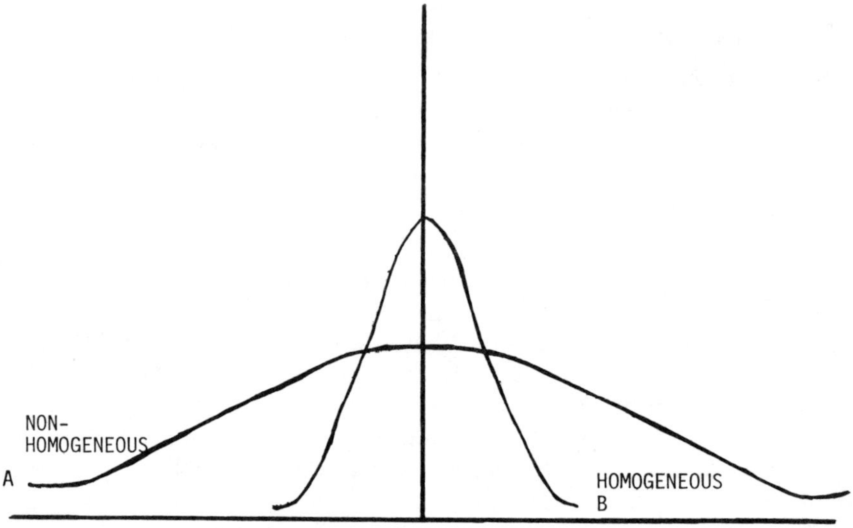

Figure 5-8. Nonhomogeneous vs. homogeneous users.

Installation A has a wide range of user CPU/connect ratios, with relatively low concentration about the mean. Installation B has heavy concentration about the mean, with almost no tail on the distribution curve. This latter case signifies a homogeneous user population. It is doubtful that installation B would have to do any surcharging at all. Subscription chargeback would be very equitable to all users.

Installation A has the choice of supporting its nonstandard workload, or of discouraging those users who deviate significantly on the high side of the mean.

Why would an installation want to keep abnormal work? Often, this work is complementary to the more normal workload, and does not significantly affect the standard user. In such cases, the CPU is actually used quite efficiently. Small users benefit from the significant cost absorption made by the large users.

But in other cases the large users can seriously degrade response times for everybody, including themselves. In such cases, the abnormal processors may be discouraged by increasing the surcharge to the point where it hurts. Under these conditions, large users may want to obtain their own, dedicated minicomputer, where they would tend to become homogeneous.

The point is that surcharge accounting is to be avoided, if possible. Because it is something extra that must be done, it becomes expensive and time consuming. If the user population can be kept relatively normal, then simple subscription fee chargeback will be adequate for accounting purposes.

Chapter 5.4
Specialized Decentral Systems

The decentralized processing installations we have been describing thus far have been generalized in nature. Although many of these computers may have begun as dedicated to a single application, most evolve into general purpose machines, supporting a diverse community of users.

There are two categories of decentralized processing that, from an accounting standpoint, are unique enough to isolate and discuss. They are: 1) turnkey systems, and 2) word processors.

TURNKEY COMPUTERS

Turnkey processors consist of standard minicomputers, or, in some cases, custom built hardware, that have been enhanced with special software and peripherals to perform specifically defined tasks. The hardware is not usually considered general purpose, and an outside user community is not solicited. The minicomputer can be considered dedicated to a specific application.

Custom software houses purchase minis at OEM discounted rates, install their own proprietary software on them, and sell a complete package of hardware plus software to the user. In some cases the supplier will actually manufacture his own hardware, also.

All the buyer need do is install the equipment, turn the power on, and begin processing. No special programming is required. Solutions are produced immediately.

Turnkey systems are particularly popular in graphics applications and accounting. But it is fair to say that virtually all areas that can benefit from off-the-shelf software have, or will have, turnkey systems that are applicable. The field is relatively easy to enter, thus competition is fierce.

A well-designed turnkey system properly matched to an application is probably one of the best bargains in computing. The reason is that expensive software development is spread over a large installation base. The buyer is getting the use of this software at a fraction of what it would cost him to develop in-house.

If the system has been well tested in many installations, then the user is acquiring a product that can be put to work immediately to solve his problems. Of course, a system that has been poorly designed or is full of software errors can turn into a nightmare for the user. Practitioners often speak in descriptive terms of the system's friendliness to users. If the turnkey hardware or software is hard to use, then it is probably worse than no system at all. Potential users will simply stay with their conventional manual methods.

A characteristic of most turnkey installations is that they are dedicated to a single task. When the software is well matched to the hardware, then there is little extra capacity left for use by the outside, casual user. Therefore, there is much less chance that a turnkey operation will become a general purpose computer center, with the resulting need for sophisticated accounting controls. Also, users who purchase turnkey systems are less likely to be DP hobbyists. They have a specific problem and need a specific solution. The turnkey system solves their problem, and they seek no further involvement with the computer. To the average user, a turnkey system is used like a pocket calculator.

When specialized support is needed, turnkey users tend to be heavily dependent on the company that developed the software. It is difficult to find support expertise in the centralized computer center, or anywhere else within the company. In fact, many turnkey software packages are proprietary and cannot be tampered with by outsiders because of copyright provisions. Thus there is no need for the turnkey user to keep a programming staff, or require systems programmers. Hardware maintenance support is also often supplied by turnkey vendors.

The cost planning matrix for a turnkey operation should therefore be quite simple. Cost accounts would primarily consist of hardware, software, and supplies, with special emphasis on vendor support. The usual company allocations would also be included.

What should be missing from the matrix are most labor costs associated with programming, operating, and managing the hardware. Turnkey systems are usually quite basic, and can be run by casual operators.

Cost pooling would be very straightforward. With only one basic application, it is senseless to calculate more than one cost pool. Utilization measurement should also be very straightforward because the user population would be homogeneous.

Most turnkeys supply one basic processing product. It may be graphics design, for example, or a basic accounting package. Users of these systems are therefore limited to a specific area within the company. Nonaccountants, for example, would have little reason to use the accounting turnkey package.

A negotiated chargeback scheme is therefore adequate accounting for most turnkey systems. The various users can get together and agree on the percentage split that each of them must bear. Of course, if there is only one user, all cost can be charged to him.

It is dangerous to assume that a turnkey system is so simple that no accounting is necessary. Total costs of a turnkey installation are much greater than the initial purchase price. Ongoing vendor support is usually quite heavy. Vendors have a way of continuously updating and improving their software. And users are anxious to acquire these improvements because they generally add to the productivity of the system.

As with other forms of computing, turnkey users eventually discover needs for improvement. They want more. The vendor is usually happy to cooperate, for a price. Modifications, improvements, and enhancements of the basic turnkey package may therefore be provided on a custom basis. But the important point to remember is that as soon as the user deviates from the basic package, costs will escalate significantly. If the vendor must supply custom programming, for example, the work will be done at very high rates.

To paraphrase Henry Ford: The basic product is cheap, but you eventually get the buyer on the cost of service. That's where the profit is.

Most turnkey suppliers operate under the same principle. The initial product is relatively inexpensive, but the inevitable upgrades are very costly.

Because of this, turnkey systems must adopt cost planning matrix accounting. This information can be used to track long-term cost trends of each turnkey installation. Cost comparisons between installations can also be made. Experience may show, for example, that vendor support costs should not exceed 10% of hardware costs per year. Any user exceeding that ratio should then be made to justify his position.

Turnkey installations will proliferate throughout all corporations. Developing uniform cost planning matrices will be the only way to subject these diverse operations to some form of cost control.

OFFICE AUTOMATION

The computer hardware used for word processing is a type of turnkey system, but is so popular that it deserves its own discussion.

A typical word processing setup includes a central minicomputer that supports a number of remote workstations, which are usually CRTs with upper/lower case characters. Workstations are connected permanently to the CPU, so that the clerk or secretary has instantaneous access to the computer without any sign-on delays.

Word processing supports various clerical activities such as typing, text editing, and text storage. In some cases, word processor computers are connected into a communications network so that documents can be electronically transferred throughout the network. This latter situation is sometimes called electronic mail.

Word processing is moving into an area that has typically been untouched by computers. The basic users are secretaries. Secretaries and clerical workers have generally been considered an overhead or indirect cost. That is, they do not charge their time to specific company contracts, products, or services.

Therefore, the tendency is to bury the costs of word processors in overhead also. This can be a mistake. There are two important reasons for treating word processing equipment costs the same way as we have treated all other forms of decentralized computing costs. They are:

- High cost equipment is replacing low cost equipment.
- The cost of word processing equipment will grow despite the declining value of semiconductor components.

High Cost Equipment

For many decades now, clerical activities have been performed by secretaries who use equipment like typewriters, copiers, and filing cabinets. Because there have been relatively few changes to the way secretaries perform their functions, it has been fashionable in recent years to criticize clerical activities as being very low in productivity improvements.

That really isn't true. There have been vast improvements in typewriter technology, to the point where all modern conventional models self-correct without manual erasure. Office copiers have eliminated the need for carbon paper, and the laborious effort required to make it work. Microfilm has greatly improved record retention capabilities. Small cassette recorders have given all secretaries the ability to take dictation without the use of shorthand. And modern telephones allow one secretary to easily handle the incoming calls of dozens of people, and to do it on a part-time basis.

All of these productivity enhancements have required little or no capital investment. Technological advancement has been made slowly, and often incorporated into new products that replaced worn out models.

It therefore can come as a jolt when these low cost items are replaced with word processing hardware costing tens of thousands of dollars per workstation. When word processors were first introduced in the late 1970s, the per station cost was around $10,000, on a fully amortized basis. As we shall see in the next section, there is little hope that these costs will ever decline, and every reason to believe that they will increase at least as fast as inflation, and even more quickly if significant enhancements are required.

The first areas to receive the benefits of word processors were the obvious high volume typing applications. If a clerk types documents eight hours each day, then a word processor provides significant productivity improvements. Full screen edit, spell checking, and document storage, all provide vast capabilities not available with older technology. It is safe to say that most of these high volume typing activities have converted to word processing technology by now. Their work volume can easily justify the heavy front-end investment.

Where do word processing vendors turn for additional markets? Those typewriters sitting at virtually every secretary's desk in the nation are an obvious market target.

But just as the average secretary does not use the typewriter all day long, he or she will not use word processing gear continuously, either. There are many other duties to perform, such as answering telephones, coordinating appointments, making travel arrangements, ordering office supplies, and acting as an interface between managers and the outside world. There are simply very few secretaries in modern corporations who do nothing but type documents all day long. Consequently, word processing can become only a partial solution to productivity improvement. And the hardware may become a large waste of money.

Typing out a memo now and then is hardly justification for a sophisticated CRT attached to a powerful minicomputer. Yet word processing vendors are out to replace every one of those conventional typewriters.

The only reasonable way to have a semblance of control over major word processing gear is to force each installation to become a responsibility center and develop a cost planning matrix, at least on an annual basis. At the beginning of the year, forecasted costs can be determined, and at the end of the year, actuals can be gathered and contrasted with the original plan. In this way, word processing administrators open their costs up to management.

For most corporations, individual word processing installations are not major financial items. The cost planning matrix should therefore be quite abbreviated and simple. Hardware and related would be the most significant cost, primarily comprised of depreciation, maintenance, vendor support, communications, data lines (if a network were used), software, and supplies. Overhead allocations would be similar to those discussed previously. As with other turnkey systems, a single hardware cost pool would adequately represent the installation.

A very good reason to enforce fiscal control over word processing is illustrated in Figure 5-9. Here we see two word processing installation configurations. Installation A could be called a low usage system, with only three active workstations attached to the CPU. Installation B, using the same type of CPU, has 10 workstations connected. Obviously, installation B has a much lower cost per workstation, assuming, as we did, that the CPU can adequately handle the additional workload. Developing a cost planning matrix for each installation will point this cost discrepancy out to anybody who is interested.

With consistent cost data from all WP installations, meaningful comparisons can be made. Cost standards can be established to help insure that all word processing groups are operating as efficiently as possible.

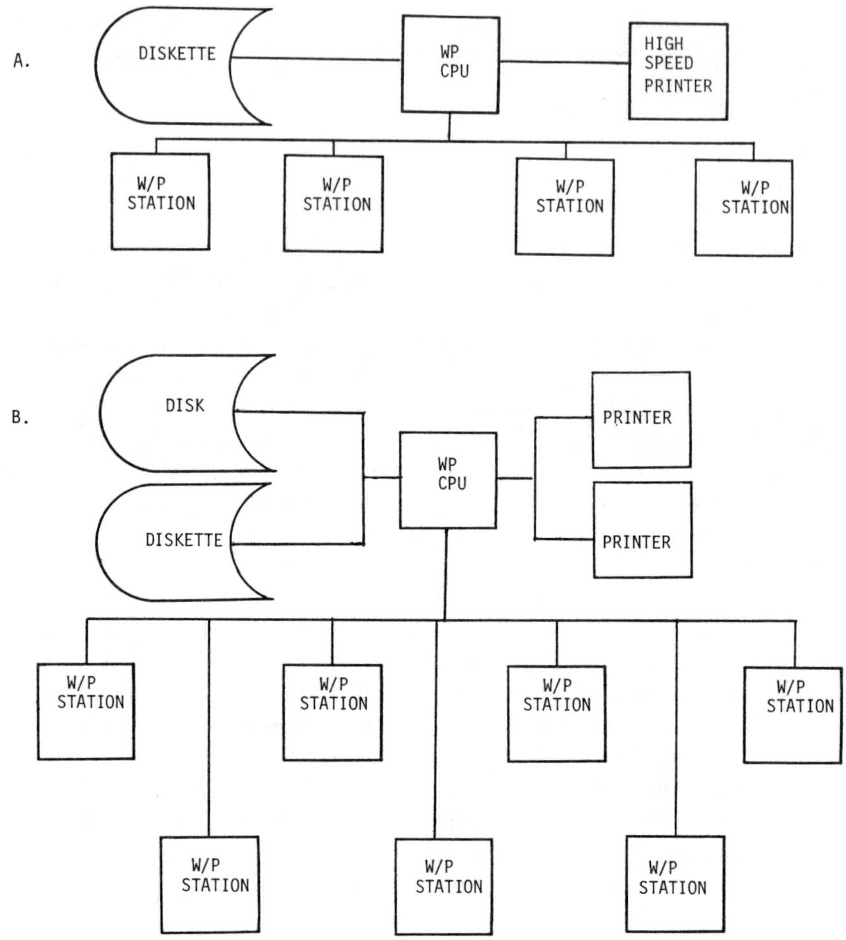

Figure 5-9. Two word processing systems.

Word Processing Cost Growth

As high technology hardware moves into the office, hardware design will almost certainly improve. It is likely that technological improvements will bring the cost of basic hardware down. It is therefore possible that word processors could eventually become as inexpensive as present typewriters. If WP gear really did did get that cheap, then taking the time and energy to develop cost planning matrices would be unnecessary. Costs would be trivial.

The problem is that we are dealing with computers. Once a baseline computer operation is installed, such as a word processor, the costs *never* decline. This phenomenon is created by the way manufacturers package and market their products. The concept can half jokingly be expressed as: You have to spend more to save more.

Once the hardware base is established, hardware prices do not come down, regardless of technological advancement. Instead of reducing prices, technological breakthroughs allow more features to be added to the basic package.

IBM and other large computer manufacturers have been using this technique for decades. They are constantly introducing new features, which cost more, but that promise to offset increased costs by improving productivity.

Figure 5-10 illustrates the point. The figure is based on very large CPUs, but is representative of all classes of computers.

The figure shows that over three decades, MIPS (millions of instructions per second), will have increased nearly ten-fold. Costs for a top of the line CPU will have increased five-fold. Productivity will therefore have grown twice as fast as cost. But costs have nevertheless grown steadily because manufacturers keep repackaging each new generation into denser and denser boxes, which, on a unit basis, are more expensive than their predecessors. Most users want these new features because they offer expanded capabilities, thus they find it impossible to downsize their CPU requirements. They cannot take advantage of the more inexpensively priced smaller units. They need more, not less.

Hardware vendors are caught in the same cost/push spiral as everybody else. Although one basic component – semiconductor chips – is becoming less expensive, the costs of everything else is inflating significantly. Manufacturers can offset some of these cost increases through better productivity. But they must continuously increase revenue. The best way to do this is by introducing new product lines with greatly increased features, but higher price tags.

Word processors established their baseline prices in the mid-1970s. When it comes time to replace the existing equipment, suppliers are obviously going to

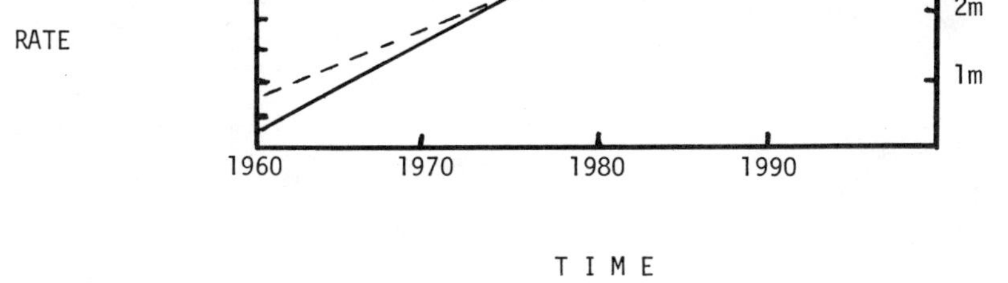

Figure 5-10. Dollars vs. MIPS rates.

try very hard to sell a new package with many more features, but a higher overall price tag.

It is therefore very unlikely that the costs of word processing will decline. In fact, when people discover new applications, they will demand increased capabilities. As with all other forms of computing, the demand for solutions will grow inexorably, and force the acquisition of more expensive equipment.

Again, the only way to fully recognize this fact is to build the cost planning matrix, and use it to monitor cost growth, and, hopefully, control it.

Chapter 5.5
Accounting Expectations

Until now, we have dwelled at great length on the "how" of cost data collection and chargeback for decentralized computing. But there is more. Once all decentralized processing facilities are identified, total costs for each installation have been calculated, and chargeback methodologies have been established, somebody has to oversee the whole thing. Somebody has to analyze the cost data, know what trends to look for, and know when the company is overspending.

There are a number of reasons for centralized cost control. They are:

- Independent decentral operations have a tendency to continuously upgrade their equipment. This is especially true of CPU, disk, printers, and software.
- They have a tendency to seek new applications within the company to fill up excess capacity.
- They have a tendency to encourage casual timesharing usage, and they use this additional utilization as a justification to expand. Hardware requirements then increase.
- They have a tendency to continuously expand the scope and size of their operation by offering new and attractive products such as graphics, custom programming, and specialized software packages.

Actually, the above points are true of any aggressive organization, including large central mainframes. But when one considers that the decentral operation was justified for specific purposes, expansion implies that the original justification was superfluous and created in bad faith. This is not a good business practice, nor should it be tolerated in any company that wants to make a profit.

FINANCIAL REQUIREMENTS

One of the nice aspects of centralized computing centers is that if they are properly set up as cost responsibility centers, they tend to be self-controlling. Standard rate trends are quite obvious measures of success or failure. Each computer user becomes an auditor of the cost performance of a central computing facility. If rates increase unreasonably, it doesn't take long before the whole company is questioning the value of the "expensive computer center." This adversary relationship between user and center is healthy.

Because decentral facilities are spread throughout the company, there is no natural control phenomenon over the entire base of installed equipment. Since there is no frame of reference, individual users do not know whether they are getting a good computing deal or a bad deal, from a cost standpoint.

The point behind cost planning matrices, and standard utilization measurements, is that uniformity is brought to the diverse decentral computer population. Management can then exert reasonable control over the decentral computer base.

We have mentioned the following points a number of times, but it is useful to summarize them again within the context of overall control. Each decentral computer responsibility center should prepare the following things:

- An annual cost planning matrix forecast, using a standardized, company-wide format.
- A quarterly summary of actual costs compared with each forecasted element of the planning matrix (this can be annual in the case of word processing equipment).
- A set of forecasted standard rates, if appropriate.
- A quarterly comparison of actual rate to standard, along with calculation of variance and revised standard rates, when necessary.

Based on this information, the parent company management should watch for the following trends in each responsibility center:

- Substantial year-to-year growth in computer cost. This is a case where rates can sometimes be misleading. That is, even if rates stay stable, costs can still be increasing at a considerable pace. The responsibility center is merely balancing cost growth with increased utilization. Regardless of whether or not the rates stay stable, equipment cost growth that is greater than inflation should be questioned. Since most hardware is purchased and put on a depreciation schedule, there is little reason for this cost to increase for at least a period of three years, unless the equipment was seriously underconfigured to begin with. Obviously, if there are sound reasons for growth, concern would be directed elsewhere. But the fact that management questions the performance of each responsibility center is enough to keep most computer operations self controlled.
- Labor costs that grow faster than inflation. Once a basic staff has been selected, there are not very many reasons for labor costs to increase much faster than inflation. If labor expenses grow unreasonably fast, hardware costs will generally follow. The increased staff has time to think up more applications and

will do more experimenting with exotic hardware. The original staff can do this too, but the point is that with more people thinking up ways to expand, the probability that expansion will actually occur is much more likely.

• Unusual increases in standard rate must be justified. Rates are a relative measure of performance. Rate increases are caused by either underutilization or rapid hardware expansion without justifiable usage. The responsibility center should be in a position to justify all unusually large rate increases to the satisfaction of controlling management.

These are all negative observations. Obviously, many processing centers will be run smoothly. They will work within reasonable cost limits, and will not seek expansion for expansion's sake. When these centers are identified, they should be used as baseline models, against which all other operations should be compared.

PULLING IT ALL TOGETHER

Decentralized computing centers are controlled by decentralized management. That is, there are managers who are closely involved with the day-to-day operation of the computer.

The next level of management, although responsible for the computer operation, is usually not very sophisticated in computing. They are not equipped to determine the effectiveness of the computer operation. Since these second level managers usually have responsibility for a single computer center, they have no baseline against which to compare the operation. Other than examining year-to-year cost trends, they have no way to tell if the computer is well-run or poorly run.

Many corporations today are setting up special organizations to oversee the general development of information systems hardware and software. A commonly used name for such organizations is Information Resources Management, or IRM. These organizations are generally not a part of the large, centralized computer center. This is recognition of the fact that there is more to data processing than central mainframes within most companies.

IRM groups attempt to develop a very broad perspective of the information requirements of the corporation. They can therefore provide excellent control points for the collection and analysis of cost data from each of the decentralized computing centers within a company.

Figure 5-11 visually displays how a group of decentralized systems could evolve in a typical corporation. In this case, there are three decentralized centers processing general applications, two turnkey operations, and five separate word processing systems. None of these operations have any reason to communicate with each other. Each is under the control of a different set of managers.

An IRM-type organization could serve as a focal point to collect the various cost reports we have discussed in this section. From the broad vantage point of

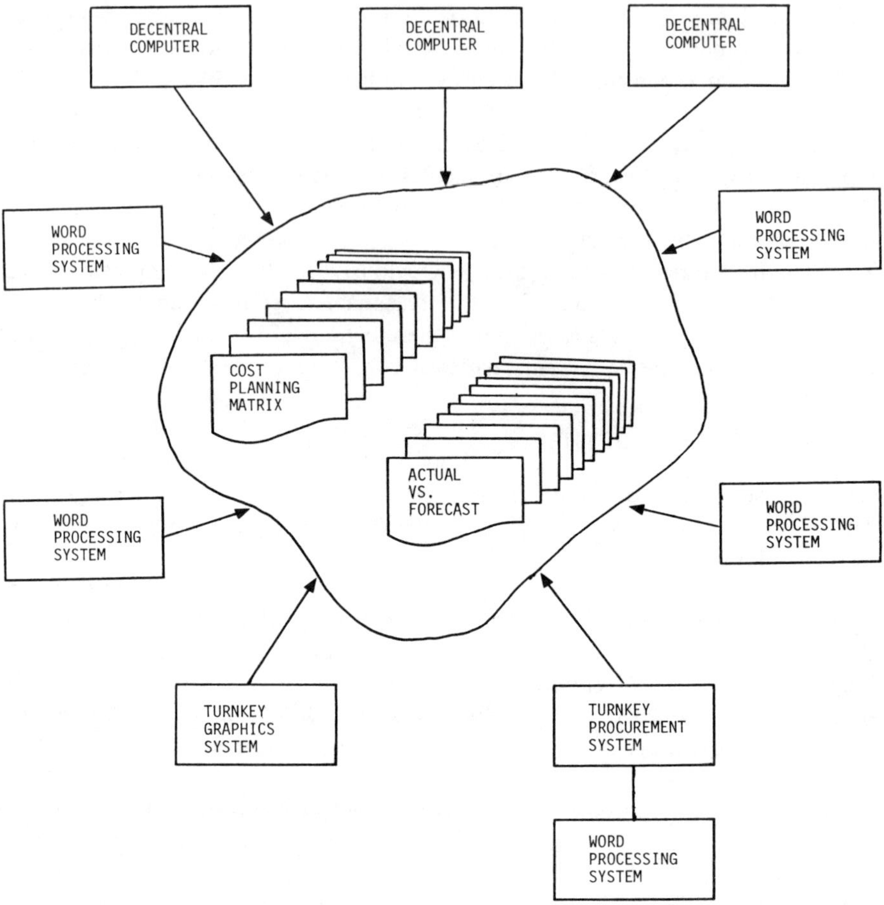

Figure 5-11. Typical decentral computing operation.

IRM, the various decentralized centers could be compared and contrasted, using common cost data. The effectiveness of each operation could be determined. Winners could be separated from losers.

An IRM type group could examine the following specific areas:

- Rate information. Each center's rates could be compared with other similar operations. Efficient groups could be isolated and studied. Their techniques could be applied to centers that were less well-run.
- Nonstandard users. Centers with heavily surcharged workloads could be identified. Surcharges on the basic rates indicate that the jobs processed by the

computer are not homogeneous. In some cases this might be desirable. But generally, if the nonstandard workload amounts to more than 15%, then another decentral computer could probably be justified. As we have pointed out before, most computer operations should strive for a homogeneous workload.

• Justification of new computers. Decentralized systems should only be authorized when they make a reasonable fit with the main centralized center that already exists. In many cases, it might not be economical to migrate work from central processors to decentral machines. But this is not something that could be determined by practitioner managers trying to make a single decentral operation run. Only a generalized, company-wide entity could make such comparisons.

An IRM-like group, by whatever name chosen, is the only logical overseer of decentralized computing. Without them, unrestrained proliferation of expensive computers could be a real possibility.

The experience such a group would build is the kind of knowledge that cannot be taught in books or gained from consultants. Each company must find its own unique mix of computer technology. No single mode of computing is right in all situations. An organization that understands the true costs of computing is in an excellent position to guide the company correctly through the maze of computer offerings that exist.

Chapter 5.6
Decentralized Computing and Advances in Technology

The accounting concepts we have developed for decentralized computing tend to be expensive to implement and maintain. Record keeping costs money, and analyzing the resulting data also costs money. Cost accounting techniques should therefore apply when costs involved are relatively significant.

Today, sophisticated decentralized computers can cost hundreds of thousands of dollars to purchase. And when ongoing operating costs are added up, we often find that additional hundreds of thousands of dollars are necessary each year to keep a computer running productively. As decentralized computers proliferate throughout a company, the obvious conclusion is that substantial company resources can be tied up in minicomputers. Without question, cost accounting techniques should be applied under these circumstances.

But do we worry about costs when a complete CPU can be put on a single inexpensive chip of silicon? Or when several densely packed chips constitute a powerful computer?

In not too many years, the typical user who today accesses large computers interactively will have all the computer power he could possibly need stuffed neatly into one of the drawers in his desk. Only his tasks will command the CPU. The computer will be his. There will be no job contention, nor slow response at peak processing hours during the day. There will be no data line problems. The simplicity of the electronic package will almost eliminate downtime, and when it occurs, a technician will simple replace the entire unit. Electricity draw will be insignificant. No air conditioning or special environmental controls will be needed. Nor will there be any operators or clerks or other support people. Just a one-to-one relationship between an individual and his computer.

Produced in sufficient quantities, the price of these compact computers would probably be quite reasonable. Complete computer packages could become as popular as telephone handsets.

When the cost of computers becomes trivial, then concern over accounting can cease. Accounting is only used when the situation is material. If the cost of any item is material in comparison with annual sales, or total assets, or some other form of meaningful value, then reasonable cost accounting rules must be applied. Conversely, if costs of an item are considered nonmaterial, then they can be grouped together into some type of miscellaneous expense account, where they disappear from all but the most curious eyes.

FUTURE ACCOUNTING

The question therefore arises as to whether or not computer cost accounting will exist in the long run. If the world of computing dissipates into a collection of tiny but powerful microcomputers that are handed out like boxes of paper clips, then accounting is clearly superfluous. Accounting costs would exceed the value of what is being tracked.

But is that truly the direction in which computing is headed? Perhaps. But a more logical direction is towards two distinct types of computers.

Any individual wanting processing power could have it, right at his desk in a compact little CPU/memory device. Computing *power* would be completely distributed.

But the storage of large amounts of data is an entirely different matter. The argument rests on whether or not data can be effectively distributed. Decentralized data files are not necessarily very attractive. In fact, they can be more trouble than they are worth.

When comparing decentral with central data bases, we often find that centralized information is more secure, more accurately updated, and can be managed and controlled more easily and efficiently.

Compare data bases with public libraries. Although libraries can be decentralized throughout the community, each branch has a relatively small number of books, usually in very generalized categories. There is still no substitute for large, central libraries, where massive numbers of books can be stored under one roof. It is more effective to have people come to the central, comprehensive library, than to disperse small numbers of books through branches.

If data bases become too fragmented and spread out, they lose their value to all but the most casual queries. If, for example, a company bills customers from each of twenty decentral branches, using twenty different computer systems, it can very quickly lose control over bad debts, cash flow, and interbranch sales. What prevents a deadbeat customer from buying at several different branches if there is no central control? The point is that there are many forms of data that must be centralized.

It would therefore appear logical that decentral computers of the future – personal computers – would still require active communications with larger central computers, where important data could be stored. Structuring and indexing large amounts of data will always require big CPUs. As computers get larger, data bases simply grow.

These large, central machines will be expensive and will require accounting. But the nature of these future data handling machines will be different, and this will require a change in accounting technique. Instead of concern with raw processing power, we will be more concerned with the quality of data, and its value to users.

The interaction of future remote computers with large central machines will occur in two different ways:

- Small remote computers will add data, in various forms of completeness, to central files.
- Small remote computers will query for data from existing central data bases.

There is a similarity here with electric utilities. Central generators produce the bulk of electricity, which is distributed to users. But there are some customers who generate their own electricity, and feed any excess back into the power grid. For this they are rewarded with payments from the utility.

In data processing applications, those who withdraw data from the central base would pay for that data, based on a predetermined valuation. Those who supplied data into the central system would receive credits, so that the cost of their data processing needs could actually be reduced.

The essential cost accounting problem would be one of identifying all data bases, and establishing values for each. Value would be a function of the data's usefulness, and how much it cost to collect, arrange, and store.

Solving these cost accounting problems is best left to the future, when the actual situation begins to materialize. But the point is that large computers will continue to exist, and their costs will most likely be amortized over smaller decentral machines. The cost of the entire system will be born by those who demand data. Those who supply data will be rewarded through lower costs.

Part VI
Distributed Computer Accounting

Chapter 6.1
Introduction

One of the problems with distributed computing is that there isn't very much of it. Authors such as Weitzman, Lorin, Katzan, and Scherr have covered the theoretical concepts of distributed computing well. As illustrations, they have used many hypothetical examples, or designs in the process of being implemented and tested.

Many of the most popular working designs used as examples were developed in an experimental manner under research oriented conditions. The acid test of bottom line profitability never had to be faced by these systems because funding was ultimately supplied by some governmental institution.

Exciting distributed concepts are introduced regularly. But most of these ideas have not been tested in the real world from an operations or financial standpoint.

If distributed computing is to have any significant impact, it must be successfully implemented down in the shop, or in the accounting department, or the remote sales office, or in a supplier's warehouse. The whole point behind distribution is to get computer hardware placed where data is actually generated and used. Most of these environments are hostile in terms of both physical surroundings and the people who are expected to press buttons.

Many people think they know what distributed processing is, but few can point to successfully implemented systems. We can not therefore be sure whether we are exploring a computer methodology that has a useful future, or a concept which will never get out of the academic laboratory.

THE ENVIRONMENT

Distributed computing is substantially different from the decentralized approach to computing. Distributed processing is a blend of minicomputer technology and communications networking. Networks are the key that separate distributed processing from everything else. The concept of distribution could not exist without an efficient way to transmit digital information over distance. We will therefore spend as much time exploring the accounting concepts of networks as we will spend on computers.

Distributed computing networks are more complex than simple point-to-point telephone lines. Using sophisticated switching techniques, messages can traverse in many different ways through a network before arriving at the final destination. In many cases the network actually has compute intelligence built into it. This allows for message switching reliability and load sharing.

The transmission of data is a relatively new technique. Computers existed for decades before considerable data communications began. Because of this, communications technology is still developing and trying to catch up with the speed and diversity of computers.

Competition is substantial within the communications industry, but suitable products are not always available for distributed networks. Even the massive AT&T had to back away from a proposed intelligent data transmission network called Advanced Communications Facility (ACF) in the 1970s because of the overwhelming complexity of the entire scheme. A highly degraded offering was made more than five years after the promised implementation date.

As is often the case when markets are controlled by a monopoly, user needs are not always met. And when outsiders attempt to fill those new needs, a bureaucratic nightmare develops around them. AT&T fought off potential competitors for many years using incredibly expensive techniques such as lobbying congress and actually writing and attempting to pass its own protective legislation. These abuses eventually led to the agreed breakup of the company based on a Justice Department suit that was pursued for more than 10 years.

The problem has been that the physical act of transmitting data requires huge amounts of capital investment. It is very hard to encourage capital formation when the competition is a monopoly.

Private companies have had mixed success competing against AT&T. The situation may be similar to the early days of mainframe computing, when such apparent giants as Xerox and General Electric dropped out of the computer business. Even their vast financial resources could not guarantee success against an entrenched monolith such as IBM.

The chances are very good that AT&T competitors will come and go. Major corporations will enter, lose a lot of money, and eventually retreat from the market.

A betting man would probably have to stack the odds in favor of AT&T as the eventual major supplier of satisfactory digital transmission facilities.

DIFFERENCES

Large centralized computing centers share many common characteristics with smaller decentralized processing facilities. But distributed computing has few similarities with any other mode of processing. Because of this, many cost accounting techniques must be created rather than borrowed. Although tools such as the cost planning matrix can still be used, the relative weight of various components changes substantially. For example, the chargeback method must take into consideration the existence of dedicated and shared components within the same computing system.

One interesting difference between distributed computing and other modes is that the entry level cost to a distributed network of computers is relatively low. With a few inexpensive minicomputers and several yards of coaxial cable, a distributed network can be created. Because of this, colleges and universities have shown a strong tendency towards adopting distributed computing techniques. The literature is therefore full of interesting and exciting experiments.

Large Computer Evolution

To understand the possibilities of distributed computing, we must first briefly explore how large computers have evolved since the 1950s.

Unlike small computers, large systems have always been more prevalent in industry than in the academic world. The present widespread usage of large mainframes in most corporations illustrates this point. Many of the important software developments have therefore evolved on large scale IBM-type processors. Applications like graphics, interactive processing, and data base systems have all reached a high state of refinement on what was once thought to be a business oriented line of computers. These so called business machines have proven to be general purpose computers capable of a wide variety of data processing functions.

Centralized computers have become so large and expensive, particularly when latched together into multiprocessors, that most colleges and universities simply cannot afford the most modern technology. This means that many professors and students use computers literally cast off from industry. The academic community therefore provides very little large system research and development. Most of it comes from manufacturers such as IBM, or from industrial users.

There is a problem when private industry provides the bulk of product enhancements. Breakthroughs can be suppressed until the current technology is fully and profitably exploited. Innovation is controlled, and there may not be much product improvement at all unless competition is healthy and aggressive.

Distributed Computing Breakthroughs

Because the availability of distributed computing components to the academic community is obvious, they have developed a strong commitment to basic research and development in this area. With increased research activity, most of it in the public domain, there is a good possibility that substantial breakthroughs will be made. And users will benefit from these breakthroughs.

This means that it will be hard to predict exactly where distributed computing can go. As any strategic planner will confess, breakthroughs are the chief enemy of planning and forecasting. A breakthrough can radically change the course of events and destroy painstakingly developed plans. Inexpensive hand-held calculators, for example, destroyed the plans of many old-line manufacturers of bulky mechanical adding machines. A sleepy industry was turned upside down within months. And think what happened to the producers of slide rules.

One area likely to be affected by breakthrough is communications. Data transmission expenses are a significant portion of the cost makeup of any distributed computing facility. And communications costs have shown a continuing and disappointing tendency to increase, in spite of glowing predictions made in the middle 1970s that network costs would drop dramatically.

Despite satellites, waveguides, microwaves, optical fiber, and increased competition, the total cost of data transmission for most corporations has continued to increase. In some cases the cost of transmitting a unit of data has declined slightly, for people lucky enough to work under special conditions, but the decreases have never come close to offsetting the costs associated with increased usage. Economies of scale have not worked for the suppliers of data transmission services.

It does not appear that common carriers were able to anticipate the significant growth that has occurred in data transmission. Carrier networks have therefore been patched together, with a hodge-podge of modern and antiquated equipment. In many cases, the cost of processing significant amounts of data is less than the cost of transmitting that data a few hundred miles. And a company unfortunate enough to be located in a remote area may find that data communications services are unavailable at any price because of very old switching facilities.

If a breakthrough in data transmission is made, the impact on distributed computing could be significant. Cost relationships would change and the justification of complex systems could become easier.

Communications today is like core memory was in the 1960s and early 1970s. In those days, the amount of usable core was so small and valuable that it was an extremely limiting resource. Millions of hours of programming time was spent in trying to optimize core usage so that computer system performance could be improved. Today, there is so much memory available on large and medium sized systems that program region size is immaterial, and people don't care how much space a job uses.

Massive availability of memory probably encourages sloppy programming. But so what? Programmers are in great demand. Many of them are consequently mediocre. But their inefficient use of memory, something that could not be tolerated in the early days of computing, is now a trivial aspect of computer performance and cost. Computers are now built to tolerate sloppy programming techniques.

So it is with communications. Network costs are high and capacity is low. Millions of programming hours will be spent in attempting to optimize network utilization.

But if breakthrough occurs and large volumes of data can be transmitted at very low cost, then distributed computing may indeed become a very popular – perhaps the only – form of computing.

Whether or not distributed computing is presently an economical computing alternative depends on the cost accounting techniques used. As with other forms of processing, there are many hidden costs that tend to be overlooked. The act of physically distributing computer power doesn't necessarily save money, as the following chapters will show.

Chapter 6.2
Distributed Computing Overview

International Data Corporation (IDC) is an organization that assembles statistics on various aspects of the computer industry. This information is tabulated and used in articles appearing in the trade press. The information is also assembled into formal reports that can be purchased by companies with a need to know industry characteristics.

IDC estimates that shipments of new minicomputers have been growing, and will continue to grow, at a compounded annual rate of between 25% and 30%. Their reports show that minicomputer growth is roughly twice that of large computer shipments, although large processor shipments still make up higher dollar amounts.

IDC also estimates that 50% of these newly purchased minicomputers end up in distributed computing networks.

Whether or not so many minicomputers are being used as distributed processors is debatable. IDC gets its data from questionnaires that are sent to various key people within the industry. If a respondent says that the computer will become part of a distributed network, IDC accepts that response.

The problem is that much of the computer industry does not really understand what distributed processing is. Many people think that two or more minicomputers loosely attached to each other, perhaps sharing common disk storage, constitute a distributed computing system. But there is much more to distributed computing than a few attached computers. Distributed computing requires a new approach to the principles of data processing.

WHY DISTRIBUTE DATA PROCESSING?

When all of the costs associated with distributed computing are added together, they are significant. It is not true that distribution of data processing automatically results in cost savings. Because of the high expenses associated with networking, this mode of computing can often turn out to be the most expensive of the three alternatives, on a cost per transaction basis. If a justification is prepared honestly, cost savings is not generally identified as the primary reason for distribution. Less quantifiable advantages such as local access to data or reliability are more likely to be used.

For example, retailers with many stores spread over a large geographic area can use distributed computing to very good advantage. Computing transactions required at the retail level, such as recording sales, keeping inventory updated, and reconciling the cash account each evening are relatively trivial. A large computer really isn't necessary to handle these transactions. A minicomputer is quite adequate for the task. The ordering of inventory can be handled through the network, using distributed techniques.

Large banks with multiple branches can also use distributed computing. Simple teller transactions such as balancing receipts and withdrawals can be handled directly at each branch. More complex transactions like updating accounts can be accomplished using the network.

Distributed Characteristics

No single computer within a distributed computing network is expected to handle all of the work that is potentially offered to it, nor does it have immediate access to all data needed to perform its assigned tasks. Work sharing, as well as data sharing, are characteristics of a distributed system. High rates of interaction between computers is typical. This is because the parent organization also has a great deal of interaction between its many disseminated organizations. Distributed computing therefore works best where it mimics the parent organization's style, which is disseminated.

Because of the high degree of computer interaction and interdependence, failure of any single piece of hardware is less catastrophic than is disruption of a centralized processor. When the central machine is down, everything is lost. The nodes in a distributed system need each other, but loss of a single node does not create a catastrophe. If any individual node fails, that node can be bypassed by telephone circuits, and the overall system can remain viable, although possibly degraded.

Distributed computing places processors with the user. Data is input directly into a computer by individuals who actually understand the data and have some responsibility for it. There are less chances for input errors since intermediaries such as keypunch clerks are not used.

The local computer can edit data, and assemble it into meaningful reports. The data can then be fed into the larger network where it is consolidated and summarized. Local nodes than tap into this large data base as needed.

We can sum up the perceived benefits by stating that the distributed computer provides local control of data processing while allowing access into a much larger network of computers. The large network of processors is often quite powerful, in terms of processing power and shared data. Thus we have computer power which can equal or exceed that of large centralized processors while retaining the flexibility of decentral processors. And the whole system tends to be more reliable than a central machine.

BASIC GROUPS

There are two basic schools of distributed processing practitioners. We can call one group the *purists,* and the second group the *mixed configuration proponents.* Purists are radical in their approach to distributed computing. Mixed configuration proponents tend to be more conventional and conservative.

Each group has its own body of literature, both in magazine articles and books. The purists do not have a substantial amount of practical field experience, and their concepts tend to push the limits of existing technology. Mixed configuration proponents have working systems as models, and do not seek radical solutions to the problems of distributed computing.

Purists

Purists embrace distribution with a vengeance. Their basic philosophy is that a distributed computing system must be made up of interconnected nodes, all of which are minicomputers. The nodes must interact intensively, cooperate closely, and practice a great deal of interdependency. It is almost as if the functions once performed on a central computer are split up into many small groupings, scattered about geographically on minicomputers, and made to perform as a whole once again through the use of communications lines.

Several network designs are illustrated in Figure 6-1. The top drawing shows a classic ring configuration. Each node is connected with two other nodes so that the entire system forms a closed loop. As the nodes intercommunicate, they may often send messages in both directions to insure reception. The form the messages take, and the way each is switched around the network, are called communications protocols.

Protocols have been mentioned before. They are formal sets of rules that must be adhered to if successful transmission is desired. There are various levels of protocols. Some are important to each user, and some are buried within the operating system and are invisible to users.

Each computer manufacturer has chosen to keep certain protocols unique. There are obvious competitive advantages to such a move. Off-brand equipment cannot be attached to the network, and a user is not likely to switch to a different manufacturer once the network has been established. This is a very undesirable state of affairs, and one of the reasons that data communications techniques are not yet mature.

A point-to-point configuration, shown in the lower portion of Figure 6-1, is also adapted by the purist school. Without the symmetry of the ring, messages must often traverse a complex route to get to their destination.

Routing of messages can be accomplished by each node, or it can be handled by a specialized set of computers that are dedicated to network functions. These dedicated computers are often called communications concentrators. Their

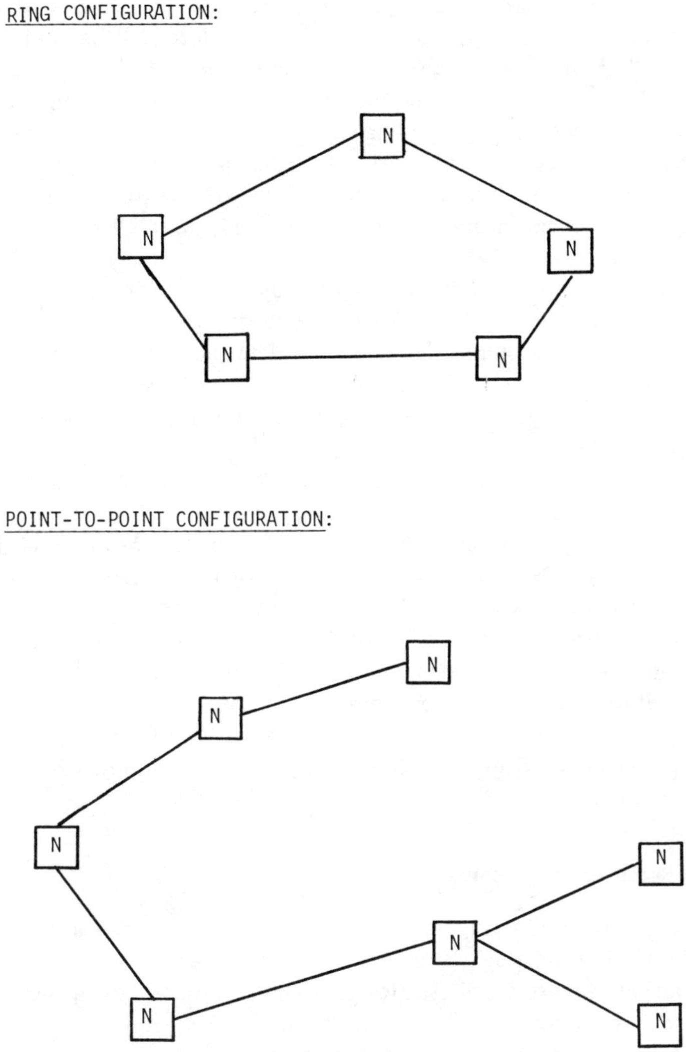

Figure 6-1. Two distributed computing configurations.

primary function is to reduce the communications coordination load on processor nodes.

Message handling functions in a point-to-point network require more processing overhead than in a ring because it is more difficult for a message to find its destination. Offsetting this is the possibility that network costs will be lower for a point-to-point configuration because duplicate lines to each node are not required.

Ring architecture tends to be implemented within the confines of a single plant site, or building, where terminals are relatively close together and data line costs are small. Point-to-point structures make more sense when nodes are interconnected over a large geographic area. In such cases, common carrier data line costs can become very significant.

Regardless of the type of network used, the purist school of distributed processing stresses that each node is heavily interdependent on all other nodes. There is no hierarchical structure, where one node may be more important than other nodes.

Interdependency means that all nodes must cooperate with each other. Processing resources can be shared when necessary, and data bases are distributed throughout the system. These shared data bases can be broken down into partitions, which are stored at appropriate nodes throughout the network. This causes the interdependency, because nodes are often in a position where they must share data.

In some cases, complete data bases can be installed at each node, so that there is no need for query activity. This is called data base replication. It can be a cumbersome method of doing business, particularly if the number of nodes is large.

One of the first developments of a purist distributed network was called ARPANET. This is a network that connects many government oriented research facilities. Any institution, or node, requiring information on specific research topics can transmit through the network to the appropriate node, acquire the data, and use it for whatever purposes required.

ARPANET was a pioneer. Many other networks have been developed using its original techniques. These techniques have also been adopted by the larger value added networks.

Mixed Configuration Proponents

The second group of distributed processing proponents favors a more mixed approach, which is almost a hybrid between straight centralized computing and pure distribution. Figure 6-2 illustrates their basic methodology, using only two examples drawn from many different possibilities.

The top configuration in 6-2 uses concentrators to bring data from a substantial number of smaller nodes into a central host. Portions of data bases may be distributed to each node. But a final, or offical, copy of the data is centrally stored by the host. Although there is some autonomy at each node, the structure tends to be quite hierarchical, because final responsibility for data integrity resides at the central host. Internode communication is still possible, but less necessary. The central processor exerts a great deal of control over each node.

In the bottom drawing of 6-2, a second approach is shown. Two large-scale centralized processors are tied together with a high-speed channel, presumably

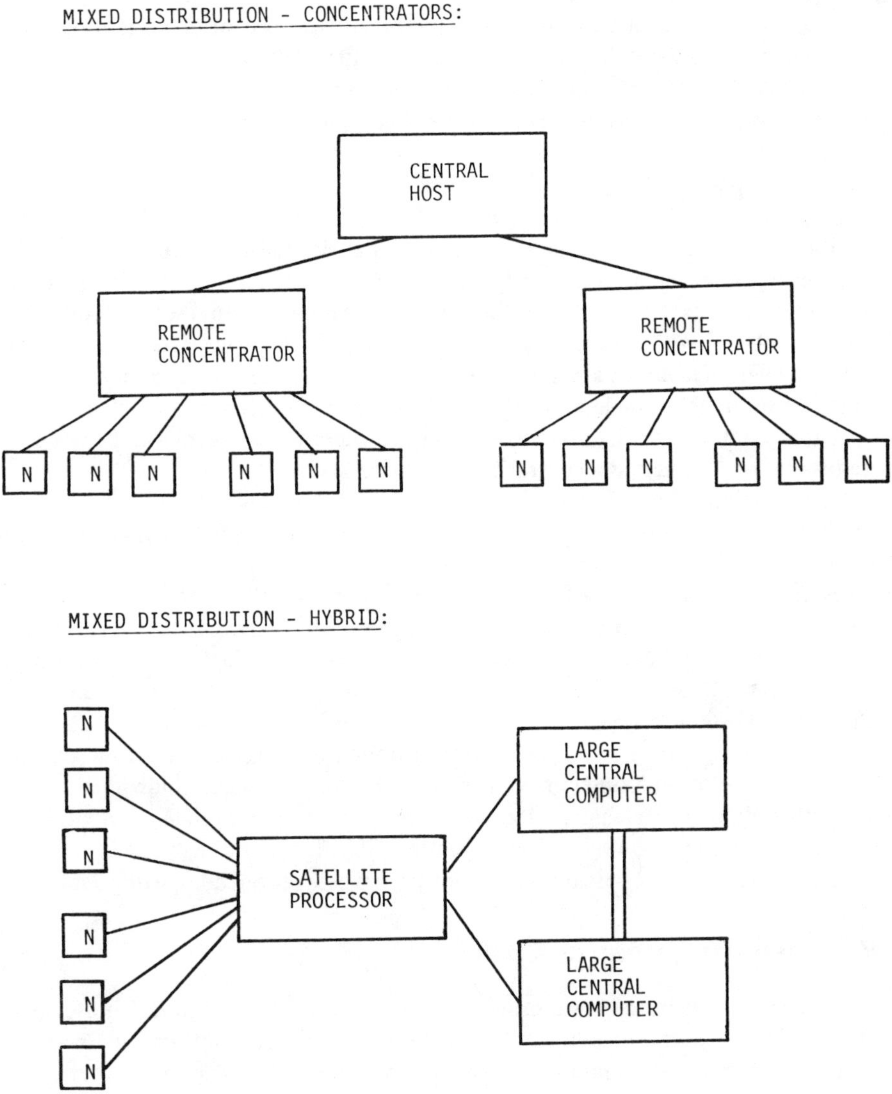

Figure 6-2. Two mixed distribution configurations.

offering backup protection and redundancy. Several satellite processors are connected to both central systems. Multiple small nodes feed into each satellite. Again, the configuration is characterized by the hierarchical structure of data flow. Computer processing can occur at any point, but the importance of the processing and data increase as one gets closer to the central computer.

The configurations in 6-2 represent a natural evolution of the centralized processing approach. The central computer still exists, but processing capability has been distributed out to users. The historical ties to central computing have not been cut, however, since a hierarchical structure still exists.

As might be expected, mixed configuration proponents tend to be made up of those with a vested interest in centralized computing.

SUMMARY OF CHARACTERISTICS

In either the pure or mixed configuration of distributed processing, nodes have basic processing capabilities. They are never used simply as terminals. To a greater or lesser extent they are autonomous. In a pure system, these autonomous nodes practice high degrees of interaction with their counterparts because data and processing resources are shared. Nodes approach each other as equals. In a mixed system, there is less autonomy. The interaction tends to be one way, with remote nodes feeding data up through a hierarchical network. Data bases are usually maintained at a central computer facility.

Pure distributed configurations have partitioned or replicated data bases that are stored throughout the network. If the data is partitioned, each node keeps a unique copy of its own data and shares that data with other nodes when necessary. In replication, each node keeps a copy of the entire data base. In these cases, messages must be sent throughout the network to continuously update each data base copy. The method chosen for data base distribution depends on cost, security, and accuracy. Data base needs and requirements will differ from system to system.

Mixed configurations do not need partitioned data bases. All of the data is eventually stored and updated at the central site. Of course, individual nodes may store data for certain periods of time, such as a complete working day, before forwarding it to the central computer. The data handling techniques used in mixed configurations are derived directly from centralized computing concepts.

MANAGEMENT RESPONSIBILITIES

The types of distributed systems we have been discussing thus far are quite complex to design and implement. Unlike decentralized computing, where mainframes can often be uncrated and running in a single day, distributed networks require a large amount of advanced planning and design. The integration of computer processing, data storage, and data transmission are quite difficult to carry off.

In addition to the resolution of technical questions, there are overall managerial concerns, such as:

• Computer acquisition must be carefully controlled. A single brand of computing equipment is usually necessary because of protocol restrictions. Peripherals should also be common.

• A communications network of data lines must be established and constantly managed. The network will probably be made up of a combination of telephone company lines and value added network facilities, thus doubling the coordination effort.

• Even though the computers are distributed, the entire organization of people must be uniformly managed. Since intense interaction is expected, each node must be operated according to specific standards. Even if operators are casual part-timers, they require indoctrination and training in a standardized fashion. Highly trained programmers must also be obtained. Not only should they program applications, but they must feel comfortable with communications interfaces and protocols. These programmers must be capable of operating in an environment that is still developing. In some cases data transmission between nodes is not fully understood. Two transactions, for example, can simultaneously request the same hardware resource. This produces a phenomenon known as deadlock. Neither transaction receives the resource, and the entire network is sometimes brought to a halt because resolution cannot be achieved. Experimental algorithms have been devised in an attempt to eliminate this problem.

• The hardware/software facility must be managed. Assets must be controlled and inventoried. Maintenance must be arranged. Equipment must be refurbished or replaced as it wears out. Hardware must be upgraded when it becomes obsolete. Software must be modified as the parent organization evolves.

• Provisions must be made for data base integrity. If data bases are distributed, constant vigilance is necessary to maintain accuracy. Since many individual nodes are involved, security becomes a problem. Unauthorized access to important information must be discouraged. Security is quite hard to enforce on central computers, and the matter is even worse on distributed networks.

• Growth in the network must be coordinated and organized.

A distributed computing system is made up of hardware, communications lines, and people. These three elements must work together effectively if the system is to be successful. Obviously, this complex blend must be managed if it is to be successful. Although each individual node is autonomous, the entire network is highly cooperative and dependent.

Chapter 6.3
Networks

Transmission of computer data over telephone lines is always a significant portion of distributed computing costs. It will therefore be useful to explore some general concepts of communications to gain a better appreciation for the cost accounting problems that must be faced.

Technological changes in the communications industry were infrequent until satellites came into commercial use in the 1970s. As the availability of satellite transponders grew, many people predicted that a new era of cheap communications would begin. It was felt that the cost of transmitting large quantities of data would drop dramatically.

This hasn't completely happened. As we pointed out before, although there have been some selected reductions in data transmission costs, these have not been large enough nor broad enough to offset the increased usage most corporations have experienced.

AT&T, the principal telephone monopoly, has constantly restructured its prices to large telecommunications users, sometimes in very confusing ways. In 1981, for example, they eliminated Telpack service, which was a discount scheme offered for many years to large corporate communications users. Telepack flat charged for bundles of dedicated circuits, and offered significant savings over all other conventional prices. At the same time, AT&T took the opportunity to significantly increase prices for conventional long distance transmission. The result was that many heavy communications users saw an overnight increase of as much as 60% to their long distance telecommunications costs. This was an unprecedented escalation, and resulted primarily from the criticism that corporate users were being subsidized by small users. This presumption has never been proven, although it is known that the phone company uses average costing techniques, which tend to benefit high volume users.

It can be concluded, therefore, that technological advances such as satellites, fiber optics, and microwave facilities will not have much of an impact on the cost of transmitting data, at least in the short run.

Value added networks, although initially cheaper (and less flexible) than AT&T, have shown a tendency to increase prices each time AT&T escalates rates. The strategy has been to undercut AT&T by just enough to give themselves an advantage that offsets the fact that they cannot supply true nationwide coverage. Value added nets also cannot supply higher speed data lines.

In the long run, when very large satellites positioned by the space shuttle become commonplace, and when AT&T replaces much of its aging equipment with high technology devices, there may be a possibility of significantly reduced prices. But it will probably take something of a major technological breakthrough before prices of telecommunications fall seriously.

The point to be remembered is that all telephone service is provided by regional monopolies. Monopolies never reduce prices unless competitors can provide enhanced services at a lower cost. And even then, reductions may not be significant. Railroads are an excellent example of this inflexibility. In the face of stiff competition for freight from truckers, railroad rates remained high and significant revenue was lost, to the point where major rail lines went into bankruptcy. The inflexibility and poor judgement of any monopoly must never be underestimated.

SOME COMMUNICATIONS DEFINITIONS

A typical distributed network makes use of many conventional telecommunications devices. Much of this hardware has been around for a long time.

The transmission of data began in the 1800s with the creation of telegraphy. The telegraph was eventually replaced by voice transmission, which incorporated the use of analog signals over copper wires to reproduce speech.

Modern data transmission must make use of these voice facilities. To do so requires special equipment, such as modems, which translate binary computer data into analog signals that are transmitted over telephone lines. The analog to digital conversion has created many technological problems over the years. In many cases, existing voice equipment is incapable of handling high-speed data transmission.

The local loop is the most fundamental unit in transmission. A local loop consists of two copper wires, called a twisted pair, that connect the individual transmission node, such as a voice handset or terminal or computer, to a central switching station. The central switching station then consolidates messages and forwards them to their destination switching station over large, high volume trunk lines. The destination switching station extracts each transaction and sends it through s series of switches and lines to the destination local loop.

For many years this entire system used mechanical switches, and even manually operated jacks. High speed solid state switches are being incorporated into the telephone system, but they require an immense capital investment and cannot be implemented everywhere immediately.

The local loop, as anyone who has a telephone knows, is billed on a flat monthly fee basis. Transmission to any point within a small surrounding area is usually included in this fee, since switching functions are trivial. Messages that must transmit out of the local area are charged on a message unit basis, or on connect minutes.

The pricing structure used for local loops can be used advantageously by many companies. If a single plant site is within the area of a local switching station, all communications is accomplished using flat-cost local loops. Transmission charges can be quite reasonable. Huge amounts of data can be sent over a local twisted pair circuit for a cost of less than ten dollars per month. At this price it is not worth looking at alternative transmission schemes.

However, as soon as transmission requirements extend beyond the immediate plant site and local switching offices, the costs increase significantly. The point is quickly reached where the basic dial-up line becomes far too expensive for data transmission.

Leased lines are an alternative to dial-up. These lines are dedicated, point-to-point lines that are priced on a flat monthly fee. Leased lines vary in cost depending on the line speed and distance.

Value added networks offer point-to-point communicating like leased lines, but the pricing structure is somewhat variable. But VANs still require a flat monthly fee as a minimum before the network can be used.

COMMUNICATIONS DILEMMA

The relatively high cost of data transmission seems to contradict the basic premise of distributed computing.

Distributed computing promises to put computer power where the user needs it, and link each user with counterparts. The concept is appealing, since computer power is distributed along with the business operation. But distributed nodes must communicate with each other over expensive data lines.

Each time a node is installed, a certain amount of fixed communications expense is incurred. Data lines must be leased for fixed monthly fees (in some cases lines are paid for based on volume of data transferred plus a fixed fee, but the end result is virtually the same as a fixed monthly fee because distributed networks have very little discretionary power over the amount of data that must be transmitted during any period). Modems must be purchased and various types of control units and communications processors must usually be bought.

Once a network is in place, there is no advantage in trying to minimize data line usage. Because so much of the cost is fixed (usually 80% to 90%), interaction must be encouraged. The network should be used to the fullest extent possible, but not saturated to the point where additional resources are sporadically required.

It could therefore be concluded that a distributed system that minimizes usage of the network is actually an inefficient system. This fact introduces some interesting design constraints that most analysts are not familiar with. The principal constraint is actually on the compute power of each node. A node cannot be too powerful or it will drain utilization from the network. Processing dollars and communications dollars will be wasted in such a situation. Not only must computers be sized to the workload, but workload and computers must be correctly sized to the capacity of the network. The sizing effort takes considerable technical expertise, as well as constant monitoring to insure that all ingredients stay matched.

DATA TRANSMISSION

As pointed out before, digital information must be modified before it can be transmitted over a standard analog telephone line. Digital to analog conversion is accomplished by a modem, and two of them are needed for each data line. At one end of the telephone line, computer signals are modulated into analog frequencies, and at the other end of the line, the analog signals are demodulated into binary pulses. Modems have been refined over the years. At lower transmission speeds they are quite inexpensive. Their costs increase with data handling capacity. Line speeds can approach the requirements of actual channels using special, but costly, modems. This means that the data line can be made to operate at speeds close to those of the computer.

Another device commonly used is a multiplexor. If a number of terminals or nodes are located near each other, a multiplexor can be used to send all signals over a single transmission line. Multiplexors are relatively expensive, and calculations are necessary to determine the breakeven between total line cost and the cost of a single line/multiplexor combination.

Other hardware devices useful for distributed networks include concentrators, line monitors, control units, and controllers. Concentrators are used in sophisticated data networks to make high-volume usage of expensive lines. Concentrators buffer data from numerous slow-speed devices and transmit packets of it in bursts. Many slow-speed devices are comingled on one high-speed line. Monitors are used by communications experts to determine utilization of data lines, and to help track down problems. Control units are needed to allow CRT type devices to connect directly to communications lines. Controllers provide the interface between data line and computer. Each line is connected to a port, and the controller buffers line input until the computer is ready to accept it.

Communications is a very complex field, and this brief description covers only the basics. The complexity of data communications has led to the need for specialized communications experts. These people are needed whenever the transmission of data is attempted. They design networks, implement them, and monitor utilization to insure that data is being transmitted at the lowest possible costs. They also work with various suppliers of data lines and hardware whenever trouble erupts. When data transmission problems occur, the vendors involved in the network will consistently point fingers at each other to try and avoid responsibility.

Communications experts are in great demand. They are costly to hire and hard to find. Their presence contributes significantly to the overall costs of data transmission.

RELATIVE COSTS

Companies lucky enough to have a single, compact location can install their own data lines if desired, using coaxial cable. Maximum transmission speeds can be obtained at a very low cost. Once installed, the cabling will last indefinitely.

Companies with locations reasonably close together (within fifty miles) can use microwave facilities for all interplant communications. Compact, low-cost units are available for commercial use. Again, the volume of data transmitted is virtually unlimited.

But if the company is decentralized, with locations spread over great distances, then there is no alternative but to use a common carrier. In such cases, the realities of communications cost become apparent very quickly.

Even though there are alternatives to common carrier usage, most companies prefer to deal with the telephone company. Several years ago the Network Analysis Corporation studied communications costs in a number of large corporations. They found that most companies spend about 75% of their communications dollars on local loop/local hardware. Of course, AT&T changed that relationship somewhat in 1981 by significantly increasing the cost of long distance transmission to major companies. But the point is that substantial costs, often hidden, are tied up in local communications activity.

It is apparent that companies probably do not pay too much attention to communications costs. Common carrier competition will undoubtedly change that attitude, as the whole area gets more exposure.

Distributed computing networks tend to have heavy costs at the local level. For example, networks such as rings require complex switching hardware to route signals through the data lines. Even if all distributed nodes are within one building, the communications hardware can build to a significant cost.

Another point to keep in mind is that the data lines used in distributed networks must be dedicated to the network. Dial-up lines cannot be used. This is because all nodes must have continuous access, and must be constantly available, to all other nodes. Nodes must therefore have dedicated communications facilities. The lines cannot be shared by nonnetwork users.

CLOSER LOOK AT DATA LINE ALTERNATIVES

The most common form of transmission line is the local, voice-grade loop, or twisted pair. Most residences in the nation have at least one local loop, as do most of the desk bound office workers in the nation.

All twisted pair copper wires can handle the transmission of data, using special equipment. As a straight, unconditioned line, they can handle up to 4800 bits of data per second, which is more than adequate for most terminals. Typewriter terminals cannot produce data faster than 30 or 60 characters per second. Alphanumeric CRTs operate in the 120 character per second range, and graphics tubes require the full 4800 BPS speed.

The twisted pair lines can be modified with hardware to handle much greater data speeds. With line conditioners spaced every 6000 feet, 1.5 megabits per second can be transmitted. This is the realm in which intercomputer communication takes place.

The special hardware necessary to boost the capacity of telephone lines insures that the line, now called a data line, is dedicated to a single user. This includes the entire distance from the sender to the receiver. No switching must be done to establish a connect, because it is permanent, 24 hours per day, 7 days each week.

Dedicated lines are very expensive. To cut costs, many users lease only the conditioned local loop. The local loop feeds into a specialized common carrier not affiliated with the telephone company. These special carriers are called Value Added Networks (VANs), and many of them only handle data.

VANs generally charge less than the telephone companies for equivalent service, but they have two disadvantages. They may not cover all cities within the U.S., and they do not offer high-speed data rates. As these companies mature, such shortcomings will be eliminated.

Another alternative, mentioned before, is to bypass common carriers altogether. If plant locations are reasonably close together, microwave units can connect each plant, and coaxial cable can be installed within each building. Such combinations can transmit data at rates up to 50 million bits per second. Speeds like this are definitely not needed for distributed computing networks, but the approach may be of value to large companies wanting to supply all of their own transmission services.

COMMUNICATIONS PROTOCOLS

We have mentioned the concept of communications protocol before, but this area needs further attention. There are a substantial number of cost considerations.

A communications protocol is the set of operating conventions that govern data transfer operations over the telecommunications facility. Protocols are software. Some of the more popular high-level protocols follow, with brief descriptions.

• System Network Architecture. SNA is IBM's networking concept. Because IBM is such a dominant presence in the computer market, anything it offers tends to become a standard. However, IBM was relatively late in entering the distributed computing area, thus its network architecture is by no means a standard. SNA tends to be designed for a hierarchical computing structure, as one would expect from the world leader in large computers. The IBM assumption is that there are central, or master components, and decentral, or slave components. This type of networking probably makes sense for centralized computer facilities wishing to move into distributed processing. But it has little value for somebody designing a system with autonomous, minicomputer nodes that do not require a large centralized machine.

• ARPANET (Advanced Research Project Agency) was created by the U.S. Department of Defense. It was one of the first truly distributed networks using the autonomous node approach. It became the basis for several value added networks such as Telenet. ARPANET does not make use of rings. It consists of randomly distributed nodes that connect into a nationwide communications network. The network uses the concept of packet switching, where data is segmented into small packets, concentrated, and transmitted over high-speed lines. Through switching devices activated by information within each packet, they eventually end up at their destination node. Packet switching tends to be most attractive to low volume users who want to minimize their communications costs. Therefore, ARPANET nodes tend to be low volume users.

• Ethernet. This network protocol was developed by Xerox, and makes use of the ring methodology. Ethernet transmits data in packets that start in both directions from the sending node. Dual transmission provides redundancy. Ethernet has provisions built into it to handle line contention and data collision. If, for example, the transmitter does not get acknowledgement of message receipt, the sender retransmits at random intervals, which are adjusted based on data collision history. By pulsing packets throughout the network, high line utilization is achieved.

• Other networks. Nearly every minicomputer vendor has its own unique network protocol. Two of the more popular ones are DECNET, by Digital Computing, and Mailway, produced by Wang. None of these protocols are compatible.

NETWORK COST CONSIDERATIONS

All communications networking schemes reqiuire substantial amounts of commitment in terms of people, hardware, and cost. A network is therefore somewhat like a centralized computer operation. The cost of entry is high for both.

Communications costs come from many different areas. Local twisted pair loops are available only through the telephone monopoly. That same phone company will also generally sell a range of modems, and sometimes terminals. These offerings may or may not be competitively priced. To determine exactly who's brand of hardware is best in a given situation requires technical expertise, which obviously won't be supplied by the telephone monopoly. It is the distributed computing network planner who must determine which brand of modem, multiplexer, concentrator, terminal, and control unit will be used.

If the network extends beyond the plant compound, as most of them do, the cost of long distance transmission must be considered. As pointed out before, value added networks undercut telephone company offerings in price.

The relationship between local loops and a VAN is illustrated in Figure 6-3. Each of three nodes uses its own local loop to hook into a VAN. The VAN then takes care of switching data between nodes.

There are a number of competing VANs. Prices, quality, and geographic coverage differ substantially. Some VANs have been around longer than others, and the industry is characterized by a significant failure rate. This is to be expected when the competition is the world's largest monopoly. Choosing the right VAN is therefore a very technical matter, and could be risky.

This continual need for technically qualified communications analysts leads us into a discussion of the use of highly trained people.

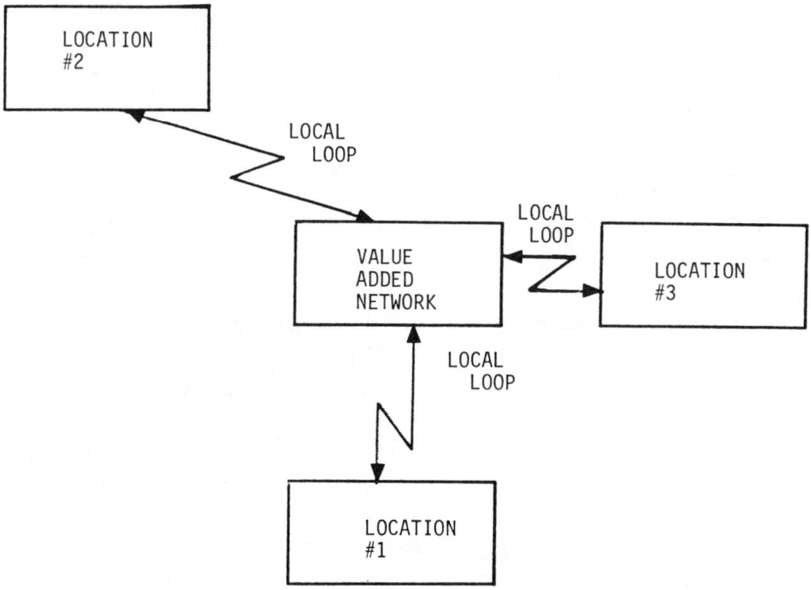

Figure 6-3. Use of value added networks.

Individuals who are qualified to handle communications problems and designs make up a new and growing profession. There is a great demand for communications technicians and planners, and the demand will obviously grow as distributed computing becomes more popular. Of course, centralized computing operations have needed these types of technicians for years, which places even more demand on their services.

Any distributed computing facility will need people in the following skill categories:

• Communications administration. Somebody should have total and final responsibility for communications decisions, such as choice of digitizing hardware and use of value added networks. These are crucial decisions that will have a lot to do with the success or failure of the distributed computing system.

• Network analysts. There are significant cost trade-offs associated with any network. They are the less significant areas that in total can add up to big costs. Decisions encompass areas such as terminal multidropping, multiplexor installation, data line speed requirements, and concentrator placement. All networks grow and evolve. So even after initial design, the analyst has a never ending task of monitoring transmission loads and making appropriate equipment modifications to meet changing needs. The analyst must also be alert to useful and cost cutting changes in technology.

• Systems programmers. Although minicomputer vendors supply network protocols, most distributed processing systems will eventually need custom modifications. Networking is a relatively young computing art. It will be years before thoroughly tested, foolproof designs evolve. Until then, each user will have to make individual modifications to the operating system as problems develop. The choice is to either pay the hardware vendor for custom work, or hire one or more full-time systems experts. The alternative chosen will depend on the overall size of the network. Small installations could probably get by with vendor support, but as size increases, the need for dedicated programmers would become overwhelming.

• Technicians. Distributed computing networks will almost certainly have several different varieties of hardware supplied by differing manufacturers. And one or more common carriers will also be involved in the project. Experience has shown that competitive vendors do not work well together, either at the time of installation, or during problem resolution. The typical large distributed network will therefore usually require one or more full-time technicians who can make simple installations, such as terminals, and trouble shoot problems to determine which vendor or supplier is at fault and should be contacted. Such an activity is mandatory if high uptime is desired.

SCARCE RESOURCES

The above discussion on various aspects of computer networks was intended to provoke thought about the magnitude of work involved when attempting to transmit data. It was not intended to be a comprehensive list of all communications requirements.

Many of the human skills required to establish a network must be developed internally because qualified applicants are so scarce. Whether or not a particular network can justify a complete complement of communications technicians obviously depends on size. As a network becomes large, it can support more and more dedicated people.

From an economic standpoint, a functioning data network is a valuable and scarce resource. Because of this, some form of network accounting will almost certainly be necessary. We will explore accounting alternatives in the next chapter.

Networks become so valuable because there is difficulty in creating good ones. The two biggest obstacles to achieving a satisfactory design are:

- Changing network requirements.
- The difficulty of working with a telephone monopoly.

When a network is first installed, it is very unlikely that an optimum design can be immediately achieved. Much fine tuning is required to balance capacity with load. Many different types of hardware may be acquired before the right combination is found. This configuration experimentation is an expensive, time consuming process, and many users of the network will be inconvenienced because of unresponsive communications during this period. And there is always the chance that problems will never be resolved, thus the network will never perform as expected.

As time passes, users and practitioners suggest new ways of doing things. Or new network features are required. These forced changes modify the nature of the network, and may make it less efficient. It is a rule of thumb that if changes were not anticipated in the original design, they will make the network less efficient and more likely to fail. If enough unanticipated changes are made, the entire network may have to be redesigned.

Dealing with telephone companies has always been and probably always will be a problem. Phone companies are monopolies as well as incredibly large bureaucracies.

There is little doubt that the reliable transmission of voice and data messages in the U.S. has few rivals in the world. But installation services are another matter.

Typical distributed processing needs, such as specially conditioned lines, often take months, or even years to install. The latter half of the 1970s saw a significant increase in telephone usage that seemed to correspond to the rising price of gasoline. This trend is continuing, which means that service levels may deteriorate even more as demand for them grows. The important thing to remember is that monopolies do not act with capitalistic greed for new revenue. They do not really solicit business. Network planners must deal with this tendency by anticipating long installation delays.

A distributed network that reaches into smaller communities has a unique set of problems because it is forced to deal with tiny, independent utilities. The relatively simple installation of a few data lines may push these small switching facilities beyond their design limits. In such cases, the user simply cannot get the capacity he needs, and will have to wait an indefinite period of time before new equipment is ordered and installed. In fact, the user may be asked to pay for the capital costs of the new equipment before the phone company will consider installation. Sophisticated data switches are very expensive.

Users should never underestimate the difficulties of dealing with a monopoly. Further, the complexity, cost, and manageability of a distributed computing network should never be underestimated. The simple existence of a smoothly running network can be considered an asset with intangible worth greater than that shown on the books. Although this value should not be formally recognized, its presence should reinforce the need for network cost accounting.

Chapter 6.4
Costing and Distributed Systems

As with the prior two modes of computing, the first step in the distributed computer accounting process is to identify a responsibility center or centers. This puts limits around the accounting effort.

A typical responsibility center would consist of a communications network and connected processing nodes. What truly defines the reponsibility center is the network.

The task, as with the prior two modes of computing, is to take general ledger costs that are segregated by account number and divide them up between cost pools. Cost pools are then used to develop standard rates.

This chapter will focus on creating cost pools, and the next chapter will discuss cost rate alternatives.

DISTRIBUTED COMPUTING COST POOLS

Since distributed computing techniques differ significantly from other modes of computing, cost accounting also tends to differ. Both the description of many pools and their content are unique in the field of computing.

Directly identifiable costs break down into three fundamental pools, as follows:

- Labor
- Network
- Nodes

Conventional overhead costs also exist, and are quite similar to those found with other forms of computing.

The first major grouping of costs, which is labor related, consists of programmers, and a new category called network planning and control. The network is very important to distributed computing, and requires staff support.

The second major grouping is the network itself. It is made up of data line costs and the expenses associated with specialized communications hardware.

The third grouping encompasses the actual nodes, which are made up of hardware and associated costs.

Cost Planning Matrix

Figure 6-4 shows a distributed computing cost planning matrix. Representative costs have been included, and their calculations are described below. In order, then, we will explain the cost pools. It is assumed that the origination of these costs, in the general ledger, is a process already understood from past examples.

• Programming – applications. Computer operating systems and communications protocols are generally supplied by the hardware vendor. But the set of programs that perform the actual work, such as inventory control or order entry, must be tailored for each distributed application. As with all other forms of computing, except for turnkey systems, the applications programmer must do this.

A good distributed computing system is not something that can be developed by the casual, hobbyist user. Multiple data sources, segmented data bases, and unique node interface requirements have to be blended together into a workable, on-line system. In our sample configuration, one full-time programmer is included. This is a conservative value that is probably significantly understated in the early development phases.

• Systems programmer. Minicomputers have operating systems that start out as relatively simple structures, but inevitably become very complex when significant networking is required. Many distributed systems actually push up against the state of software art. In these cases, vendors, with their off-the-shelf programs, may not be very useful. There is a critical, hard to define point where it is simply too risky to depend on vendor support. Whether this point is reached at three nodes or thirteen nodes depends upon the network manager, and his perception of risk. Even a relatively large distributed network is small to most major minicomputer suppliers. Their responsiveness during times of catastrophic software failure may therefore be quite unsatisfactory. The only solution is a systems programmer. In our case, one full-time systems programmer is charged to the distributed system.

• Network analysis/support. We specifically isolated networking in the prior section to point out that it is an activity which should not be underestimated. The network and its operation may be the most complex component of the entire distributed computing system. Because of problems with common carriers and equipment suppliers, a number of people will be required to make things work. In this case we have included three people as follows:

One Network Manager
One Network Analyst
One Network Technician

COST PLANNING MATRIX
DISTRIBUTED COMPUTING
THOUSANDS OF DOLLARS

COST POOL / GENERAL LEDGER ACCOUNT	BILLABLE LABOR	ALLOCATED LABOR	ADPE LEASE	ADPE DEPRECIATION	COMMUNICATIONS DEPRECIATION	DATA LINES	VENDOR SUPPORT	SOFTWARE	SUPPLIES	GENERAL SERVICES	OCCUPANCY	OTHER OPERATIONS	G&A	TOTAL
DIRECT COSTS														
LABOR														
PROGRAMMING – APPLICATIONS		40												40
SYSTEMS PROGRAMMING		45												45
NETWORK ANALYSIS/SUPPORT		120												120
OPERATIONS/SUPPORT		60												60
TOTAL LABOR		265												265
EQUIPMENT														
NETWORK COMPONENTS														
PROCESSORS				5			2							7
DASD				2										2
NETWORK				1	20	96	5	5						127
SUBTOTAL				8	20	96	7	5						136
DEDICATED COMPONENTS														
PROCESSORS				30			5	10	5					50
DASD				10										10
NETWORK														
SUBTOTAL				40			5	10	5					60
TOTAL EQUIPMENT				48	20	96	12	15	5					196
INDIRECT COSTS														
MANAGEMENT/STAFF		45												45
OTHER OVERHEAD										20	25	10		55
G&A													50	50
TOTAL OVERHEAD														150
TOTAL		310		48	20	96	12	15	5	20	25	10	50	611

1M72116

Figure 6-4. Distributed computing cost planning matrix.

The network manager is responsible for major design decisions and ongoing planning and implementation. For example, he must set response time goals, negotiate maintenance contracts, and authorize equipment acquisitions. Because a distributed network is ultimately a network of people, much of the manager's job is simply dealing with them, and keeping them happy. The manager must insure that people can use the network in an efficient and cost effective manner.

The network analyst designs the basic network to the specifications of the manager. The analyst must optimize common carrier data line usage. He must also insure that network hardware and software meet the needs of the user population.

The network technician installs equipment and cabling, or oversees vendor installation. He also troubleshoots problems to determine who is at fault, then contacts the appropriate vendor with a trouble call.

As a network matures, and the growth curve becomes less steep, the importance of network management and network analysis generally decline. These two functions may even be consolidated into a single person. But the workload of a network technician will often grow as the network ages and becomes more prone to failure, and as hardware must be replaced.

Mature users develop increased expectations. They demand better response times and longer operating hours. These requirements can push a network beyond its designed limit, placing additional pressure on the technician. Thus it is unlikely that the labor costs incurred during network development will ever decrease, even after all of the problems have been worked out of the system.

• Operators/support. Interactive nodes probably don't require full-time operators, unless they handle extremely large volumes of data. The whole point of distributed computing is to get computer power out to the ultimate user. He can then perform data input and hardware operation.

However, in any system there are housekeeping activities. Many of these, such as data base update and backup, must be performed during nonpeak hours, when system activities are at a low point. These functions are best performed during the second or third shift, which means that a full-time operator will be needed. User-operators cannot be expected to consistently devote extra hours to such activities.

We have included one operator, and a second clerical individual to perform activities such as ordering and delivering supplies, arranging for special equipment maintenance, and carrying out miscellaneous housekeeping functions.

• Network processors. Most sophisticated networks make use of intelligent controllers and data concentrators, used to send data efficiently over communications lines. Equipment is also needed as a link between the various protocols used by public networks, and those of computer hardware manufacturers. All of this equipment is usually purchased, thus we show only depreciation costs, along with a small amount of vendor support. On our simple matrix, the costs in this category are not very large. Expenses would depend on the number of nodes, communications sophistication, and data speeds required.

• Network DASD. Sophisticated networks can make use of DASD for storing and transmitting data. Disk can also be used to buffer data during peak transmission periods. In the case of our matrix, the costs in this area are insignificant, and the category is included for reference purposes only.

• Network transmission costs. All costs associated with the actual transmission of data are displayed in this section. Everything between sending modem and receiving modem is included. The largest contributers to this area are the common carriers, such as telephone companies and value added networks. In-plant networks made up of coaxial cable or other owned facilities may also be included.

The cost of data transmission is quite significant, as can be seen on the matrix. They exceed other hardware costs by a large amount. The largest single expense on the matrix is data lines. Communications hardware depreciation is next most significant. It is comprised of modems and multiplexors purchased for the network. Other less significant costs include hardware vendor support and software.

• Dedicated processors. This is the equipment located at each node. It consists of all data processing equipment up to, but not including, the modem. This is essentially node hardware.

The principal component of any node is the CPU, which processes the actual data. Processors are normally purchased, and this causes the high depreciation value. On the matrix, we have included annual depreciation for six nodes, each costing about $150,000, purchased price. Although minicomputers can be purchased at much lower values, the kind of power most sophisticated interactive networks need requires relatively expensive CPUs.

Along with CPU cost comes vendor support, software, and supply charges. These are standard costs we see with all computers.

• Dedicated DASD. DASD costs represent the storage of data. We choose to itemize these costs because DASD is a significant cost element and can easily grow to the point where it is out of control. All computer installations experience an unending demand for more DASD capacity. The best that most operations can do is slow the growth by discouraging sloppy storage usage habits. Unused files should be eliminated or archived on tape or detachable disk.

Computer operations should develop a ratio of storage costs to CPU costs. This ratio can be used each year to measure the relative growth of disk usage. Each installation must determine when disk is growing too fast.

• Management and staff. We have already point out that the communications network needs a manager. The entire distributed system, including the network, also needs an overall top manager. This manager can settle problems between conflicting nodes, or between nodes and the network. He can determine when a new node is needed or when a node can be eliminated. He can insure that standards are being maintained by all users, thus keeping processing and transmission quality high. And, most importantly, he can control costs of the network and of individual nodes. The manager should have ultimate responsibility for the distributed computing system and be its principal representative to the parent company.

• General services, occupancy, other operating, and G&A. These costs have been discussed in depth in earlier sections. They are just as applicable to distributed computing as they are to centralized and decentralized operations, and should not be overlooked. All companies should make an honest attempt to develop equitable allocations of these costs to each distributed computing responsibility center. Failure to do so gives distributed computing an unfair financial advantage over other modes of computing. Such an advantage would lead to incorrect cost justifications.

General Comments

Once again, the cost matrix uncovers substantial amounts of expense that are not directly associated with computer hardware, but nevertheless exist. Node hardware is only 10% of total cost, in our example matrix. Total hardware, including nodes, network equipment, and data lines, is 32% of all costs. Nearly half of total costs are labor related.

The costs of processing hardware placed at each node are actually relatively trivial when compared with total costs. This is because network costs and labor support expenses are so significant.

The matrix reinforces the observation that a distributed computing network is a complex and expensive blend of computers, transmission lines, and people. Labor costs are large because many people are needed to fit the various components together and keep them working day in and day out.

It is an interesting observation that an automated solution can end up requiring many operational type people, whose costs far exceed the expenses of visible minicomputer hardware at each node. And these people are not mere clerks, but highly trained technicians and managers, who are not cheap, and who will become more and more expensive as inflation continues its inevitable upward spiral.

Distributed computing systems are an expensive way to process data. These systems can seldom be sold on the basis of cost savings because they generally increase costs to the parent company, rather than reducing expenditures.

Chapter 6.5
Developing Cost Rates

The six node distributed network introduced in the prior chapter, and detailed on the cost planning matrix, has costs that rank as follows:

Major Pool	Percentage of Total
Nodes	10%
Network	20%
Labor	40%
Overhead	30%
	100%

As pointed out in the previous chapter, it is a remarkable conclusion that the most visible part of the entire system – the minicomputer hardware at each node – is such a small portion of total cost.

The most tangible aspect of any distributed computing system is the equipment at each node. Users can relate quite easily to costs of this visible equipment. Other costs, such as the network and labor support are hidden from the average user. Because of this, it is hard to convince users that transmisstion costs are significant. In our sample matrix, they are twice as large as node costs.

Making matters worse is an observation about the different nature of the cost makeup of nodes and networks.

The minicomputers acquired for each node are normally purchased. Their costs are therefore fixed, and depreciated over a certain amount of time, such as five years.

Network costs consist primarily of leases and service charges. These costs are subject to inflation as well as the price changing whims of monopolistic common carriers. Network costs are definitely not fixed. They will therefore increase each year, at least with inflation, and in some years will go up much faster than inflation.

The user is therefore faced with the dilemma of visible minicomputer hardware costs remaining relatively stable, while invisible network costs increase steadily, as if they were out of control.

The costs of labor exceed the total of all network and hardware costs combined. One reason for this is the relatively small size of our six node sample network. The same labor base could probably support a network somewhat larger. On the other hand, as network size and complexity increase, technical support tends to follow. It is dangerous to generalize about labor other than to point out that its costs are always significant for distributed computing.

COST POOLING

The four basic cost pools identified on the distributed computing matrix were:

Labor
Network
Nodes
Overhead

To simplify matters, these costs can be collected into two pools, which will then be used for chargeback. The two pools are network costs and node costs.

Reallocating labor to the pool that it supports, and then charging overhead to all costs produces a cost distribution as follows:

Major Pool	Percentage of Total
Nodes	30%
Network	70%
	100%

Analysis will show that the network pool picked up a large share of the labor. This is because so much labor is required to maintain a network.

Network costs therefore dominate the distributed computing responsibility center. Because of this, any chargeback scheme developed must give significant influence to transmission chargeback.

NATURE OF DISTRIBUTED USERS

Before developing chargeback alternatives, it will be useful to explore how distributed users tend to function.

The user population is obviously distributed. The degree of distribution depends on how the parent company operates. However, there is a limit to the distribution options. There are only three basic ways that a distributed system can be implemented.

- A decentralized corporation that has plants throughout the country or world could have a distributed system with identical range. Each plant could have one or more nodes tying into a network. Although data could be transmitted freely throughout the network, there would be little or no association between actual nodes. Only information would be made available and transmitted.
- A second option would be distribution between company and customers or suppliers. In this case, the network of distributed processors would extend outside the corporation. But, once again, each node would tend to operate independently of all other nodes, and only seek information as needed.
- And finally, a company could place nodes within a single division, perhaps in all branch offices, or in each production department. The combinations are limitless. Still, the nodes have little in common with each other, and merely require data from the network.

The point of this is that distributed nodes are autonomous, and not very dependent on other nodes. Each node enters and receives data by interacting with a common network. But, other than data transfer, there is little relationship between nodes.

Because of this, there is no discretionary use of the distributed network. Nodes are locked into processing business transactions, servicing the network, and drawing needed information from it. There is no time or capacity left at any node for nonbusiness usage, as there is on a generalized computer.

A good example of a discretionary data handling device is the common telephone handset. Although it can be used for business purposes, it can also be used for personal or nonbusiness activities. Individual users control how each handset is used. There is very little that companies can do to control telephone usage, and insure that handsets are used for business purposes only.

Distributed computing nodes have no such option. They are locked into a closed network and transmit business oriented data back and forth. There is nothing else that they can do.

It makes sense to charge telephone handsets on a utilization basis, such as through connect hours and complex algorithms relating time of day, duration of call, and distance. Such charges are necessary to discourage nonbusiness use. The assumption is that individuals will not abuse the phone system with too many personal calls, because there is always the threat that a large cost will show up against nonbusiness telephone numbers.

Usage oriented charges make no sense in a distributed computing network, however. Each node is trapped into an autonomous business relationship with all other nodes. Detailed accounting is of little value if each node has no control over the utilization that it builds up. Because of the independence between distributed nodes, individual nodes can do nothing to influence the overall cost of the network. Yet the network makes up 70% of total costs.

The network must be charged back to users equitably, but without unnecessay detail.

CHARGEBACK ALTERNATIVES

As with all other modes of computing, distributed system chargeback alternatives range from simple to complex. The distinct division between node costs and network costs adds even more to the accounting complexity.

Node Chargeback

Hardware making up a node can be as simple as a CRT with some intelligence, and as complicated as a full scale minicomputer configuration, with disk, tape, and printers. The cost of an individual node is insignificant when compared with the total network.

Because the value of each node is small, sophisticated accounting techniques such as CPU measurement are unnecessary. Another reason for discouraging complicated node accounting was developed in the preceding section. It was pointed out that distributed nodes have no discretionary use. They are tied continuously to a network, and must perform assigned tasks. The distributed node should operate a fixed number of hours each day, must transmit and receive based on business activity, and has little or no value when the network is shut down.

After considering the negatives associated with complicated accounting, the only two alternatives left are as follows:

- Charge the total cost of each node to the identified user, on a fully amortized basis.
- Bury the cost of the node into network costs, where it would be distributed out over whatever chargeback method was chosen for the network.

The first option is simple and direct. Each user pays for the equipment he has. This is sometimes called dedicated costing.

The disadvantage of the first option is that the corporation may not want users to pay directly for equipment. This would be particularly true if nodes were placed with customer or supplier facilities. In these cases, the corporation would want to encourage the use of computers, and chargeback could potentially alienate the user or inhibit implementation of an effective distributed network.

The second choice states that all node costs are absorbed by the larger network. Whatever chargeback method is chosen for the network will also allocate node costs. This method is also simple and direct. However, there is no assurance that each node will be equitably charged for the equipment it has because chargeback will be based on utilization. A low utilization node could conceivably pay much less each month than the equipment it actually uses. Inequalities like this are inevitable as cost pooling increases.

The physical act of charging back costs to users is complex and hard to control. In the case of the centralized computer facility, the issue can be resolved by setting up a small accounting department within DP that can be given the responsibility for insuring that each user is appropriately charged for services performed. But the central facility has economy of scale that gives it the luxury of forming its own accounting department. A distributed computing operation has no such size advantage, since responsibility, authority, and cost are disseminated with users.

Assuring that the cost of each node gets charged back to the proper user, and making sure that acquisition of new hardware or software also get back to the benefiter, are not simple tasks. This is why the direct chargeback of node hardware to each user is often considered more trouble than it is worth. There is no doubt about direct chargeback's accuracy, if done properly. But the question is: Does that accuracy have any meaning to the ultimate user? Will he change his method of operation based on those costs? The answer is no. Each node must use a certain equipment configuration so that it can effectively communicate with all other nodes. Whether we charge for hardware or bury it somewhere else has absolutely no bearing no what equipment gets installed.

The argument can be advanced that the entire distributed computing system is one entity that can be apportioned out to users based on some form of utilization measurement. Each node benefits the entire network because it participates in the distributed system. Each node is a member of a team. We can therefore conclude that discrete accounting chargeback of node associated costs is probably unnecessary. These costs can be piggybacked onto network costs, for final accounting disposition. This saves in clerical expense.

Network Chargeback

There are several different ways that transmission costs occur.

The standard telephone is charged to users based on distance, elapsed time, and data rate. If a network was comprised entirely of voice grade phone lines, then total system costs could be charged back to each user in the same manner as the phone company billed. Some users, of course, would pay more than other users because of the distance factor.

But there are a number of different alternatives to basic phone services. First, there are leased lines and WATS lines provided by the telephone companies. A flat monthly charge is made for these services, based on distance and data rate.

Or satellites can be used. Here a complete transponder, which represents multiple circuits, can be purchased for a flat monthly fee. Value added networks come and go, and various pricing schemes will be introduced. There is little likelyhood that standards will be developed.

As network planners lay out the basic distributed transmission system, a number of different alternatives may be considered. Many VANs, for example, extend only to the largest cities in this country. If access to smaller cities and towns is necessary, then conventional telephone lines must be interconnected with the VAN. The mix of transmission alternatives used will mean that actual costs could be incurred in a number of different ways – some dependent on volume and some dependent on time. And as the network grows, the mix might change. WATs lines could be replaced by leased lines, for example.

The mixture of transmission alternatives makes it very difficult to discretely assign costs to each individual node. It is nearly impossible to determine which nodes are incurring heavy transmission costs.

And there is a more fundamental concept here. Should any node be penalized because of location? Or should all nodes share equally in transmission costs? Since there is no alternative to being connected the prescribed number of hours each day, it seems unfair to single out any particular node and charge it more heavily than others because it happens to be separated from the center of activity. The node must remain connected regardless of what the transmission costs are. Again, if any single node has high transmission costs caused by its remote location, what can that node do to lower those costs? Nothing.

The network chargeback system must therefore take into consideration that:

- Data transmission will be accomplished in a number of different ways, some more expensive than others.
- Since no central node exists, it is not possible to penalize any node because of transmission distance.
- Nodes do not make discretionary use of the network.

We will discuss three different approaches to chargeback, but will conclude that only one meets the tests of simplicity, understandability, and reasonable equitability.

Subscription Fee Chargeback. This concept has been discussed before. Each node would be charged a flat monthly expense for connection to the network. There would be no penalty for distance, utilization, or the time of day during which the network was accessed.

If node hardware costs are included in the network, as was suggested earlier, then it is a simple matter to add a surcharge to each subscription fee to cover monthly equipment costs.

The advantage to subscription fee charging is that a single rate represents the costs assigned to each node. Network growth and increases in complexity can be handled adequately, since accounting is so simple. If costs are not to be charged back to some users, such as customers or suppliers, then those subscription fee values can be absorbed in parent company overhead accounts.

Developing the subscription fee is as simple as taking total forecasted network costs and dividing by number of nodes. The fee can be adjusted whenever significant variances begin accumulating. If the fee must be increased, it is an indication that costs are increasing faster than usage.

The principal disadvantage to subscription fee chargeback is that it makes no attempt to encourage efficient usage of the network. There is no cost restraint placed over individual users. Since everybody pays an equal amount, there is no incentive to come up with cheaper ways of doing things.

But, as we pointed out before, it is very difficult for individual, autonomous nodes that have a specific job requirement to act in any way that differs from network designers' and managers' dictates. Each node must meet prescribed standards, regardless of cost.

That is why network design and planning are so important for a distributed network. Analysts must determine the most cost effective way of getting the communications job done. Any savings are passed on equally to all users.

A summary of the characteristics of subscription fee chargeback are as follows:

- Nodes are not penalized for location.
- Nodes are not penalized for hours of operation or amount of utilization.
- Costs and savings are born equally by all nodes.
- Costs of dedicated node hardware can be added to the basic subscription fee.

Connect Time Chargeback. The simplicity of subscription fee chargeback can lead to inequitability. This is a characteristic of simple accounting.

Networks are not always homogeneous. Distributed systems can be devised that require unbalanced workloads, with some nodes carrying more processing load than other nodes. Figure 6-5, as an example, represents a network made up of two different types of nodes. The active nodes are interconnected between themselves continuously. They could represent corporate headquarters and several major subdivisions. The less active nodes are interconnected only at certain times, when pertinent data must be transmitted between them and their control node – in this case corporate headquarters. Otherwise, the passive nodes remain disconnected from the network, and perform local processing activities. These passive nodes could represent small branch offices.

Clearly, subscription chargeback would tend to be inequitable because some nodes are much more active on the network than other nodes.

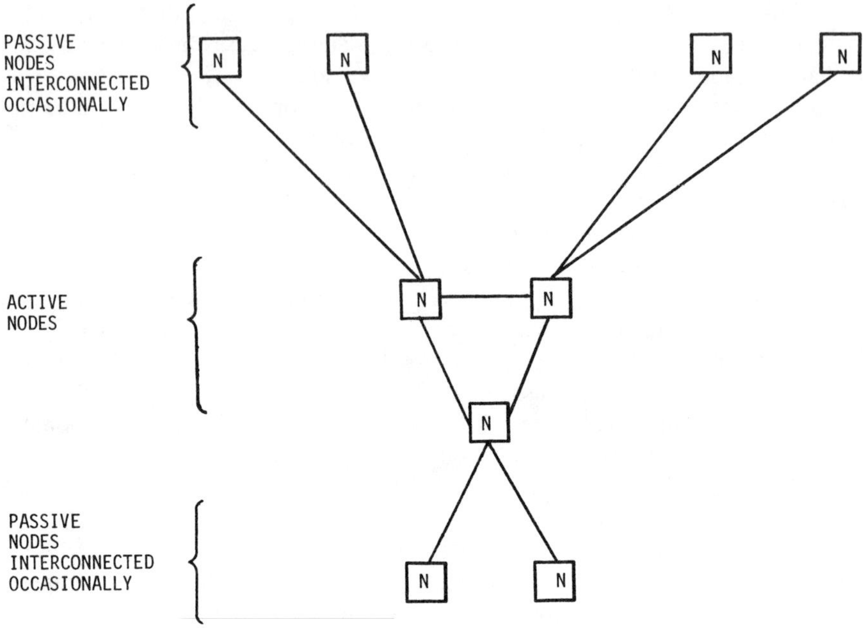

Figure 6-5. Passive vs. active nodes.

A workable alternative would be to adopt connect hour chargeback. Connect hours are a reasonably good measure of network utilization, particularly when all nodes process at the same data transmission rate.

To collect connect hours, an accounting program would have to be included as part of the basic network operating system. Connect hours are usually generated to calculate performance statistics, thus using the same measurement for accounting would be a trivial additional exercise.

A problem with connect hour chargeback is that it does not lend itself well to chargeout of dedicated node hardware. Fluctuating usage of each node would make it quite difficult to recover hardware costs consistently. High volume nodes would pay more than their equitable share of hardware expense.

Without the ability to absorb node hardware costs in the network, direct chargeback of this hardware would be necessary. This additional accounting burden could be time consuming and expensive to administer.

Connect hour chargeback therefore requires a considerable amount of clerical support. Rates must be continually monitored because utilization can fluctuate based on business volume. When additional nodes are added to the network, their impact must be estimated and standard rates adjusted appropriately. And the collection of accounting data can be difficult to perform accurately, because node hardware must be charged back separately.

User perception of connect hour costs may hinder the effectiveness of the distributed network. Users may try to cut back expenses by reducing connect hours. If a user is not attached to the network, his lack of participation might reduce the overall quality of the system.

The characteristics of connect hour chargeback are:

- It is a reasonably equitable method of determining usage of any network.
- It is most effective when there are substantial differences in usage between various nodes.
- There is a high administrative overhead, because of accounting, incurred if the method is to be run properly.
- There may be a negative incentive causing users to reduce network connect time so that their costs can be lowered.

Algorithm Accounting. Distance is a contributing factor to network cost. Most common carriers include distance in their rate structure.

When nodes are scattered over a wide geographic area, some nodes will contribute more communications cost to the pool than other nodes.

A form of message unit can be adopted. Its makeup is similar to that used by many telephone companies. A typical formula could be:

$$\text{Unit} = \text{connect hours} \times \text{distance in miles}$$

Connect hours could be accumulated as in the prior method, using network monitor information. A factor, representing miles from some base point, could then be developed through analysis for each node. The node's connect hours would be multiplied by its distance factor to develop utilization. A standard rate could be calculated and applied against these units to accomplish chargeback.

Establishing distance factors would be somewhat arbitrary. If all nodes are autonomous, then what point of origin would be used for mileage calculations? Squabbling between nodes could make such a method troublesome and unworkable.

The method does have merit, however, in distributed networks where nodes are connected for short periods of time, and are primarily in a seek mode. Florist delivery systems and travel agent reservation systems represent this type of network. Individual nodes are small and usage is relatively low. Adequate recovery of resources must be based on discrete utilization, and a distance factor makes sense because information is usually being obtained through a central source. Such networks tend to be hierarchical.

Since the unit method of accounting is quite complex, the overhead associated with it is high. Processing cycles will have to be set aside to handle accounting tasks.

The characteristics of algorithm accounting are:

- A high degree of equitability for each user.
- A large cost to accomplish accounting.
- A hierarchical network with some central source, which establishes a base point from which distances are measured.

CONCLUSIONS

As with all forms of accounting discussed to this point, there are cost trade-offs to be considered when choosing any one method.

As the degree of equitability and accuracy increase, cost and complexity of accounting systems also increase. The question to ask is whether or not increased accuracy is worth the trouble and expense. Relatively inexpensive computer systems cannot be burdened with complex, high-cost accounting methods.

Connect hour accounting, and the use of algorithms, have the advantage of equitability and accuracy. But these methods add substantially to the complexity of the operating system, and they are expensive to maintain and control. Is the equitability worth all the trouble? The answer must come from the system manager.

In all but the most unusual cases, subscription fee chargeback seems acceptable for distributed computing. The methodology is simple, easy to administer, and reasonably equitable.

The largest problem with subscription chargeback is its tendency to average. Because all users pay an average fee, large customers benefit and small processors are penalized. If this problem is considered significant, the subscription fee can be modified into a semivariable charge. A basic fee could be established, with escalating values as the complexity of the network usage increased.

Figure 6-6 shows a distributed network divided into three distinct groups. These are not hierarchical groupings, but merely represent the degree of interactivity and connect volume. Low-volume users pay one tenth the amount that high-volume users pay, with moderate users right in the middle. This method solves potential inequities associated with a flat, uniform fee. But it means that each node's utilization must be monitored to insure that a user classified as low volume hasn't migrated to a higher category without telling anybody.

Subscription chargeback is desirable from a user's standpoint because it is so predictable. The user knows precisely what his charges will be each month, and can predict them into the foreseeable future.

In short, subscription chargeback has just about everything going for it. Careful consideration should be made before any other technique is adopted.

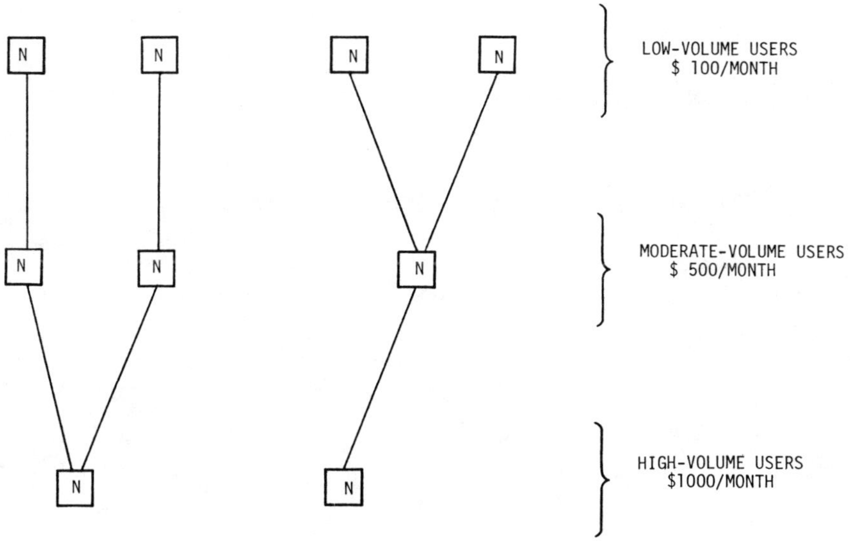

Figure 6-6. Hierarchical pricing scheme.

Part VII
Uses of Accounting Data

Chapter 7.1
Worst Case Accounting

Before we look at the many uses to which computer cost accounting data can be put, it will be useful to explore several cost accounting problems that must be overcome by data centers.

In previous chapters we have reviewed how accounting should be – simple, understandable, and equitable. But most modern computer installations today have a very different type of accounting. It is complex, convoluted, and difficult to understand. In many cases, it isn't even equitable.

For each of the three modes of computing we have described simple accounting solutions that are just as effective as their complex counterparts. But why do so many computer centers practice complex accounting? An answer to this question will help us understand where computer accounting came from, who developed it, and where the vested interests lie that tend to thwart moves to simplicity.

TECHNICAL EXPERTISE

Systems programmers are generally recognized as the people who keep modern computers performing up to expectations. The services of programmers are sometimes offered by the computer manufacturer, but more often they are under the direct control of the data processing department or decentralized computing operation.

Systems programmers are a very specialized breed of people. Their skills are not very transferrable. They generally must work on only one brand of computer since architecture differs between most major manufacturers, with the exception of plug compatible machines such as products produced by companies like Ahmdahl.

The specialized nature of systems programmers allows them to develop intricate knowledge about a particular type of computer. They become expert in computer architecture and understand many of the actual inner operating functions. This knowledge separates these people from all other workers, and tends to put them on a pedestal. Knowledge, retained by an elite group of specialists, breeds power. With power comes a basic disrespect for the views of anybody without this specialized knowledge. This disrespect can be viewed as a form of technological bigotry.

When accounting was first proposed for computers, it was generally assumed that the intricate makeup of these machines would require complex accounting. Since systems programmers had apparently mastered the intricate nature of computers, it was logical to turn to them to solve the problem of machine accounting.

But realistically, large computers are too complex for any single systems programmer to comprehend. Within a complex computer operation, systems programming must specialize in areas such as utility programs, timesharing systems, data base systems, and global operating systems.

Because accounting had to embrace the entire machine, a committee of systems programmers was usually assembled to create a workable methodology. Accounting was therefore placed into the hands of people who felt very comfortable with complexity.

Systems people approached the problem of accounting by assembling usage statistics. This is a logical first step. The data could be found under the generic category of *performance measurement statistics.*

Usage data was first introduced by computer manufacturers for performance purposes, rather than accounting. To optimize performance, the user needs data on how jobs are running through the system, and what the usage requirements of these jobs are. An analogy can be drawn with the design of an automobile. A designer must understand the characteristic of an automobile, both in aerodynamic shape and engine performance, before optimum mileage per gallon of gasoline can be achieved. Likewise, a computer operation must understand what kind of jobs it processes as well as the operating characteristics of its mainframes before determining if jobs are being efficiently processed. Once jobs and hardware are understood, software and equipment can be modified, or tuned, for optimum performance.

Computer users wanted to achieve optimum performance. Computer manufacturers did not attempt to tell each installation how to optimize, but, rather, supplied vast amounts of performance data. This data tracked every conceivable aspect of computer operation.

IBM collects performance information under the title of SMF, which we have discussed before.

There is a distinct possibility that manufacturers created these vast data banks of job performance statistics more to confuse than to help. A technical expert could spend a lifetime (and some do) searching around through this data, looking for correlations and meaningful trends. All too often the analytical results merely point out the obvious. But people seem to feel more comfortable with statistical analysis than with common sense.

When systems programmers reviewed these performance statistics, they were able to reach two preliminary conclusions:

- On a gross basis, job profiles could be developed and scarce resources identified.
- The large array of performance statistics available proved that computer accounting had to be complex. In other words, if the data is available, why not use it.

Detailed performance data revealed utilization for CPU, memory, channels, switches, disk, tape drives, and printers. As computer systems evolved, additional statistics showed up for the transmission of data.

To encompass this vast array of resources, all of which were considered significant, a complex accounting scheme had to be developed. Thus came techniques such as algorithms, which we discussed earlier. By grouping many measurements together into a single formula, the algorithm gave the appearance of simplicity to apparent chaos.

What appeared to be an elegant solution was actually very unsatisfactory. The components of the algorithm, and their relationships, were so tangled that what attempted to be precise was actually quite imprecise.

Suppose, for example, a computer installation has an algorithm such as the one displayed in Figure 7-1. This is a fairly complex formula. Constants were added based on calculations made by systems programmers to give relative weight to each of the elements of the formula.

The algorithm has five variables. A given job can change any of these variables from run to run. And the accuracy of items such as CPU time and I/O time are questionable. So the accounting units for a programmer's job may vary from run to run for no apparent reason. The variability is not predictable because each of the algorithm elements can go up or down randomly.

The point is that an algorithm created by technical experts can generally only be understood by technical experts. Unless system programmers are given specific instructions to keep the formula simple, they will strive for complexity under the assumption that it is more accurate. This is a mistaken assumption if the complexity cannot be comprehended by the average user and if utilization measurement is nonrepeatable.

```
UNITS = 5 x CPU min + 1.5 x memory + .5 x tape + .7 x setup disk
```

Figure 7-1. Typical CPU algorithm.

USER RESPONSE

One of the basic tenets of accounting is repeatability. If periodic data cannot withstand the test of repeatability, it loses credibility.

For example, think how you would react if, when your automobile's gas tank was close to empty on two different occasions, the first fill-up took twenty gallons of gasoline, and the second fill-up took thirty gallons. A small variability is expected, but a 50% variance is unreasonable. You would suspect that the pump measurement device reading at the local gas station was nonrepeatable. You would either complain or, more likely, take your business elsewhere. But you probably wouldn't buy gasoline from that particular pump again because you would be highly suspicious of its accuracy.

Nonrepeatability, under any circumstances, creates distrust and dissatisfaction.

If the computer accounting algorithm results are nonrepeatable, there are two basic responses from the user community.

The first response is one of rejection. The user simply runs his jobs and gets his work done and pays absolutely no attention to the chargeback accounting system. The user has no respect for the accounting system and, if asked, will make his negative views known. When nobody pays attention to accounting, then the accounting system is a waste of money and resources. It would be better to use the resources consumed by the accounting system on work that was more productive.

The second response to nonrepeatability and complexity is gamesmanship. Using intuition and experimentation, individuals with the right kind of inclination will find ways to take advantage of the accounting system to their own benefit. They will experiment until they find a combination of job characteristics that reduces their cost. For example, the programmer may find that by squeezing his job into small amounts of memory he reduces his cost, but the CPU actually thrashes away inefficiently. Users play various parts of the algorithm against each other until they hit upon a cost saving combination. But resource consumption may be far above what it would be had the job run with conventional default parameters.

The second user response points out another danger. The accounting algorithm can have poor or even bad assumptions built into it that lead people into inefficient use of the computer. As computer hardware and software architecture changes, what began as a good assumption might turn into a very poor accounting concept. The charge for memory is a good example. In the mid-1970s, stiff charges for memory made sense, because it was a critical resource. Today, memory is abundant, and charging for its use is not very meaningful.

Whether the user disregards the accounting system or tries to game it, no useful purpose results. The accounting is useless, and may lead to inefficient use of computers.

No group of technical experts, such as systems programmers, can ever foresee all of the variations that will be caused by a diverse group of users. Although complex accounting concepts and algorithms give the appearance of understanding, from the user's viewpoint they generally lead to misunderstanding and confusion.

If users cannot predict their future processing costs with some degree of accuracy and confidence, or if they cannot understand how costs will change if they modify a program parameter, then accounting is of no value to them.

The solution is to put accounting oriented people in charge of computer chargeback. Utilization schemes will inevitably be simple and straightforward because these people do not have a very deep understanding of exactly how a computer operates.

To price any item, whether it is a good or service, all the practitioner really needs to know is what the ultimate user perceives as value. Value perception made by the person who builds the product or performs the service has no meaning. The final user is the only one who really counts.

Chapter 7.2
Who Benefits from Cost Accounting?

Parts four, five, and six of this book went into much detail to describe how cost accounting can be applied to all major forms of computing. We have attempted to devise methodology that keeps accounting techniques uniform within a company, so that there is comparability between different modes of computing.

THE PRICE MECHANISM

The consumer marketplace practices the concept of uniformity and comparability through the price mechanism. Automobiles are a good example. They come in all shapes and sizes, with an infinite variety of operating characteristics. But most of the differences between vehicles are perceptual – that is, any given characteristic will be perceived as having different value to different individuals. Roominess is important to one person, but trivial to another. Styling and practicality are other opposites, each having its proponents. The one equalizing factor in the marketplace that everybody can agree upon is price. As cars increase in price, their value increases because it takes more money to acquire them.

By forcing computer operations to cost their services, they are opened up to the price mechanism. Value is established so that various services can be compared, contrasted, and evaluated. As more computer options become available, the price mechanism can help determine which option is best for the company, at least in terms of dollars.

But the problems associated with the price mechanism on the open marketplace must be eliminated from industrial decisions. The most significant problem has to do with whether or not the cost truly represents the value of the service.

The price of any particular automobile may not be a true representation of its actual value, because it may include intangible items such as prestige and status.

Eliminating intangibles in the computer world can be accomplished through accounting uniformity. As a start, all computer operations must count up total costs – all costs. Many of these costs are hidden within the company's accounting system. Devices like the cost planning matrix must be applied uniformly to all computer applications.

Although we have covered them before, once again we shall list the various cost categories that are applicable to all modes of computing:

- Hardware
- Communications
- Software
- Supplies
- Operator Labor
- Systems Programming Labor
- Management and Administrative Labor
- Occupancy and Facilities
- Company Overhead
- Other Allocations

By displaying these items on a planning matrix, and then using the basic form for all modes of computing, a uniformity is brought to the cost gathering process. No cost will be overlooked in any computer installation, either existing or planned. The method also brings a logical shape to the broad range of costs that make up a computer installation.

The centralized computer facility is probably in the best position to produce a representative cost matrix. Central organizations have usually been around for quite a long time. They have a reasonably good understanding of their costs, and they can afford to establish a full accounting group.

Decentral and distributed operations are not large enough to justify hiring accountants and clerks. Large clerical staffs would defeat the purpose of these small installations. Their accounting task, therefore, is not quite so simple.

Standardization in the cost collection process can help. Uniform, company-wide rules for developing cost planning matrices should be developed. Detailed instructions for developing each cost category can be prepared. Standard allocation percentages can be worked out for those overhead items that are not direct charged. All the practitioner need know is his direct costs, such as hardware rent, supplies, software, and labor. Using standard allocations, a single person could cost out an entire distributed or decentralized operation, using a "fill in the blanks" approach. And uniformity would be guaranteed.

STANDARD RATES

After the cost matrix is completed, the rate building process begins. Standard rates – rates that are based on future projections rather than history – are recommended, because they force financial people to look into the future and attempt to forecast what they think will happen. The process of forecasting is as important or even more important than the final results. Trying to predict future events produces an understanding of the computer operation that no other activity can replicate. When people think in terms of future cost and future utilization, they are less likely to pursue technology blindly. Their computer installation is managed more like a business and less like a hobby shop.

To help in the rate building process, the company should develop common utilization measurements for each mode of computing. This eliminates reinventing the wheel and insures compatibility within each mode.

Decentralized users might choose the user connect hour as the basic accounting unit. Distributed networks might adopt the subscription fee. Once established, the same utilization measurements should be used by all new computer systems.

ACCEPTANCE

Cost accounting methodology eventually benefits all people associated with computers. Those who actually manage the computer benefit because the accounting technique helps them better understand the equipment they have, and the relative value of various components. It helps them realize that there are more costs than basic hardware rental. And those who use the computer benefit because they learn what the true costs of computing are. They are also given a measurement tool to use when comparing alternative services. They can then shop around for the best processing deal.

But to achieve acceptance within the computing community, the cost accounting system must be simple. If the system is too complex and convoluted, then many of its benefits will be lost. After all, the principal reason that computers are acquired is to provide automated solutions by processing data. Accounting for the processing is an afterthought. People are not going to take the time to sift through intricate accounting schemes. If the methodology is too tangled, they will ignore the results.

We could have developed a much more complex cost planning matrix. For example, the column titled ADPE Hardware Rent could have been expanded into the following categories:

Hardware Rent
Scheduled Maintenance
Nonscheduled Maintenance
Installation Expense
Freight
Overtime (extra shift rental)
Use Tax
Property Tax

But to keep the matrix simple and workable, we assumed that these costs could be consolidated under the general heading of ADPE Rent. Most of the above items vary in direct relationship to rent, so itemizing them would serve no useful purpose.

Simple structure, and consolidation wherever possible, kept the cost planning matrix to a workable size. Nobody could get overwhelmed with detail.

Simplicity extends to the choice of utilization measurements, as we have pointed out a number of times. Simple utilization helps the user understand his bill, and helps the practitioner forecast future usage.

If the entire cost accounting system is simple, then it is more likely to gain wide acceptance. Getting a cost accounting system accepted by users is the single most important goal within the entire field of cost accounting.

COMPARATIVE EVALUATION

Once a uniform method of standard costing is developed, rates throughout the company become very meaningful because they can be compared and contrasted with each other.

Suppose, for example, a company has ten minicomputers installed in the plant as decentral, standalone configurations. If each of these operations can develop a standard rate, using uniform cost accounting practices (which could be audited from time to time to insure compliance), then a quick glance at each of the rates would indicate which installation was run best, and which installation was having problems. In general, a poorly run installation would have high rates, and a well run computer would have low rates. Most operations would fall somewhere between the best and the worst.

Installations with rates that were significantly higher than average would be candidates for close scrutiny. Perhaps legitimate justification could be produced for an operation's unusually high rates. But management wouldn't be doing its job if it was not aware of this type of condition and hadn't at least asked a few investigative questions of the appropriate practitioners.

This example represents one of the key provisions of a standard cost system. Cost accounting highlights potential problems through the technique of deviation from normal trends. It also provides backup information, in the form of the cost planning matrix, which will help isolate the exact cause of the variation.

Although we have been using small computers in our examples, large centralized installations can also be effectively measured using standard rates. Their rates can be compared on a year-to-year basis to determine whether they are trending up or down. Increasing rates are an indication of problems, and should be challenged by upper management.

Standard rates are a simple, effective tool for cost control. They may not offer the final word, but they are very powerful indicators of underlying problems or successes. Without them, management is only guessing at the effectiveness of computerization.

Chapter 7.3
A General Cost Model

Before managers who have responsibility for computer installations can make judgemental decisions on cost or rate, they must understand the basic pattern that all computer operations follow. An acceptable cost rate at one stage of a computer center's development may not be reasonable during a future time period. Neither costs nor rates are constantly stable. They change with the life cycle of the installation.

The evolution of any computer operation breaks down into the following segments:

- Justification of the computer installation.
- Evaluation and approval.
- Installation of hardware/initial staffing.
- Implementation problems/burn in period.
- Problem resolution/cost increases.
- Post resolution/fine tuning.
- Maturity/cost control.

Figure 7-2 displays these seven stages of development graphically, and relates them to standard cost rate. As the graph shows, during the installation and implementation periods the standard rate increases. During fine tuning, the rate stabilizes, and during maturity the rate actually declines.

Over time, the entire nature of the data processing installation changes. Even the people associated with the computer tend to change, from entrepreneurial types in the beginning to routine managers in the mature stages. The kind of people connected with the operation have a great deal to do with the way costs are controlled, or not controlled.

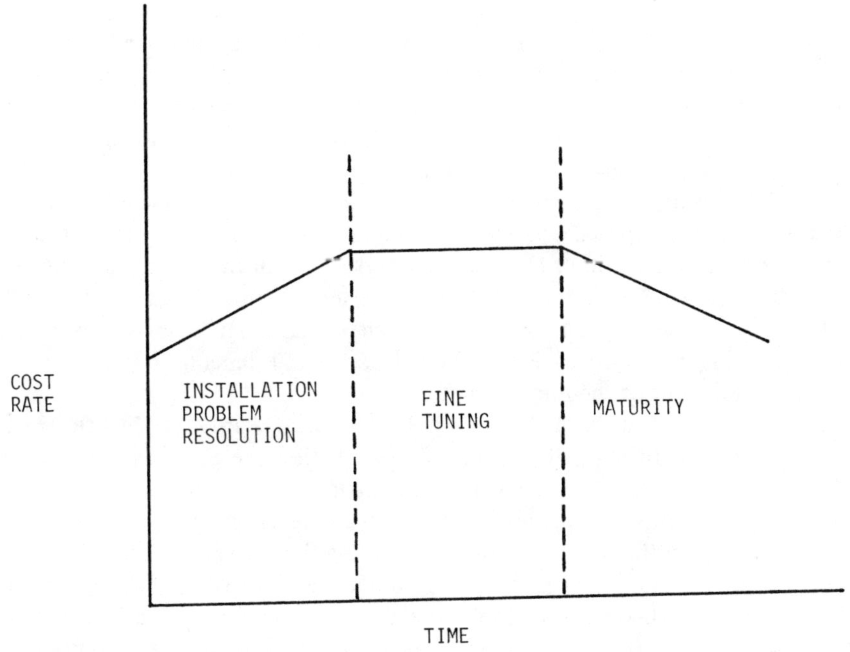

Figure 7-2. Evolution of a computer center.

DEVELOPMENT STAGES

Justification

There are many reasons behind the desire to create a computer operation. But it always begins with people who want something.

Centralized operations were usually begun haphazardly, starting with card handling equipment in the early days and evolving through many phases of hardware, as manufacturers came out with larger and more sophisticated computers. In most companies there was probably no clearcut plan to computerize. It simply happened, by starting small and growing larger and larger as the company became more dependent on data processing. A few corporations undoubtedly tried to plan computer growth. But, remarkably, the end result was usually the same. All companies were swept along with the tide of computerization. By the late 1970s, most large corporations had major computer centers centralized under one management. The justification was economy of scale.

Most large computer centers never received much of an initial justification. They just seemed to happen.

The acquisition of more recent decentral and distributed minicomputers indicates the possibility of a much greater tendency toward some kind of justification. The justification is often inadequate or misleading, but it is much more than what went into acquiring many early centralized processors. The justification of smaller computers is probably forced, to a large extent, by the central facility, which doesn't want to see its processing base erode.

For minicomputers, an individual or group of individuals first perceive the need for a small computer or network of computers. This perception leads to discussions with one or more hardware vendors. A team may eventually be set up to study the issue and make recommendations. Or, individuals may be left on their own to develop and present to their management a justification. In either situation, the approach is usually free form, and depends a great deal on the ability and talent of the minicomputer proponents.

Managers presented with these highly technical hardware justifications usually have a very difficult situation to resolve. If they are good managers, they realize that everything has been slanted in favor of the acquisition. Why else would the justification be made? Proponents are certainly not going to come forward with a plan that discourages the very thing they are proposing.

Good managers also realize that they understand little or nothing of the technical jargon sprinkled throughout the proposal. The cost data is probably quite misleading, particularly if comparisons are made with centralized computing facilities.

A manager's reactions to the justification can range between two extremes. He may authorize blanket approval of all such justifications because the individual dollar amounts seem trivial and he doesn't have the time to crawl through all of the confusing detail. Or, he may disapprove all such requests because a central computer already exists and because he intuitively feels that minicomputer installations rarely show savings caused by actual reduction of people. That is, if it cannot be clearly shown that the computer will eliminate people, then costs haven't truly been eliminated and the proposal is without merit. The manager in-between these two extremes probably vacillates between approval and disapproval, never quite sure why his decisions end up the way they do.

Evaluation and Approval

Evaluation of proposed computer systems can be made in a number of different ways.

Managers can rely on intuitive feel. For example, deciding that the acquisition of a small computer is a trivial situation, and should therefore always be approved, is an intuitive approach. The danger to such an approach is that, in the long run, the small computer may grow into a very large computer, with costs far in excess of trivial amounts.

Another technique, more scientific, is called Return on Investment, or ROI. The life cycle savings of the installation are turned into an annual yield. The yield, in percentage terms, is compared with a target return, called the hurdle rate. If the project has a return that is less than the hurdle rate, then it is not worth investing in because the necessary money could earn more elsewhere. Think of return on investment as annual compounded interest. The savings, or return, grows at a compounded rate. The hurdle is also a compounded annual rate.

The problem, of course, is that the analytical methodology may be far more accurate than the data actually analyzed. All projections of cost savings are arbitrary and slanted in favor of approval, since numbers were developed by people who really want the hardware. Whether the analytical technique is sophisticated or unsophisticated, the results will inevitably show that hardware acquisition should be made.

Proper evaluation should start with consistently developed cost numbers that are realistic. Here is where the value of the cost planning matrix becomes apparent. The matrix provides a consistent way of itemizing all cost values, including those that are somewhat hidden, such as allocations.

Using the full cost approach, techniques like ROI become much more meaningful.

Installation

After official approval, hardware and software are ordered. Facility modifications are usually necessary to house the new computer. For all but the very smallest computers, separate housing, with fire proof walls, sprinklers, and air temperature control are necessary. In all cases, conditioning of the power supply to prevent power surges is absolutely necessary. Separate areas must be provided to securely store supplies. And a terminal room may be necessary.

As the equipment arrives, people are hired. Startup begins fitfully. There are always hardware and facility problems to be worked out. Startup is a very expensive period. Substantial amounts of time pass before any productive work is done.

Problem Resolution

When the computer or computers are actually powered up and begin running, a whole new set of serious problems begin. Those who work a lot with minicomputers have coined the term *burn in period* to describe the problem resolution period. Beginning with the point when a computer is first powered on, and extending for a period of several weeks to several months, random outages inevitably occur. Once the problem components have been isolated and replaced, the electronics usually operate for a long and trouble free service life.

Mechanical hardware such as disk devices and tape seem to have the reversed situation. They are extremely reliable when first turned on, and continue like this until a certain threshold of wear occurs, after which they seem to be prone to a constant series of problems.

During the initial problem resolution period, users obviously attempt to perform productive work. There are many delays and frustrations caused by hardware downtime. It is wise not to expect too much from the computer during burn in.

A characteristic of this period is sudden, poorly justified acquisition of additional equipment. The terms "killing the problem with hardware" and "panic buying" are appropriate. When operating problems become particularly frustrating, one obvious solution is to get more hardware, and continue to acquire equipment until the problem is resolved. Once a commitment to a computer has been made, it becomes much easier to justify additional equipment to make the system work as intended.

This problem resolution period is an important test of the adequacy of the original proposal, and of the team implementing the new system. Responsible management should monitor activities very closely because costs can easily get out of hand.

Post Resolution

Problems are eventually resolved. The time period can be anywhere from a few weeks to a few years, but eventually, managers get their hands around the anomalies and solve them. The installation moves into a period of fine tuning. Small, incremental changes are made to improve performance or productivity. More features are added to the hardware and software. Costs don't increase as fast as they once did, and tend to be more closely matched with workload changes. The standard rate stops increasing and may actually level off.

Maturity

After a period of stability, the system becomes mature. Utilization tends to increase as the user community builds confidence in the system or systems. The increased utilization combined with stabilized costs usually results in lowering cost rates. Users are able to get more work done for the same amount of money, or fixed applications actually become cheaper.

Hopefully, this period of maturity is long and productive.

Eventually, technology changes so much that the current hardware solution is obsolete. The manufacturer may threaten to discontinue maintenance support of the aging hardware. A significant change must be made. Justification begins for new equipment, and the whole process begins all over again.

Because we know that this cycle of justification through maturity will occur over and over, it makes sense to standardize justification and acquisition of computers. Further, standard measurements must be adopted so that system productivity can be determined. This sums up the purpose of implementing the cost planning matrix and a standard cost system, with standard rates.

Chapter 7.4
Managing the Cost of Computers

All computer installations, regardless of size, are responsible to some member of upper management. We are discussing here not the people who actually operate and manage the computer, but that level of management which has overall responsibility for the aspects of a computer operation.

A management strategy must be developed if computer installations are to be effectively controlled. That is, managers who have ultimate responsibility over computers must adopt a consistent, cost effective approach to the justification and operation of computers.

The next chapter will discuss who these managers should be – whether they already exist or must be created. This chapter will introduce strategic tools that can be used to monitor the performance of processing pools.

EXPECTATIONS

In the preceding chapter we introduced the concept of a computer installation life cycle. The life cycle can be measured both in terms of total cost and historical rate change. Standard rates are an important indicator of the health and productivity of each computing operation, providing there is consistency in how each operation developed its rates.

How does a manager insure that every computer operation is following the rules – collecting costs and developing rates just like everybody else? The manager must assume an adversary role and act like an accounting auditor.

All professional auditors know that regardless of how closely they examine any accounting system, such as accounts payable, or petty cash, or payroll, they will never completely understand it or comprehend all of the possible anomalies that lie hidden below the surface. The only people who truly understand what is going on in any system are the actual practitioners – those who perform the work.

During an audit, if practitioners care to open up and explain the problems and possible deviations within the system, the auditor has gained an important advantage. He has been given an insight into the workings of the system that would probably be impossible to achieve in any other way.

But, the more usual case is that the practitioner has no desire or vested interest in completely explaining the problems within his system. Problems reflect badly upon him. It would be like airing dirty linen.

So the auditor must make standard accounting tests, such as gathering a sample of data and analyzing it to insure that everything has been performed properly. If accuracy within the sample appears to be poor, then the auditor digs more deeply into the operations of that system. But when the test shows that everything has been performed correctly, then the auditor assumes that the entire system is satisfactory, and goes onto some other endeavor. The hope is that the sample is representative. That may be a questionable hope. For example, a major corporation can process invoices through an accounts payable system totalling two or three million dollars each day. An auditor examining such a system might actually examine payment records covering only several hundred thousand dollars, or about two tenths of one percent of total, on an annual basis. Many, many errors and improprieties could be missed in such a small sample. That is the risk involved in auditing. There is never enough time to retrace every single transaction.

Top managers must face their computer groups like the auditor. The manager must remember that technicians are obviously well aware of what is going on in their operations. For example, these technicians know whether or not users are satisfied and throughput is acceptable. But these local managers will filter information in such a way that only the good operating results reach top management. Technicians will pass on the good news and gloss over any adverse information.

The manager simply doesn't have the time or ability to verify the claims of technical practitioners. But there are two areas where he can make himself felt and exert significant control:

- Annual budgets
- Review of standard rates

If the budgetary process is standardized for all computer installations, the manager can review year-to-year changes in budget and compare and contrast the budgets of different installations. He may even institute annual zero base budgeting techniques, although the payoff might not be worth the effort. Many small installations are simply unprepared for such sophisticated budgeting.

But it is a strong management tool to make each computer center manager sit down once each year and justify expenditure levels for all controllable expenses.

The problem with budgets is that they represent only half of the picture. Sudden increases or decreases in budget may look strange, but may be quite legitimate because of workload changes. What start out as identical computer installations, for example, may eventually diverge substantially in total costs, because one installation operates a more complex set of application programs than the other. With complexity comes higher cost.

What makes budgets meaningful is the standard cost rate. If all computer centers develop rates in the same way, then an average, or composite rate will appear. Deviations from the average highlight anomalies, and bring even more meaning to the budgeting process.

When budgets are submitted, a set of projected standard rates should also be included. The top manager then has an excellent frame of reference to use in judging the adequacy of budget demands.

STANDARD RATE CONSIDERATIONS

In the last chapter we saw that there are justifiable reasons for the standard rate to change over the life cycle of a computer operation.

From the user's viewpoint, the most important portion of the cycle occurs when rates stabilize and begin to decline. There are therefore several questions that can be asked about this period:

- How long should an installation run before rate declines are to be expected?
- How much decline can be expected?
- What are the alternatives if no decline occurs?
- Will rate declines end, and what happens then?

We saw that rate increases could be expected from initial computer installation until the point where major problems were resolved and fine tuning began to pay off. The length of time encompassed in the initial phase obviously depends on the complexity of the computer installation, the ability of programmers and practitioners, and the reliability of hardware and vendor support.

In general, it is advisable to expect the worst of computer performance. The principal "if things can go wrong they probably will" is applicable. Computers are complex devices and there will always be problems associated with startup. But there are some hardware configurations that literally ask for trouble, while others are within the area of proven technology. For example, it would probably take longer to start up a distributed computing network having nodes spread throughout the country than it would to obtain a single decentral minicomputer and bring up an off-the-shelf accounts payable package. In the first case, intricate network technology must be designed and implemented before processing can begin. In the second case, proven hardware and software have been around for years, and the self-contained system should be up and running with only minor problems during the first few days.

Problem resolution, and the amount of time it takes, is therefore unique to the application. There is no set standard. It is management's duty to decide how much time is reasonable to get the bugs ironed out. Some projects will obviously take longer than others. But it is also management's duty to realize that this whole period is transitory and must eventually come to an end. There is a point where enough is enough, and if standard rates haven't smoothed out, then a general reorganization of the operation is in order. There is no textbook formula that can identify the point where change is necessary. Good management simply knows when the time is right.

How much rate decline can be expected? Rate declines should eventually be reasonably healthy. These declines occur because users, who begin to feel confortable with the system, process more and increase overall utilization. If the system was properly designed, this usage would have been anticipated and could be handled with little or no increase in hardware cost.

Managers often call this phenomenon the *learning curve.* People and systems get better over time, as tasks are endlessly repeated. Productivity improves and rates go down.

There is no reason why standard rates can't at least be cut in half over the course of several years. This trend has proven itself out over decades of experience with large computer systems.

What are the alternatives if no decline occurs? The answer to this question involves judgement. But it generally becomes obvious when a computer is not progressing as smoothly as anticipated. The failure of the standard rate to stabilize or decline after a certain period is an indicator of trouble. Other problems begin to surface. There is generally turmoil within the ranks. People turnover is significant. Additional equipment is constantly being acquired. At review time there is much finger pointing. People admit that there is some kind of problem, but nobody will stand up and take responsibility. Tangible results *never* seem to be accomplished.

At this time, a reorganization is probably in order. The only other alternative is to discontinue the operation, and go back to the old way of doing the job. Risk managers call it "stopping losses." The old way may not have been very bad, after all.

If rates do stabilize and then decline, will the reductions eventually come to an end? There is obviously a point in time when no further reductions can be made to cost, and further utilization increases are impossible to achieve. Capacity limits on the basic configuration of equipment are reached. If any further increase in utilization occurs, the acquisition of a large increment of hardware will be necessary. Until reasonable utilization levels are reached on the new hardware, rates actually rise. In some cases, technology might help with new hardware devices that are significantly better price/performers. But technological obsolescence eventually sets in, and no further enhancements are offered for the existing equipment.

The obsolescence problems is aggravated by the relationship that most practitioners form with a single vendor. Installations tend to become locked in with one major equipment supplier. It is natural for people to seek out these types of relationships. Users find that a good, supportive vendor can make life a lot easier. IBM learned this many years ago, when it began supplying all computer needs to most clients.

There is a price that is payed for single vendor support, however. Instead of helping the user find cheaper and more efficient ways of performing his work, the vendor attempts to continually "trade up" the installation. Hardware is forced into obsolescence as equipment with more flexibility and capability is offered. But the cost is always higher. The supplier is simply not willing to reduce his account revenue. When a substantial upgrade is made, rates do not decrease, but increase. The vendor justifies the situation by pointing out that the new configuration has significantly improved features and capabilities.

There is a pattern here. As the practitioner improves productivity on his existing system, rates decline. Then, technological obsolescence forces an equipment upgrade or change. The rates suddenly shoot up, stabilize, and finally decline as the new equipment is mastered. The cycle is then repeated as new equipment is introduced.

The only way to break the planned obsolescence pattern is to start all over again, with a redesigned system and new, creative hardware configurations. But there is a stiff price associated with this alternative, also. Front end development costs, consisting primarily of labor, may be much greater than the projected hardware savings. And a whole new series of implementation problems will inevitably arise.

The pattern should be clear. A stable equipment configuration is capable of significantly reducing standard rates. Rate reductions end with technological obsolescence and hardware changeover. A new round of rate stabilization and reduction then occurs until the next equipment changeover.

Chapter 7.5
Consolidation

Corporations today have a broad mix of computer installations. This has not always been the case. During the 1960s and 1970s, computerization was basically represented by the centralized machine room. Especially during the 1970s, corporations encouraged this trend by consolidating all computational power under one roof and one set of management, to achieve economy of scale. During that time the computer industry wasn't offering many alternatives to the large mainframe. Although minicomputers existed, they were generally not taken very seriously.

Towards the end of the 1970s and into the 1980s, smaller computers have become quite prevalent. While most companies contimue to make a major commitment to the central computer facility, there is a growing base of decentral minicomputers and an occasional distributed network. The central facility was relatively easy to control. But the haphazard method of installing small computers generally means that there is little or no centralized control over them.

Lack of central computer control is dangerous. Although we cannot be sure of the exact course that computing will take in the future, we can be sure that rapid technological change will occur. This change will affect both computers and communications networks. This change will often be beyond the grasp of the average small computer practitioner.

The pace of overall change, and the proliferation of computing hardware, suggests that the coporation should develop some form of centralized control over the entire base of installed computers and communications networks. The spread of computers throughout the corporation is putting serious pressure on technologically unprepared managers. Local managers who suddenly find their employees acquiring minicomputers may not be up to the task of understanding the company-wide characteristics of computing.

The goals and objectives of minicomputer users are often in direct conflict with those of the central computer operation. If the central computer facility can provide adequate service to users, then a minicomputer certainly tends to be redundant. On the other hand, the small computer gives local control to the user, and this is something on which a price tag cannot be put. The value of local control depends on the atttide of users. Some may feel it is absolutely mandatory, while others may feel it is an unnecessary burden, better left to specialists.

It is nearly impossible for a middle manager to assess all of these conflicts and make a rational decision on the necessity of installing minicomputers. The manager needs help.

Because computing has broken through the old centralized boundaries, new controls must be instituted. A central management group should be formed to control the acquisition, use, and disposition of computers and related items. This central control is the only logical way of insuring that a company's important assets are protected and properly managed. And the expertise that will be developed by central managers can help when wading through the claims and counterclaims of technical practitioners.

Although there are many activities that could be performed by a central computer control group, we will focus on those functions that relate to computer cost. Three important areas of concern are:

- Establishing the degree of justification that will be required from potential computer users.
- Evaluating justifications in a consistent manner.
- Monitoring the cost performance of ongoing installations.

THE DEGREE OF JUSTIFICATION

We have touched on aspects of justification a number of times. It will now be worthwhile to study justification of computer systems from a corporate-wide viewpoint.

The basic attitudes of a centralized control group must begin with the premise that minicomputers of substantial power are extremely attractive to many users, and quite available. As we have pointed out before, anybody who wants a small computer can quite easily put together some sort of justification that will show how acquisition is cost effective.

Corporations, of course, have limited resources and limited amounts of investment capital. Some very large companies could probably afford to give nearly every employee a computer, but such an act would be needlessly expensive and of questionable merit. Alternative investments in plant and equipment would usually be much smarter.

If computers are to be justified, we must first determine the degree of justification that is reasonable for a particular company. In a sense, we must ask ourselves how serious we want to get about the whole process. Do we want to put each justification through a bureaucratic wringer, or do we want to be very lenient and ask for little or no written justification.

The answer depends on two elements:

- Is the corporation centralized or decentralized in its basic operation?
- Is the corporation value driven or cost driven?

Degree of Centralization

The degree of company centralization has a large bearing on whether minicomputers are welcome or unwelcome. If a minicomputer fits quite easily into the basic operating pattern of the company, then less justification will be required than in a company offering a poor minicomputer fit.

When a company is highly decentralized, with factories and branches spread throughout the country or world, minicomputers are probably already used quite extensively. Diversified companies have learned through hard experience about the high cost of data transmission. They have found how difficult it is to keep separate operations standardized and confined within a central computer system. Decentral organizations usually operate with a high degree of delegation. It makes sense to delegate computing, also.

In such cases, a company should probably look harder at decentralized computing than at the central approach.

At the other extreme is the nondiversified company centered under one roof. Here, a centralized computing approach is appealing. If computer power is as close as the nearest terminal, then it is hard to argue that decentral or distributed minicomputers could be any better, at least from a cost standpoint. These companies should normally require significant justification for equpment that will end up in decentral facilities. Conversely, the company would be less inclined to argue over enhancements or changes to the existing large computer facility.

Companies in-between these two possibilities have no clearcut mandate. For example, a corporation may consist of one or two very large plants, with a number of smaller satellite installations scattered throughout the country. What mix of central and decentral computers is prudent? The rule of thumb would tend to be that the large plants should use centralized computing approaches and the satellites could implement minicomputers.

Another factor that influences the kinds of computers that a company feels comfortable with is managerial style. If management decisions are centralized, then computers should be, too. But if managers in the field have a high degree of autonomy and authority, then these managers should probably have their own small computers, if so inclined.

Proposed acquisitions of computers that do not fit with normal organizational and managerial patterns must be studied very carefully. Required justification for each computer should not depend so much on the cost involved as on the degree of fit that the proposed acquisition has with organizational style. Computers that deviate from the assumed management style should be inherently more difficult to justify than machines which fit the organization.

Value Versus Cost

Although this book is dedicated to the principles of cost accounting, we would be naive to assume that all organizations and all people base judgements strictly on costs. There are organizations that are not particularly concerned with cost. We call these organizations *value driven.*

Value driven organizations are more interested in building for the future than controlling the present. They are not constrained by the need to make immediate profit. Such organizations may be heavily involved in product research that they feel will place them on the verge of a significant breakthrough. But, most importantly, their operating funds come from outside investors, or from some governmental agency. Outside funding relieves these companies of the normal pressures associated with a free market economy.

Under value driven conditions, computerization can proliferate in a way that produces what is perceived to yield the greatest value. Perception need have nothing to do with reality.

Value, like beauty, is in the eye of the beholder. Without cost constraints, it can take an infinite variety of shapes. From a computing standpoint, most value driven companies probably tend to choose decentral or distributed forms of computing. These methods provide local control and hands on operation, and are fashionable enough to convince most people that they have great value.

There is very little reason for the value driven company to keep substantial cost accounting records. The extra effort would be needlessly expensive and would distract workers from whatever their goals are.

In some cases, profit oriented companies may also be value driven in the short run. Corporations involved in high technology fields might choose to put more current effort into achieving a product goal than in creating net income. Again, under these conditions computers may be allowed to proliferate in any way that enhances goal achievement and perceived productivity. The point is to keep the highly sophisticated knowledge workers happy. If a minicomputer here and there will do that, then it would be foolish not to indulge the employees.

Most companies are privately held, for-profit institutions. Because of this they are *cost driven.* Their stockholders expect them to maximize profit, so they must watch costs carefully and learn to allocate scarce resources in a way that produces the highest net income and return on investment.

A cost driven company should normally apply some form of justification requirement to the acquisition of all forms of computers. By acquiring only that equipment which fits with overall cost objectives and goals, the company attempts to maximize its deployment of scarce assets to produce the highest yield.

If a cost driven company is not closely controlling the acquisition of computers, then it is acting like a value driven company. The result will be an unsatisfactory return on assets, and a large inventory of marginally valuable minicomputers.

EVALUATIONS OF JUSTIFICATION

We will not consider the evalutions of computer acquisitions within a value driven company other than to make the following observations.

Equipment justifications made by value driven companies are obviously not going to be very comprehensive. They tend to stress noncost items such as productivity improvement, better job turnaround, higher reliability, and the benefits of local control. These are abstract concepts that are very hard to quantify. If such a justification is approved, the approval is based more on gut feel than on anything else. Value driven managers are forced to act intuitively because cost is of little significance.

Central Facility Justification

If a central facility exists, it is probably in constant need of additional hardware and labor resources. Central installations seem to grow simply because they exist. And every three to five years a new generation of mainframes comes along, causing significant disruptions to the center. Major equipment upgrades are inevitable, and are primarily caused by technological obsolescence.

If the central computer operation has a reliable cost accounting system in place, acquisition justification is a relatively straightforward endeavor. Historical rate trends effectively measure the productivity of a center at any given time. As we have pointed out before, consistent rate increases indicate the possibility of problems.

Acquisition of additional resources should be judged primarily on how they impact standard rates. No equipment, software, or related assets should be acquired if they cause the standard rate to increase faster than inflation. That is a strong general statement, but it is really quite sensible. When cost rates increase faster than inflation, it is an indication that something is out of control. Acquisitions that constantly increase rates are simply bad business moves.

Justifications of additional equipment should therefore include historic rate trends along with projected rate trends. The assumptions used in the forecast should be studied carefully. They should include a reserve for inflation, a forecast of future utilizations, and an assessment of the changes in operating characteristics that will occur as a result of the new acquisitions.

A significant purchase of disk drives, for example, should be justified by showing projected growth of storage requirements based on historic trends. Capacity increases should be closely tied to expected needs, so that cost increases will be offset by utilization increases, and the rate will remain unchanged. If technological improvements mean that more data can be stored for less money, then basic rates should decline, or at least not raise as fast as inflation.

Analyzing the impact on standard rates eliminates the need for a strong technological background. This is an important observation, because at some point in the approval cycle, those with the authority to approve or reject the acquisition are going to be technically naive.

Decentral and Distributed Justification

In most corporations, decentral and distributed computers coexist with the central mainframe computers. Because of this the justification of minicomputers must always include consideration of the central computer. The judgement to be made is whether or not computing can be accomplished more cheaply on a central or decentral computer, assuming that no mode of computing has an overwhelming technical advantage. How far a company wants to push this attitude of cost comparability depends on issues just discussed, such as organizational style and cost versus value.

It has often been observed, and not just with computers, that a basic dilemma arises whenever new technology is compared with existing, older technology. In almost all cases, the new technology looks better. The newer hardware has advanced engineering concepts and features that inevitably makes it look like an appealing cost performer.

But we must be very careful when comparing new equipment with older equipment. This is because of the effect of something that accountants call *sunk cost.* Care must be taken when comparing costs that have already been incurred with potential future investments.

A practical example will illustrate the effect of sunk cost.

When oil first became very expensive in 1974, the American public suddenly began trading in their large automobiles for small, fuel efficient cars. Such a tremendous demand developed for compact cars that their prices quickly rose to the point where small cars were more expensive than many big cars.

Eventually, people began questioning the intelligence of trading in perfectly serviceable large cars for overpriced compacts. Individuals began to intuitively realize that a three or four year old full sized car that was fully paid off was actually cheaper to keep and continue filling with expensive gasoline, when compared to the initial high price for small cars.

The reason for all of this was that most of the value of the large car was sunk, or already incurred. There were very few additional costs to incur, other than fuel and maintenance. But if a new compact was purchased, the entire high price would have to be paid with real dollars. At the bottom line, we had a large, fully paid for car consuming gasoline which then cost $.50 per gallon at a relatively high rate, with a small car which consumed much less gasoline, but also cost many thousands of dollars, out of pocket.

If the new 1975 compact cost $6000, then it would have to consume 12,000 gallons of gasoline (at $.50 per gallon), which is the equivalent of roughly 360,000 miles, before breakeven with the older car could be reached. Obviously, very few cars reach that mileage, thus breakeven seldom occurs.

When comparing a new minicomputer acquisition with older centralized technology, the same problem of sunk cost can occur. The minicomputer will consist of real dollars that the company must pay out. But the centralized operation, particularly if many of its computers have been purchased, has substantial amounts of sunk cost. The large computer's value exists on the books, and appears as periodic depreciation. But depreciation does not represent cash. Depreciation represents sunk cost. Acquisition of the minicomputer represents real cost, which will reduce cash flow and working capital.

The sunk cost phenomenon shows that investment in minicomputers is a serious undertaking. And it helps justify the need for a cost planning matrix that adequately represents the minicomputer. Costs such as support labor, systems programming, networks, supplies, vendor support, management and staff, occupancy, general services, and company overhead allocations must be loaded onto the basic minicomputer hardware costs.

If any company is serious about controlling the overall costs of computing, then justification of small computers should only reach approval when it can be shown that the minicomputer can perform the work for less cost than the centralized alternative. And this is only after both methods have been full-costed.

This may seem like a harsh conclusion, perhaps weighting the odds in favor of centralized processing. But to the degree that a company allows acquisition of minicomputers without proving cost savings, it is moving away from the cost driven and towards the value driven mode of operation. From a profit standpoint, that is not a wise move.

MONITORING INSTALLATIONS

We have already discussed the cost expectations of each computer installation within a company. Hardware managers should be expected to construct cost planning matrices that show forecasted annual costs, and they should follow these up with periodic displays of actual costs. Managers should also develop consistent sets of standard rates for their installations. Only acceptable accounting guidelines that are consistent for everybody should be used.

Some person or group of people should be in a position to analyze and compare the various cost documents prepared by each computing facility. The control group is normally set up as a central corporate function. A commonly used title for these types of groups is IRM (Information Resource Managers). If they ultimately approve the acquisition of all computers, then they can follow up by monitoring the performance of each computer installation.

Performance monitoring can help in the following areas:

- Indicate poorly managed installations.
- Provide information to aid in evaluating requests for additional hardware or labor.

The simple function of monitoring standard rates can certainly help to uncover poorly managed installations. Whether or not something is done about computers that do not appear to be operated properly is obviously a company policy decision.

Another important function of this central group would be to evaluate requests for additional equipment. These requests are inevitable, and they must be handled carefully. The cost of additional peripherals and support gear can very quickly equal that of the original equipment.

Because most of the serious evaluation effort occurs at the beginning of an acquisition, there is a tendency to allow follow-on purchases of hardware with little or no analysis. The requestor uses terms such as "performance improvement" and "enhanced capability" rather than hard cost numbers to prove that the additions are necessary. There is always the threat that if the acquisitions are not made, the existing system will suddenly fall apart.

Individual managers faced with such a decision would probably quickly cave in and meet the practitioner's demands for additional equipment. But a central organization, making many such evaluations, has a better chance of determining the truly legitimate needs.

In the long run, an IRM type organization is not so much a policeman as an educator. By forcing practitioners to accumulate and analyze all costs, a form of indoctrination is achieved. Each practitioner develops a better understanding of his costs and their relationship to the overall objectives of the company. He ceases to make unsupportable demands. His needs become more realistic and manageable.

Chapter 7.6
Determining Rate Correctness

Standard cost rates are generally meaningful only when there are several different computer installations generating comparable rates. If, for example, a company has only one computer, its standard rate does not have a great deal of meaning, in the short run, because there is no reference against which to compare. In the long run, of course, the rate can be compared against itself. But there is still no assurance that the rate is as low as it could be.

Large, centralized computer installations have had this kind of problem for years. Because they have been standalone, one of a kind operations, nobody has ever known if their service rates were equitable or inequitable.

Compounding this problem is nonstandard accounting. Very few installations within this country account for their computers in a similar way. It is therefore impossible to compare operations.

Large computer service bureaus, such as Cybernet, SBC, Martin Merietta, BCS, and McAuto, each account for their computer systems in different ways. They all use forms of the unit algorithm, but the terms in each of these algorithms, and the resources actually measured, differ significantly. To this day, a prospective purchaser of computer time from a service bureau must run a controlled benchmark at each installation to determine the lowest cost. There is simply no accounting standard, nor does there seem to be any desire to standardize.

The federal government has been frustrated by this situation for years. The government sends a team of investigators to the computer sites of most major suppliers periodically. Their goal is to insure that contractors are supplying computer services at the lowest possible prices to the government. These teams review computer cost accounting practices and algorithms. They have never found a meaningful comparison between computer installations around the country. They have found that benchmarks are the only acceptable means of making intercenter comparisons. Consequently, if a service bureau wants government work, it must be willing to compete with benchmark runs.

There is a very legitimate question that arises from all of this, and that is: How does a user know whether or not the price for computer processing is too high, too low, or just right?

Suppose the computer organization has developed a good accounting system that very carefully passes all costs back to users. At some high level the user organization summarizes these computer costs. Let's suppose the vice president of engineering receives one of these annual summaries of data processing expenditures for his total subdivision. He sees that in the prior 12 months engineering spent a total of $26 million for computer services. His response to this information might be: That's a lot of money; am I getting my money's worth?

Who can correctly answer such a question? The computer center that generated all of these costs would probably suggest that $26 million was a relative bargain, considering the range of computer services supplied. Minicomputer proponents might suggest that the price was much too high, and that a switch to smaller machines would save a considerable amount of money. Because there is no baseline against which to compare, quantifiable cost comparisons cannot be made. Proponents and opponents would both be speculating.

HISTORICAL DEVELOPMENT OF RATES

Centralized computer operations had a monopoly hold on data processing services for nearly three decades. Without competition, they were able to dictate what services were offered, the performance levels that would be provided, and the overall cost charged to users. This is a very nice position to be in. It is also very dangerous because the center tends to operate outside the realm of normal, market-type controls.

A monopolylike central computer facility can trick itself into believing it is doing a good job at a fair price when it is actually failing on both counts. Without competition there is no feedback to the center. User complaints can be ignored with no repercussions. This is because computer users in most corporations are fragmented and unorganized. Without central representation, users have no control over the computer operation.

Minicomputers are a form of competition to centralized facilities. However, it is difficult to directly compare a minicomputer with centralized processors from the standpoint of productivity. As we have seen, standard utilization measurements for large computers are very different from those used on minis. Minicomputer advocates are not likely to scoop up their applications and benchmark them on the central machine. Nor is it an easy task to transfer a central application directly onto a minicomputer. So much program modification would be necessary, because of different operating systems, that the nature of the application would probably change.

So we must conclude that even with the apparent competition created by alternative modes of computing, and with the ability to develop meaningful cost accounting schemes, the most inexpensive form of computing is very difficult to determine.

But if we have a handle on basic costs, and if the users are charged back for computing services, there are techniques available that can help to determine relative value.

A SOLUTION

It would be very embarrassing if the computer cost accountant, after developing a precise and meaningful cost accounting system, could not answer the simple question: Is the current mix of computers worth the cost?

On the other hand, how many companies ever consider this point? Computing tends to be accepted without challenge. And, in fairness, we must point out that accounting is a measurement tool. It provides the means for analysis and justification, not the final answer.

We must approach the issue of overall computer value with the assumption that too much detail can be misleading. It is almost a truism to observe that the more precisely anything is measured, the less important it is. Although relatively precise accounting systems are necessary on minicomputers and large machines, this precise information doesn't help very much in determining just how cost effective various modes of computing are for the company. We are never going to determine the true value of computing by looking at individual units of hardware. We must analyze costs from a higher perspective. But we must always be sure that the costs we analyze come from a workable, believeable cost accounting system.

Economists are faced with a problem similar to ours when they try to determine the value of certain social programs. One of their techniques is applicable to computing.

What, economists may ask themselves, is the value of clean air? Or equal opportunity employment? Or a completely safe automobile? If value cannot be placed on these social programs, then it would be hard to quantify just how much society wanted them.

Clean air's benefits are primarily psychological because the health implications are impossible to quantify. Equal opportunity employment has social benefits for various minority groups. And automobile safety deals with the value of human life. None of these areas can be easily quantified, yet their consequences must somehow be valued. It is senseless to pursue goals that people place little or no value on. And it is just as senseless to disregard goals that the public favors.

Economists solve this dilemma by using a technique called *shadow pricing.* Its essence is that it attempts to find what a representative indivdual would be willing to pay for absolute perfection – or full attainment – in the area under consideration. This value is called the shadow price.

Investment costs that are below the shadow price are acceptable. Any investment above the shadow price is unacceptable.

AVERAGE PURCHASE PRICE OF NEW AUTOMBILE	$10,000
SHADOW PRICE OF A TOTALLY SAFE AUTOMOBILE	$10,100
SOCIALLY ACCEPTABLE VALUE OF SAFETY	$ 100

Figure 7-3. Value determination.

A practical example of shadow pricing is displayed in Figure 7-3. In this case, an attempt is made to place a value on automobile safety. If, after sample interviewing of a representative population, we find that the average person is willing to pay $100 more than the basic vehicle cost for an absolutely safe car, then we have valued what the average perception of automobile safety is. It is irrelevant that necessary safety devices could cost thousands of dollars to achieve a reasonably safe car. If the shadow price indicates a perceived value of $100, then that is all society feels safety is worth.

If a governmental institution mandates that safety equipment installed on the average car will cost $500, for example, consumers will clearly rebel. Their frustration will be taken out on their elected officials. Government will have no choice but to lower its safety goals, or risk dissatisfaction of its constituents.

Shadow prices are not fixed in the long run. Special interest groups desiring a change – in our example this could be the federal government -– can therfore try to raise the perceived value of the item in the general population's mind until an adequate shadow price is achieved. In the case of auto safety, perhaps advertising and widespread dissemination of safety information could eventually increase the value that the public places on it from, say, $100 to $500. Government could then achieve its desired goals through a willing and coopertive public.

Shadow Prices and Computers

The shadow pricing concept can be used to help determine if a company is getting reasonable value from its installed base of computers.

The vice president of engineering who is concerned about the $26 million he spent last year on computers can use shadow pricing to help determine if he got adequate value for his investment.

He could ask himself the following question: How much more or less than $26 million would he be willing to pay for total computer automation?

To answer this question he must resolve issues such as:

- Does he understand what he is currently getting for his automation dollar?
- Is he satisfied with the automation he is receiving?
- Can he perceive what total automation would be like?

After deliberating the situation, he can reach one of the following answers:

- Complete automation can be achieved, using better techniques than currently applied, for less money than is now being spent.
- Complete automation can be achieved for about the same amount of money as is currently being spent.
- Complete automation will require a sum of money larger than current expenditures.

Complete automation is a goal that will probably never be achieved. But that is not the point. If the executive has thought honestly about the situation, he has developed his shadow price. In the first instance, he feels that he is spending too much money on computers. In the second instance, expenditures are about right. And in the third case, his need for computers has not yet been satisfied.

What is the most likely shadow price for computers? In a competitive economy it is hard to justify increases in expenditures that are not clearly associated with profitability. As we pointed out before, tying computers directly to profits is difficult. It is therefore very likely that the chief manager of engineering would not want to see computer costs increase, and might even want a decrease.

The shadow price of computers tends to decrease as the level of management review increases. This is probably because the upper levels of management are more concerned with profitability than lower supervisory levels.

The people with the most to lose from the effects of shadow prices are centralized computer operations. And this situation is worsened when the center has poor accounting. If the center cannot show in simple, clear terms how it has controlled costs over the years, parent company management becomes very distrustful and suspicious. Without good accounting, the center has no baseline to use in raising the perception of management to the point where they realize that the centralized computing operation is providing a highly valuable service at a reasonable price.

Shadow prices are perceptions. These perceptions can be changed, and improved. If a clear financial road map has been laid out to management, their basic attitudes towards computing will improve (assuming these attitudes were low to begin with). The center is in a position where it must continuously attempt to raise the shadow price of its services in the minds of parent company top management through believable accounting, good financial reporting, and honest cost control.

Minicomputers are in an excellent position to take advantage of the central site's dilemma. Small computers have the appearance of being inexpensive yet highly adaptive, giving the user more computer power for the dollar. These machines can also offer small increases in processing capabilities, which avoids the large front end investment necessary for a central machine. Solving computer problems with small incremental increases in capability can appear to be very attractive, financially.

If services provided by the central facility have a relatively low shadow price within a company, then that company is literally ripe for a conversion to minicomputers. Negative attitudes have lowered the value of central computing, and the first apparent solution that comes along is enthusiastically embraced, without a great deal of analysis, and without the realization that alternative solution costs may also be significant, in the long run. The situation, clearly, must be more fully quantified before an intelligent decision can be made.

TOWARDS COMPUTER EQUITY

There is little doubt that most centralized computer operations are at a disadvantage when superfically compared with minicomputers. In addition to points already raised, these smaller machines have a mystique about them because they are relatively new.

Central computer operations, on the other hand, have had many years to build up bad reputations. Looking back, many of the earliest third generation computers had incredibly poor performance records. With more and more companies depending on data processing, these performance problems became visible sore points to corporate management. Although modern computers are significantly more reliable, the damage has been done. Centralized computing has a bad reputation.

But central facilities owe it to their parent corporations to develop meaningful comparisons between themselves and minicomputers. Bad reputations are based on past performance, and may not be representative of the future. This must be pointed out before the corporation adopts too many different modes of computing, and needlessly squanders its assets.

The first, and most important, step for the central facility is to develop an understandable cost accounting system. Concepts introduced in this book should be considered. Cost accounting helps at the user level, and provides a framework that can be used in communicating with top management. At the same time, all other emerging modes of computing should adopt similar, uniform cost accounting practices.

Secondly, the computer center must sell itself. Its simple goal should be to increase the perception of its shadow price in the minds of management. That is, convince management that higher investments in centralized data processing are acceptable.

Raising the perceptual levels of management can only be achieved through continuously displaying financial information to any manager who will listen. These top managers understand summarized accounting data. They live with it daily. The computer center must provide the same kind of accounting information, professionally prepared and presented, on a periodic basis. The format of this information, within reports, depends on what managers are accustomed to seeing. If they like a column of budget data on the left, and actual data on the right, then that format should be followed. The object is not to confuse, using complex reports, but to illuminate with simple truths.

Summarized cost accounting data should be included in any financial presentation. Standard rates for major resources are useful. These rates should be compared on a historical basis, to show the center's cost control abilities.

Most managers don't realize that the cost per unit of computing work has been declining steadily for a number of years, even after the effects of inflation. These top managers generally only see total computer cost, which is usually rising. Declines in standard rates put those total cost increases in a better perspective.

The goal of the center is to increase the shadow price of central computing until it reaches an equilibrium with minicomputers. That is, until there is no perceived financial difference between data processing on minicomputers or large centralized mainframes.

When all costs are considered, there is simply no evidence to indicate that any mode of computing is substantially less expensive than other forms. Claimed advantages are based on gut feel, not on quantitative facts. By equalizing computer shadow prices in the minds of top management, no single form of computing will be given a cost advantage. Managers can then choose the form of computing that makes the most sense for the organization, using a clear mind that is unclouded by emotion or intuition.

THE RIGHT AMOUNT OF COST

When the value of all forms of computing has been equalized, we can go on to determine whether or not the current cost for computers is reasonable.

From a purely academic viewpoint, one would have to say that each additional dollar invested in computers should yield a percentage of its cost to the bottom line. If the internal rate of return is set at 20%, then every dollar of incurred computer expense should yield at least twenty cents of profit on a compounded basis. This concept of internal rate of return is used by most corporations to analyze acquistions.

But how can a general purpose computer increase profit? The answer does not appear obvious. Only by reducing some other expense in an amount greater than the computer's actual expense, will profit be improved. And the most likely expense to be reduced is labor.

However, we have already shown that the labor force is very seldom impacted substantially by computerization. Computers may replace a few low paid clerks, but they bring in many highly paid professionals needed to operate, program, and manage the hardware.

Without a clearcut relationship between computer expense and profit, we must come back to the concept of shadow pricing. The investment in computers is right when management feels comfortable with the total cost. If management believes that more investment will be better for the company, then such investment will probably occur.

Since the shadow price is not a fixed quantity, various computer advocates can increase it by using well thought out arguments and meaningful quantitative data presented in readable form. This is why it is so important for all computer proponents to get their financial houses in order. If each mode of computing presents clear, solid financial data to management, then decisions on future computerization are placed squarely on upper management, where they belong.

It is not appropriate for individual practitioners to decide the course of computing within any company. It is a major decision that should be made by senior managers.

If all modes of computing compete for management's attention, the best method will presumably win. If each mode presents itself well from a financial standpoint, intelligent choices can be made by management.

Part VIII
Rational Computer Accounting

Chapter 8.1
The Need for Accounting

Computers come in a variety of sizes with various costs. There are large computers for the organization wishing to centralize. There are small computers to support specialized applications or decentralized organizations. Large computers can be linked to small computers. The variations are endless for anybody with a bit of creativity and money.

This diversity of computers is a relatively new phenomenon. Many companies find that practitioners are still experimenting with various computer combinations. The use of computer hardware has not yet been perfected. The experimentation will continue, and spread so that very few areas within any company will be untouched by computers.

Using computers is already easy and will become easier. Hardware is being designed to fit comfortably into the daily activities of most workers. Much software can be used by nonprogrammers. This user friendliness, as it is called, can turn everybody into a computer practitioner.

Some people must have computers to augment their jobs. Others, who don't really need a computer, will find themselves using them anyway. The price we pay for computer proliferation is that many applications are dreamed up for computers when they really belong elsewhere. In a kind of perverse Parkinson's Law, the work expands to fill the available computer capacity.

Short of going out of business and closing everything, most companies find that computer usage has no relationship to the normal business cycle. Companies have prosperous periods followed by periods of decline. But computer usage and cost continue to grow, regardless of whether business is active or slack.

The growth of computer usage during busy periods is logical. Computer use grows during bad times primarily because many people don't have very much to do and fill their idle hours by playing on computers, or developing new, questionable applications. This kind of activity is sometimes termed training, but regardless of what it is called it has little productive value. Nor is the computerized output useful to anybody.

When will the proliferation of computers end?

It won't end. Companies must reconcile themselves to the fact that hordes of computer salesmen are out there, anxious to sell a machine to anybody who can sign a purchase order. To broaden the market, manufacturers are packaging computers under different names, like word processors and turnkeys. This brings nontraditional users into the ranks of computer users. These new users are unsophisticated and easy marks for the hardware enhancement and trade-up game played by salesmen.

Regardless of what they are called, all machines that process data have a similar architecture and must be considered computers. The most fundamental piece of any computer, known as the Central Processing Unit, comes as close to mimicking the human brain as anything ever invented by man. It is this concept of a device that can be programmed in an infinite variety of ways that gives any computer its wide flexibility and adaptability. Computers are truly general purpose devices. Because of this, they can be applied to an unending variety of applications.

This characteristic of computer flexibility means that every computer ever produced, from the smallest minicomputer up to the largest centralized mainframe, can be fitted with a wide variety of features and options. These peripheral additions can increase total system costs far beyond the basic price. With computers, the initial price is only a small portion of what eventually is paid to manufacturers. And all manufacturers of computer hardware want a steady stream of revenue coming from their user population.

The habits of computer users complement manufacturer desires very well:

- People always seem to want more computing capability.
- Computers can be expanded to provide more capability, but always at a price.

Corporations must be very prudent when acquiring computers. No company has unlimited capital. Although it would be nice to give a computer to everybody who thinks he needs one, there are generally better uses for the capital that would be necessary for such an act.

The only way to insure that scarce capital is not squandered on computers is to introduce some form of price mechanism. Prices work quite well on the open market in allocating capital to its most efficient use. This same basic technique can be used to monitor and help control computer proliferation.

Computer accounting provides information that can be used to intelligently manage computer growth. By placing value on the solutions that computers produce, people can choose the most inexpensive method of processing data. All forms of computing are placed in a competitive environment, where they must bid for the user's dollar.

When good accounting systems are developed for computers, two things occur:

- Financial data is produced for the computer user, and this allows him to evaluate his data processing requirements and uses.
- Those who develop and implement the accounting system reach a comprehensive understanding of their computer operation.

That is, both the user and the operator benefit. This understanding that accounting creates is a very significant byproduct of the entire process.

Suppose, for example, we study two individuals, each operating a decentralized minicomputer. One manager develops an accounting system for his computer and the other does not. What if upper management then asks the following logical questions of both DP managers:

- Is it more expensive to process on-line programs or batch jobs?
- Which could be more effective when job turnaround is poor: a memory upgrade or the purchase of a larger computer?
- Is it less expensive to store data on floppy diskettes or rotational packs?
- What is the value of the physical reports produced – how much can be saved by eliminating a particular report?
- What is the cost of data communications, and is it more or less than the cost of physically processing the data.

Anybody, including the minicomputer manager who has no accounting system, can attempt to answer each of these questions using intuition. But are such answers correct? We generally find that intuitive answers are strongly influenced by computer vendors. A practitioner with no accounting background or system turns to his major hardware supplier each time a cost question comes up. Answers may be legitimate, but they also may be strongly influenced by whatever hardware the vendor happens to be pushing at the time.

Lack of accounting data creates a knowledge vacuum. Hardware salesman are good at using it to their own advantage.

A manager who understands the cost of each computer component *and* the additional costs incurred to keep the equipment operating, doesn't need anything more from a vendor than his current price list. Accounting has taught the practitioner the relationships between various hardware components. He also understands which activities are labor intensive and he can conceptualize the true cost of people. Perhaps, for example, timesharing costs more in raw equipment than batch processing. But batch processing is labor intensive, requiring operators to mount disk and tape and sort output. These labor costs often exceed hardware investment by a substantial margin. Thus timesharing can cost less in total than batch processing.

The accounting oriented manager has knowledge and is in a position to exert much more control over his operation. If he needs additional equipment, he has a better chance of acquiring the right equipment at a reasonable price. Users respond to his cost rates by forcing him to develop a cost efficient operation.

In the consumer marketplace it is commonly observed that "you get what you pay for." In the business world, this concept isn't quite as applicable. Equipment designed for professional use is generally of very high quality. Manufacturers have big reputations at stake, and can't risk producing shoddy hardware for important corporate clients. But we can make the observations of industrial buyers that "you get what you deserve." If you purchase computer components based on brochure advertising and a salesman's recommendation, then you will probably acquire needlessly expensive and marginally useful hardware. But if you have the background accounting information to develop cost analysis of various options, and can understand the financial implications of different modes of operation, then acquisitions will be of solid value. When a manager is armed with accounting data, he can approach computer vendors in a more professional way.

A final benefit of computer accounting is that it helps data processing users understand the true cost of automation. Computing is not free. Whether the job is run on a huge central mainframe or a tiny minicomputer, there are many costs that must be incurred before the first instruction can be executed. The user doesn't have to know what these costs are, but he must be made aware of their existence. Job accounting and chargeback accomplish this. We have a value oriented world. People are willing to pay for anything that is perceived as having value. Computer solutions fall into this category. Very few users are therefore willing to fight against the concept of computer chargeback.

Because of the wide diversity of computers available in most corporations today, it is important to set up accounting standards. That is, costs must be accumulated in the same way for large central mainframes and decentral and distributed minicomputers. This consistency helps when comparing the various modes of computing, and it insures that users pay equivalent costs for data processing. No form of computing should have an inherent financial advantage caused by accounting methodology differences.

The execution of a program instruction is handled in essentially the same way on every computer manufactured. Large computers have faster cycle times than minicomputers, but their basic functions are identical. By costing in similar ways, users can shop around for the best data processing value with the assurance that all costs have been included in the rates for each offering.

Universal computer accounting brings competitiveness to data processing. It is not overwhelmingly clear that any one form of computing has a cost advantage over other modes. But the only way to prove this is to implement consistent accounting on all computers.

Chapter 8.2
Understandability

Cost accounting is an activity used throughout the industrial world to track and control expenditures. It is a very specialized form of accounting. This specialization can bring complexity. Complexity, of course, is not desirable. Companies should strive to keep cost accounting simple and clean. A very practical test is to ensure that the results of the cost accounting system can be understood by nonaccountants *and* those who do not specialize in computers.

There are two points to consider in the accounting process:

- Accounting is a necessary evil.
- Accounting costs money to develop, implement, and maintain.

Cost accounting is a necessary evil because while it is very difficult to work efficiently without its benefits, it does not contribute directly to the productive process. Accounting actually drains resources away from production and into record keeping. The accounting process requires people who must gather and interpret information.

Cost accounting also requires computer resources. CPU cycles and memory are used to gather accounting statistics. Additional machine time is needed to process all of this data into recognizable reports. So both people and machine resources are needed to produce good accounting information.

It is therefore very important that companies constantly ensure that computer accounting provides a maximum amount of data for a minimum cost. This is best achieved by keeping the accounting process simple and straightforward. Simple systems are inexpensive systems.

The users of accounting are obviously the most important people to consider when developing any financial system. Users can be defined as:

- Those who possess computers.
- Those who use computers.

On very small computers, a single individual may both possess and use the computer. This is the only situation where cost accounting can be disregarded.

Most often the computer is used by a number of different individuals, many of whom have no relationship to the computer possessor. It is in these situations where cost accounting becomes mandatory.

Even the single user system should not be completely ignored when considering accounting. Although these systems start small, they have a tendency to grow through the addition of features and attachments. Growth opens up more capacity, and the capacity must be filled. More users are attracted onto the system to fill the capacity. Suddenly the computer is a multiuse, general purpose machine and needs accounting.

No cost accounting scheme is successful unless it can be understood. Understanding mainfests itself in two ways:

- Understanding the costs involved in processing data.
- Understanding what alternatives exist to change those costs if they are at an unacceptable level.

Getting users to understand that there are substantial costs associated with using a computer is a noteworthy achievement, but only half an accomplishment. The user must also understand his charges well enough so that he knows what changes can be made to his method of operation to lower his costs. This can be done if there is a direct relationship between the various aspects of processing data and the generation of costs. The automobile operator knows, for example, that if his monthly gasoline bill is too high, he must drive less miles to reduce it. Computer cost accounting must provide similar direct relationships.

Although there are many forms of computer accounting, most of them are similar in that they are quite complex and hard to understand. Large, intricate accounting algorithms are an excellent example. These accounting methods are unacceptable because they violate the two principles of understandability mentioned above. Complexity is inherently difficult to comprehend. Busy practitioners generally do not have the time or inclination to get their hands around convoluted accounting methods. These people have many other problems, such as getting their jobs run, dealing with computer downtime and system errors, and trying to please their management. Worrying about computer cost accounting is probably one of their lower priorities. Accounting schemes must be made to fit the user, and not the other way around.

Those who possess and operate computers also have very little to gain from complex accounting methods. These systems are hard to develop and hard to maintain. Because of complexity, there is a tendency towards nonrepeatability, which causes confusion and mistrust within the user community. And some technical experts must always be available to explain the intricacies of the accounting method to new or confused users.

The solution lies with simple accounting. As any engineer knows, there is elegance to simplicity. The best design is always the simplest. Initial creations are usually complex and hard to understand. But as they are refined and modified, a simple structure generally results. A similar goal is necessary for computer cost accounting.

Accounting must be straightforward. It must be reasonably equitable to those who use it. It must be made up of measurements that are easy to gather and of low demand on computer resources. The accounting must be simple to understand by those who created it and easy to comprehend by computer users. And the accounting scheme should be built in such a way that it is impervious to changes in hardware, software, or organization. Change is inevitable but it should not impact accounting.

Simple cost accounting designs do not normally come from those who understand computers best. It is very hard to synthesize a computer down into a few simple functions. To most people, the makeup and operation of a computer appear complex. Attempting to simplify brings scowling criticism from technically oriented practitioners. They come up with numerous reasons why the simple approach is inequitable. But complexity in accounting is a sign of immaturity and not representative of how things should be done.

Most goods and services sold on the open market today come from complex backgrounds. From the way the marketplace handles these goods and services we learn that when there is honest or competitively induced concern for the ultimate consumer, the pricing structure is relatively simple. This can be observed for most consumer goods. But when there is little or no concern for the consumer, the pricing structure is convoluted and complex. Government, for example, has little concern for individual taxpayers. Income tax is a form of pricing structure. The calculation of tax is so complex that most people hire specialists to fill out the forms.

Computer practitioners must decide whether they belong on the side of those who favor the consumer with simple accounting, or on the side of bureaucrats who have little or no concern for the ultimate user.

A final observation is that bureaucrats have the advantage that there is no alternative to their presence. Those who wish to deal with these bureaucrats must learn to live with the complex intricacies of the system.

But when there is competition for the product or service, complex accounting can actually hinder sales. Consumers would rather buy simply priced items.

There is competition in the sale of computer services today. Users have the choice between large centralized mainframes and smaller minicomputers. This competition should make all practitioners think carefully about the kind of accounting system they wish to adopt. Simplicity seems to be the only alternative available, if long term survival is desired.

Chapter 8.3
Computer Modes and Accountability

It is easy to preach simplicity, as we did in the last chapter, but it is much more difficult to implement such a concept. Simplicity implies elegance, and this is something that takes time and thought to develop. We have a dual problem of developing methodology *and* convincing people that the simpler methods are still equitable. The lessons we have learned over the years from large computers can be used to enhance both large computer accounting and the newer small computer accounting.

There are three distinct modes of computing and each has its own unique characteristics that must be considered during accounting development.

Centralized computing, which has been around since the 1950s, is a form of computing that most large companies have today. This mode of computing requires large, environmentally controlled machine rooms filled with powerful CPUs and peripherals. Central machines are supported by a big staff of operators and systems programmers. Centralized machines give the user much flexibility because so many different hardware and software options are available. The large size of the CPU brings a certain richness to the user, particularly through the use of software. Of course, size has its disadvantages. Each user is relatively small and has little ability to influence how the system is operated and supported. And when large systems fail, the effect can be devastating on a company.

Decentralized computing consists of standalone minicomputers. These machines can be general purpose and patterned after centralized machine rooms. Or they can be dedicated to a specific application. In the latter case the computer is often called a turnkey system. Decentral computers do not typically start out with large support staffs of people. But as they mature and the user population grows, professional operators and other technicians are often hired. Decentralized computing has become very popular in most corporations.

Distributed computing consists of multiple minicomputers tied together with data lines. There is a high degree of interaction between processors, and intelligence is often built into the network. The data communications aspects of distributed computing are often more complex than the actual computing.

Regardless of the form of compuuting, there are certain accounting standards that must be adopted uniformly. These standards ensure that there is comparability between the different modes. A lack of accounting standardization can give a financial advantage to one mode of computing over other forms. This can lead to erroneous managerial decisions.

The most common example of poor accounting standardization occurs when a centralized machine is fully costed and decentral minicomputers are counted at hardware expense only. A unit of work provided by the central computer is burdened with hardware, labor, and overhead costs. This can make the large computer appear substantially more expensive than the smaller machine. Such cost comparisons are obviously incorrect.

If various modes of computing are desired by a corporation, than a standardized *cost planning matrix* must be implemented. The matrix, displayed in earlier chapters, ensures that each computer installation counts up all costs associated with operating a computer. The exact elements used on the matrix are not as important as the fact that all computer operations follow the same rules. By using the matrix approach, consistency will occur. Each computer operation forecasts its costs by expense account and by cost pool, thus providing information necessary for the development of standard rates.

After the computer installation develops costs, utilization must be determined. This is an area where complexity can hurt, as we have previously discussed.

Large computers generally have some form of utilization already developed, but it is usually inadequate. Before choosing a usage measurement, the nature of programs processed on large computers should be examined by the installation. In most cases it will be found that 80% or more of job steps process in a trivial amount of CPU time. Rather than using sophisticated algorithms to generate usage for this work, a flat job step charge should be implemented. For example, the installation could charge $.75 per job step for all jobs running in less than two seconds of CPU. Whether the time parameter is two seconds or some other number depends on the type of equipment used and the nature of the workload. The important conclusion is that most jobs are small and should be treated appropriately by the accounting system.

The few job steps left, usually less than 20%, are generally very large and constitute the bulk of installation cost recovery. These jobs can be charged using a simple algorithm, such as CPU time, or CPU time plus setup I/O. In some cases even a simple form of transaction costing can be used if there are only one or two major applications.

Large processing jobs represent major activities of the corporation, like payroll, inventory control, and work scheduling. These applicatiions were not created by those who wanted to "game" the accounting system or take advantage of it. These systems are used by people willing to pay a fair price for services rendered. Charging them based on a few simple measurements will accomplish everything that a complex accounting algorithm would, for a lot less money.

Decentralized minicomputers are much less expensive than central machines, and do not have the processing capacity to run sophisticated accounting. Still, users must be charged. A straightforward method is to use a monthly subscription fee, billed to each user. This is a flat charge, and does not recognize variations in utilization between users. The assumption is that users are quite homogeneous and basically do the same types of things. If this is not the case, users can be divided up into several homogeneous groups, and charged graduated subscription fees based on activity. Or, if there is too much variability in the user population, nonstandard users could be moved to another minicomputer, where they would become normal.

Some decentral machines grow very large. They get caught up in a never ending spiral of hardware enhancements that entice new users onto the system. In such cases subscription chargeback may be inequitable. It may be necessary to supplement subscription fees with another simple accounting measurement, such as connect hours. The point is that unusually large users must be penalized since they tend to take advantage of the available resources. Connect hours can be used as a surcharge over the basic subscription fee.

Distributed computing is usually made up of minicomputers that essentially become slaves to the network of interconnected data lines. That is, there is no discretionary use made by any node. There are specific tasks performed at each node that benefit both that node and other members of the network. Because of the nondiscretionary activity, subscription chargeback is a very realistic form of accounting. More effort than this would have very little payback or increase in equitability.

Job accounting on large computers and subscription fees on minicomputers are two chargeback methods that clearly meet the tests of simplicity. In so doing, they recognize the following points:

- Computer power is becoming less expensive and accounting at the individual user level is of relatively little significance.
- Computer architecture is being designed in ways that are leading to less and less repeatability in finite accounting measurements.

Blending consistent cost accumulation with simple chargeback methods gives the user the information he needs to control his computing costs and seek the most cost effective processing alternative. No mode of computing is inherently or obviously cheaper than any other method. Effective computing is a combination of convenience, price, and compute power. Price is therefore not tne only consideration when choosing a computer. But it is certainly one third of the equation and important enough that we must insure its consistency between modes of processing.

Discrete, algorithm type accounting is becoming a computer anachronism that is more and more meaningless as the power of computers increases. It is conceivable that at some point even CPU timing measurements will be non-repeatable and meaningless. By exposing outselves to the concepts of subscription fees and connect hours, we are, in a sense, preparing for the inevitable future. Eventually, subscription chargeback may be the only alternative accounting method available for any computer.

Chapter 8.4
Disseminating and Using Accounting Data

Cost accounting, as it comes directly off the computer, is of little value. This detailed information must be accumulated over a period of time so that a broad perspective can be developed. Accountants call this type of information *historical,* because it takes a certain amount of time before the information has value.

The best way to disseminate accounting information is to develop various levels of reports and distribute them to interested individuals throughout the company.

There are three distinct levels of people within most organizations who need computer cost accounting data:

- The actual computer user.
- Those who manage computer users.
- Top management within the company.

The cycle begins with the computer user, who is often a programmer or sophisticated practitioner. He writes or submits programs that consume processor resources. These resources are measured and costed. The computer user must understand this accounting data. The data will influence the way he writes future programs and the way he maintains current programs. If he is told that his computer expenditures are too high, he will use this accounting data to determine how he can lower his charges.

The user can be provided with information at two levels. The first is at job termination. Accounting usage and cost can be displayed as the job ends. This information has immediacy and may have some impact, but it is doubtful that it has any lasting value. Unless the programmer keeps some sort of log to accumulate job utilization data, the information is soon forgotten because, quite simply, there are more important things to worry about, such as the processed data that the program has provided.

Job utilization and cost data should be accumulated into weekly and monthly reports, and distributed to these same users. The important thing is to accurately identify all computer users and supply them with detailed job accounting data. To this level of user, detail is meaningful.

The second level of accounting data usage falls on middle management. This level of management directly controls those who use computers. These managers have the advantage of a larger company perspective than most programmers. Managers generally control a number of computer users so they need information that makes comparisons between programmers. And these managers are tied into the budgetary constraints of the full company. They must weigh computer expenditures against many other costs, such as labor, facilities, manufacturing and raw material.

These managers are not interested so much in job accounting data as in system cost data. They want to see what an entire application is costing, on a periodic basis.

Their accounting needs can therefore be considered more conventional. They do not need detailed computer utilization information, but need cost data. The computer organization must therefore supply them with concise, summarized financial information. Information that can be digested easily and quickly.

The most common mistake made by data processing operations is that they try to overwhelm these middle managers with information. Consequently, much of this data gets tossed.

It should be remembered that the manager is in a position to turn to his specialists if something doesn't look right. He is mostly interested in broad trends, not in the detail behind these trends.

The third organizational level potentially interested in computer costs is top management. This level of management may not even know that computer organizations exist, so it is up to data processing groups to open up channels of communication with them.

Companies should create an intermediary between the various computer organizations and top management. While the central operation is probably big enough to represent itself before top management, various decentralized and distributed operations are too small to directly contact top officers. The intermediary can represent these various groups. He can assemble cost data into meaningful summary reports and, along with key members of the computer establishment, periodically report cost trends to top management. Data should be summarized and displayed in understandable terms, with technical jargon eliminated.

Periodic reports to top management are as useful for computer practitioners as they are for top management. This is a forum that can be used to keep management appraised of the state of computer technology within the company. Management can be continually sold on the overall corporate benefits of computers. And top management can use the meetings as a way of understanding computers better. They can also scrutinize expenditure levels to determine whether or not full value is being received for money spent.

What does.reporting of cost information attempt to convey? Answering this question will help in understanding exactly what kind of reports must be prepared. Failure to consider this concept can lead to the development of meaningless and unused information.

Accounting reports attempt to establish *value.* Value to a programmer is different from value to a corporate vice president. These differing perceptions shape the content and structure of reports.

The programmer is generally interested in getting the cheapest possible cost per job execution. He is interested in the cost of each individual job. He has probably come to rely on the computer to do his debugging. Rather than completely analyzing each failed job execution, for example, he would rather fix the obvious errors and resubmit to let the computer find further errors. This could be called a lazy way of programming, but it may be the most efficient use of valuable programmer time, particularly if job turnaround is good. A smart programmer will weigh the cost of his time against the cost of frequent job submittals. He must therefore identify cost to the job level.

The corporate vice president perceives value as the total cost of data processing for the computerized systems under his cognizance. He is generally looking at a very large total cost for computing. Value to this executive is made up of much more than raw computer hardware. All of the elements contained in the planning matrix become cost to him. Based on these total costs he must determine if data processing is underpriced, priced about right, or overpriced. He needs very summarized cost information to make this determination.

Value to the programmer has as much to do with getting his job done as with cost. But the top executive is not interested in individual jobs. He sees the entire computer operation as a single set of figures. He must use this information to evaluate the solutions his organization gets from computers. He must ultimately conclude whether or not the solutions are worth the cost.

Reported information must coincide closely with the perceived value each level of the organization places on computerization and its benefits.

Chapter 8.5
Accounting and Reality

We began this book with the description of a Chief Executive Officer who found that a subdivision within his corporation had quickly and quietly adopted an alternative form of computing through the use of minicomputers. He was sensible enough to check into this situation and attempt to synthesize the matter into dollars and cents. But he really did not have enough accurate financial information with which to judge whether or not the computer conversion was worthwhile for his company. Whatever conclusion eventually reached would be based on intuition.

Many companies find themselves in this same position today. Over the years they have made substantial comitments to cenralized processing. They have allowed huge, data base oriented systems to be created on these central machines. They have invested substantial amounts of capital in the purchase of hardware and facilities and software.

Computers have allowed companies to optimize everything from raw material inventories to scheduling airplane seats. But these activities have meant that, little by little, corporations have become more dependent on computers, to the point where major mainframe outages are intolerable.

The long association between people and central computers has lead, perhaps inevitably, to dissension. Many members of the corporation have become unsatisfied with the centralized approach. Their concerns and apprehensions have been lessened since the widespread introduction of minicomputers. With these small machines, individuals can control their own destiny. They need not contend with arbitrary rules set up by a central bureaucracy. Minicomputers give people the chance to become information entrepreneurs. They can build their own systems around their own standards and run the machines as they see fit. They lose economy of scale, but they gain the enthusiam and motivation of the small businessman.

The swift and inevitable introduction of minicomputer systems has left many corporations in a state of disarray. So many computers exist within the company that any attempt to control them seems overwhelming and impossible.

It is like suddenly inheriting a multimillion dollar fortune. Do you have the sophisticated financial knowledge to control the money, or will you squander it through mismanagement and carelessness?

Have we gone too far with minicomputer proliferation? Are the principles discussed in this book therefore unrealistic? The case can be made that things have gone beyond reasonable boundaries. That there are too many minicomputers, and they have made substantial inroads into the central computer base. Why not just let the central organization slowly die off, and give everybody a minicomputer or personal system?

But who is kidding whom? Central DP organizations aren't simply going to slink off into a corner and disappear. The company that has built 60% of the installed computers in the entire world happens to be a proponent of centralized processing, along with many other imitators. IBM is not going to write off the entire concept. Large computers are constantly becoming more flexible and easier to operate. We must remember that the same technology that went into building compact, powerful minicomputers also goes into centralized mainframes. Every advance in minicomputers is generally preceded by advances in large computer architecture and software. A 5 MIPS central machine becomes a 10 MIPS machine, which is soon followed by a 20 MIPS system. The versatility and power of these huge processors is too great to ignore. Major advances in capability are being introduced every three or four years. Semiconductor technology hasn't even reached a mature stage of development, and there are technologies waiting that promise to dwarf the silicon chip.

Things are moving with great speed in the field of computer technology and they are not going to slow down. Even IBM cannot slow the pace of technology because it is confronted with some very healthy competition. Advances cannot be hidden within corporate laboratories for very long. Manufacturers often tend to rush new products to the marketplace prematurely.

If any corporation is not in complete control of its computers today, it is almost certainly headed for bigger trouble in the future. This technological turmoil can cause a company needless expense. What happens, for example, when 100 recently acquired and poorly justified minicomputers become obsolete overnight because a major manufacturer introduces a whole new line with better price performance? How long can users sit on old technology? Perhaps a dominant firm in some sleepy industry can get by with obsolete computers for a decade. But most competitive corporations can't. If their competition automates, they must automate. If their competition upgrades, they must upgrade.

Computer acquisitions and modifications must be managed. This requires information. The most meaningful, trustworthy information is always in terms of cost. And the only logical and proven way to gather costs is by using techniques such as cost accounting.

Few of us in the computer industry really know where we are today. It is a useless cliche to observe that we are in a state of transition. Everybody knows that. We have been transitioning for twenty years, and will continue that way for many decades into the future.

If you are not sure of where you are, the first thing you must do is quantify. Never mind that some of the elements may seem small and hardly worth counting. These elements will probably grow in size just because it is human nature to want more and more.

From the quantification of computers, using cost accounting techniques, come the tools that will lead to understanding. Once we understand the value of those computers, and how that value affects the corporation around us, we can implement effective control.

If accounting analysis teaches us anything, it is: Don't ever assume that minicomputers are inherently cheaper than large computers, or *visa versa.* There is no mathematical theorem or proof or rule of thumb. A sloppy operation will lead to high costs and a well-run computer will process information for a low unit cost. Computer size is meaningless.

To achieve understanding, accounting values must be accumulated in a consistent way. Each mode of computing can then stand on its own financial feet and prove its own comparative worth within the company.

Every corporation has its own unique way of doing things, and this includes the acquisition and operation of computers.

Use consistent, evenhanded cost accounting techniques and decide for yourself which is the best form of computing.

References

Baker, C.T., "Logical distribution of applications and data." *IBM Systems Journal,* Vol. 19, No. 2, 1980.
Bell, J.D., "Future directions in computing." *Computer Design,* Mar. 1981.
Bell, T.C., "Allocating data processing costs." *Proceedings of the CMGX International Conference,* Dec. 1979.
Bernard, D., "Management issues in cooperative computing." *Computing Surveys,* Vol. II, No. 1, Mar. 1979.
Brandon, D.H., *Data Processing Cost Reduction and Control.* New York: Van Nostrand Reinhold Co., 1978.
Champaine, G.A., "Perspectives on business data processing." *Computer,* Nov. 1980.
Chen, P.P., Ahoka, J., "Optimal design of distributed information systems." *IEEE Transactions on Computers,* Vol. C-29, No. 17, Dec. 1980.
Clifton, H.D., Lucey, T., *Accounting and Computer Systems.* New York: Petrocelli Books, 1974.
Dooley, C.R., "How to develop a data communications chargeback system." *Data Communications,* Nov. 1978.
Eckhouse, R.H. Jr., "Issues in distributed processing." *Computer*, Jan. 1978.
Emery, J.C., Gilchrist, B., "Managerial and economic issues in distributed computing," *Information Processing 77 (IFIP Conference Proceedings),* Amsterdam, Netherlands: North-Holland Publishing Co., 1977.
Enslow, P.H. Jr., "What is a distributed processing system?" *Computer,* Jan. 1978.
Ferrari, D., *Computer Systems Performance Evaluation.* New York: Prentice-Hall, Inc., 1978.
Frank, H., "Tommorrow's people to determine DDP's price tags." *Data Communications,* Sept. 1977.
Gligor, V.D., Shattuck, S.H., "On deadlock detection in distributed systems." *IEEE Transactions on Software Engineering,* Vol. SE6, No. 5, Sept. 1980.
Hankison, R.L., "MVS transaction charging." *Proceedings of CMGX International Conference,* Dec. 1979.
Head, R.V., *Strategic Planning for Information Systems.* Wellesley, Mass.: QED Information Sciences, Inc., 1979.
Henke, E.O., Roderick, H.L., Conway, L.G., *Managerial Use of Accounting Data.* Houston: Gulf Publishing Co., 1978.
Horngren, C.T., *Cost Accounting, A Managerial Emphasis.* Englewood Cliffs, N.J.: Prentice Hall, 1972.

Howard, P.C., *The EDP Performance Management Handbook,* Vol. I. Phoenix, Az.: Applied Computer Research, 1980.

IDC Corporation, *EDP Industry Leaders (IDC #1973).* April, 1979.

IDC Corporation, *IBM Data Book (IDC #2044).* Dec. 1979.

Input, *Distributed DP Systems: Applications, Performance and Architecture (Input #10).* Menlo Park, Ca., 1978.

Input, *Trends in Delivery of Remote Computing Services.* Menlo Park, Ca., 1980.

Input, *Trends in Computer Services Pricing (Input Report #30).* Palo Alto, Ca., 1980.

Katzan, H. Jr., *An Introduction to Distributed Data Processing.* New York: Petrocelli Books, Inc., 1978.

Kollaritch, F.P., *Cost Systems for Planning, Decision and Controls: Concepts and Technologies.* Ohio: Grid Publishing, Inc., 1979.

Lorin, H., "DDP: how to fail." *Datamation* Feb. 1981.

Lorin, H., *Aspects of Distributed Computer Systems.* New York: John Wiley and Sons, 1980.

Martin, J., *Future Developments in Telecommunications.* New Jersey: Prentice Hall, 1977.

Morino, M., "Transaction accounting – its role, implementation and use." *Guide 45,* 1977.

Niswonger, C.R., Fess, P.E., *Accounting Principles.* Cincinnati, Ohio: Southwest Publishing Co., 1977.

Nolan, N.J., "Standard costing for data processing." *Proceedings of CMGX International Conference,* Dec. 1979.

Nolan, R.L., *Management Accounting and Control of Data Processing.* New York: National Association of Accountants, 1977.

Nolan, R.L., "Controlling the costs of data services." *Harvard Business Review,* July-Aug. 1977.

Noran, R.W., *Computer Architecture: A Structured Approach.* New York: Academic Press, 1979.

Osterhout, J.K., Scelpa, D.A., Sindhi, P.S., "Medusa: an experiment in distributed operating structure." *Communications of ACM (Vol. 23),* Feb. 1980.

Ross, R.G., "IBM found not inclined to 'star' nets." *Computerworld,* March 9, 1981.

Scherr, A.L., "Distributed data processing." *IBM Systems Journal, Vol. 17, #4,* 1978.

Slenn, M.F., Lehman, H.R., "Data communications using the telecommunications network." *Computer,* May 1981.

Specthrie, S.W., *Basic Cost Accounting.* New Jersey: Prentice Hall, 1963.

Strassman, P.A., "Managing the costs of information." *Harvard Business Review,* Sept.-Oct. 1976.

Streeter, D.N., "Centralization or dispersion of computing facilities." *IBM Systems Journal,* Vol. 12, No. 3, 1973.

Sullivan, K.M., "Does distributed computing pay off?" *Datamation,* Nov. 1980.

Swan, A.J., *Data Communications Protocols.* Manchester, England: The National Computing Centre Limited, 1978.

Thruow, L.C., *The Zero-Sun Society.* New York: Basic Books, Inc., 1980.

Truett, L., Truett, D., *Managerial Economics.* Cincinnatti: Southwestern Publishing Co., 1980.

Weitzmann, C., *Distributed Micro/Minicomputer Systems.* New Jersey: Prentice-Hall, Inc., 1980.

Weizer, N., "A history of operating systems." *Datamation,* Jan. 1981.

Wenig, R.P., "Prepare for the switch to distributed processing." *Data Communications,* July 1979.

Index

Index